C000007919

£17·50

THE VALUES DEBATE

Woburn Education Series

General Series Editor: Professor Peter Gordon
ISSN: 1462–2076

For over 20 years this series on the history, development and policy of education, under the distinguished editorship of Peter Gordon, has been evolving into a comprehensive and balanced survey of important trends in teaching and educational policy. The series is intended to reflect the changing nature of education in present-day society. The books are divided into four sections – educational policy studies, educational practice, the history of education and social history – and reflect the continuing interest in this area.

For a full series listing, please visit our website: www.woburnpress.com

Educational Practice

Slow Learners. A Break in the Circle: A Practical Guide for Teachers
Diane Griffin

Games and Simulations in Action
Alec Davison and Peter Gordon

Music in Education: A Guide for Parents and Teachers
Malcolm Carlton

The Education of Gifted Children
David Hopkinson

Teaching and Learning Mathematics
Peter G. Dean

Comprehending Comprehensives
Edward S. Conway

Teaching the Humanities
edited by Peter Gordon

Teaching Science
edited by Jenny Frost

The Private Schooling of Girls: Past and Present
edited by Geoffrey Walford

International Yearbook of History Education, Volume 1
edited by Alaric Dickinson, Peter Gordon, Peter Lee and John Slater

A Guide to Educational Research
edited by Peter Gordon

International Review of History Education, Volume 2:
Learning and Reasoning in History
edited by James F. Voss and Mario Carretero

International Review of History Education, Volume 3:
Raising Standards in History Education
edited by Alaric Dickinson, Peter Gordon and Peter Lee

THE VALUES DEBATE

A Voice from the Pupils

Leslie J. Francis
University of Wales, Bangor

WOBURN PRESS
LONDON·PORTLAND, OR

First published in 2001 in Great Britain by
WOBURN PRESS
Crown House, 47 Chase Side
Southgate, London N14 5BP

and in the United States of America by
WOBURN PRESS
c/o ISBS
5824 N.E. Hassalo Street
Portland, Oregon 97213-3644

Website: www.woburnpress.com

Copyright © 2001 L. Francis

British Library Cataloguing in Publication Data:

Francis, Leslie J. (Leslie John), 1947 –
   The values debate: a voice from the pupils. –
   (The Woburn education series)
   1. High school students – England – Attitudes
   2. High school students – Wales – Attitudes
   3. Values – England
   4. Values – Wales
   I. Title
   373.1`8`0942

          ISBN 0–7130–0209–3 (cloth)
          ISBN 0–7130–4029–7 (paper)
          ISSN 1462–2076

Library of Congress Cataloging-in-Publication Data:

Francis, Leslie J.
   The values debate: a voice from the pupils/Leslie J. Francis
   p. cm. – (Woburn education series, ISSN1462-2076)
   Includes bibliographical references and index.
   ISBN 0-7130-0209-3 (cloth) – ISBN 0-7130-4029-7 (pbk)
   1. Middle school students – Great Britain – Attitudes.
   2. High school students – Great Britain – Attitudes.
   3. Values – Great Britain
   4. Educational surveys – Great Britain.
   I. Title. II. Series.
   LA635.F73 2001
   373.18`0941–dc21

                                                    2001016137

*All rights reserved. No part of this publication may be reproduced,
stored in or introduced into a retrieval system or transmitted, in any
form or by any means, electronic, mechanical, photocopying,
recording or otherwise, without the prior written permission of the
publisher of this book.*

Typeset in 11/12¹/₂pt Times by FiSH Books, London WC1
Printed in Great Britain by MPG Books Ltd, Bodmin, Cornwall.

CONTENTS

TABLES

PREFACE

Nearly 34,000 young people participated in this study. Their commitment to me was to take the survey seriously. My commitment to them was to make their voices heard. This book sets out to do precisely that.

The organisation of a database of this magnitude has been no small challenge. I am grateful to the teachers and headteachers who administered the survey in their schools and to members of the research team who have prepared the responses for analysis, checked the data, searched the literature, prepared the manuscript and compiled the index: Diane Drayson, Mike Fearn, Susan Jones, William Kay and Mandy Robbins. I am also grateful to Peter Gordon who commissioned the book and displayed helpful patience throughout its long gestation.

INTRODUCTION

This book presents the findings from a new values survey conducted among young people between the ages of 13 and 15 years throughout England and Wales. The aim was the ambitious one of assembling a database of over 30,000 respondents. There were two reasons behind this ambition. First, a database of this size would allow confidence to be placed in the findings and allow the analysis to claim proper authority. Second, a database of this size would ensure a good representation of young people from minority backgrounds. This whole database of 33,982 young people is now used for the first time.

The current work sets out to make the voices of these 33,982 young people clearly heard at a time when there is considerable interest and debate in society at large over the question of values education and education for citizenship. The research has been undertaken and the book written in the belief that good educational practice and relevant educational policy are best shaped in the light of and in dialogue with the views of the pupils themselves.

Some of the findings from the research presented in the book will clearly confirm well-founded opinions about young people's values shaped by personal experience and professional practice. Other findings from the research will, with equal clarity, challenge cherished opinions and long-held views. From time to time all who work with young people, both in the statutory and the voluntary sectors, need to stand back from their immediate concerns and listen with fresh ears to the voices of a generation of young people who are actively shaping their own futures. It is for such people that this book has been written.

In Chapter 1, 'The Values Survey', the context for this new study is provided by discussion of three main issues. This chapter begins by focusing on the renewed interest in values and education following the 1988 Education Reform Act. It is argued that values education needs to be grounded within the context of empirical research into the values of young people. Second, this chapter addresses the problem of shaping a conceptual and empirical map of values relevant to the latter years of secondary education and into adulthood. Attention is drawn specifically to the series of studies begun in the late 1970s on which the present survey builds. Third, this chapter presents the necessary technical information regarding how the values survey was conducted. Attention is given to the development of the questionnaire, the nature of the sample and the description of the respondents.

In Chapter 2, 'Values Profile', an overview is provided of the responses of the whole database of 33,982 young people. Each of the 15 value areas targeted by the survey is taken in turn and full use is made of the range of information given in response to each individual question. These 15 areas are defined as personal well-being, worries, counselling, school, work, religious belief, church and society, the supernatural, politics, social concerns, sexual morality, substance use, right and wrong, leisure and the local area. In one sense this chapter is looking for a consensus in the values held by young people.

Chapter 3, 'Age', begins the process of exploring behind the apparent consensus offered in Chapter 2 in order to identify the factors which predict individual differences in the values held by young people. Although comparisons can be made only between year-nine and year-ten pupils, age emerges as a significant predictor across many value areas. Year-ten pupils see the world in a different way from year-nine pupils.

Chapter 4, 'Sex', continues the process of exploring behind the values consensus in order to examine the distinctive world-views held by young women and by young men. The data make it clear that sex emerges as a significant predictor across many value areas. Young women and young men not only inhabit different bodies but structure their value systems in significantly different ways.

Chapter 5, 'Social Class', turns attention to a third key demographic variable. In this chapter information about paternal employment is used in association with the social-class classification system prepared by the Office of Population Censuses and Surveys. This system distinguishes between three grades of non-manual and three grades of manual occupations. The data make it clear that the social class classification of paternal employment remains a significant predictor of individual differences across a range of values. England and Wales are by no means classless societies.

Chapter 6, 'Parental Separation or Divorce', sets out to assess the extent to which this key difference in home background functions by itself as a predictor of individual differences in values. The data make it clear that almost one in four 13–15 year olds now come from families which have experienced parental separation and divorce. Moreover, significant predictions can be made about the young person's world-view on the basis of this information.

Chapter 7, 'Church Attendance', employs a generally accepted index of religiosity in order to examine the extent to which religion makes a difference to the values which young people adopt. Religion has become an oddly neglected variable in empirical research among young people. The data demonstrate, however, that church attendance functions as a strong predictor of individual differences across a wide range of values.

Chapter 8, 'Television', proposes an analysis between two groups of young people. One group, defined as the young television addict, watches more than four hours of television on an average weekday. The other group watches less television than this. The data make it clear that the young television addict has adopted a world-view distinguished by a number of significant differences in values in comparison with other young people.

The conclusion draws together the key findings from each of the chapters. It highlights the main values profile of young people in today's society, and draws attention to the key individual differences in values associated with age, sex, social class, parental separation or divorce, church attendance, and excessive television viewing. It is against this background that developments in values education and education for citizenship now need to be assessed.

For teachers directly concerned with the delivery of values education among year-nine and year-ten pupils, the statistical profile published in this book can provide a benchmark against which the values climate within their own classrooms can be assessed. The author welcomes enquiries from teachers and headteachers about how such comparisons can be made within specific schools.

1

THE VALUES SURVEY

This book presents the findings from a new values survey conducted among more than 33,000 young people between the ages of 13 and 15 years throughout England and Wales. The present chapter provides the context for the new study by discussing four issues. The chapter begins by focusing on the renewed interest in values and education following the 1988 Education Reform Act. It is argued that values education needs to be grounded within the context of empirical research into the values of young people. Second, the chapter addresses the problem of shaping a conceptual and empirical map of values relevant to the later years of secondary education and to young adulthood. Attention is drawn specifically to the foundation set by a group of studies generated from a Leverhulme-sponsored project in the late 1970s and early 1980s. Third, the chapter describes how the present values survey was designed and conducted. Finally, an outline of subsequent chapters is provided.

VALUES AND EDUCATION

The 1988 Education Reform Act addressed education's concern with promoting the spiritual, moral, cultural, mental and physical development of pupils and of society. The importance of these concepts is reinforced by their place in the inspection framework for schools established by the 1992 Education (Schools) Act. This Act requires Her Majesty's Chief Inspector of Schools to keep the Secretary of State informed about the spiritual, moral, social and cultural development of pupils. Registered inspectors have also been required to comment on these matters.

These requirements of the 1988 Education Reform Act have resulted in the question of values moving higher up the educational and political agenda through the 1990s and into the twenty-first century. This growing emphasis on values can be illustrated by reference to four approaches: the National Forum for Values in Education and the Community, the Personal and Social Education Framework, citizenship education and current central initiatives. The wider discussion about values and education and the relevance of research to that discussion has been documented, for example, by Taylor (1994a, 1994b, 1998, 2000), Halstead and Taylor (1996, 2000), Christie, Maitles and Halliday (1998) and Stephenson *et al.* (1998).

The National Forum

In a discussion paper entitled *Spiritual and Moral Development* the School Curriculum and Assessment Authority (1995) challenged schools to see that the dimensions of spiritual and moral development applied not only to religious education and collective worship but also to every area of the curriculum and to all aspects of school life. This discussion paper clearly spoke in terms of the 'ethos of the school' and in terms of 'values' and 'attitudes'.

Following from the discussion paper, the School Curriculum and Assessment Authority launched a high-profile national symposium in London on 15 January 1996 under the heading 'Education for Adult Life'. The seminar was organised under four themes. The first theme on relationships embraced education for family life and education for self-knowledge. The second on work and commercial life embraced becoming employable and the subject of ethics and work. The third on personal and community life embraced the notion of citizenship and the common good, values and the spiritual dimension. The fourth on looking to the future embraced science and technology, politics and economics, and religion. The questions raised under each of these themes hinged on the debate about values.

After the National Symposium on Education for Adult Life the School Curriculum and Assessment Authority established the National Forum for Values in Education and the Community in March 1996. The values debate was well underway. The stated aim of the forum was to demonstrate the support of society for the promotion in and through schools of 'a set of commonly-agreed values, attitudes and rules'. In accordance with this aim the brief of the forum involved four tasks:

- to investigate whether there was common agreement on the values, attitudes and rules of life which schools promote on society's behalf;
- if so, to identify and formulate these values, attitudes and rules;
- to recommend ways in which schools might be supported in promoting these values, attitudes and rules of life and in fulfilling their role to contribute generally to spiritual and moral development;
- to suggest ways in which the groups and the constituencies they represent might ensure that these values, attitudes and rules of life are promoted generally in society.

In the course of its work the National Forum for Values in Education and the Community consulted widely among groups representing teachers and headteachers, people working in the media, youth workers, the world of work, those concerned with the law and its enforcement, educational researchers, religious groups representing the Christian churches and other world faiths, those involved in initial teacher training, parents and governors, local education authorities, and specialist organisations like the British Humanist Association and the Sex Education Forum.

The National Forum for Values in Education and the Community also commissioned a survey from Market and Opinion Research International (MORI). A total of 849 men and 929 women responded to this survey. The findings demonstrated that for younger children under the age of 10, respondents were split between those who felt that they should be told what is right and wrong (51 per cent) and those who felt that they should be guided to develop their own sense of right and wrong (47 per cent). A higher proportion of respondents felt that older children aged 11–16 years should be guided (59 per cent) rather than told (24 per cent). A further 15 per cent felt that 11–16 year olds should be allowed to decide for themselves what is right and wrong.

According to the School Curriculum and Assessment Authority (1996) MORI also presented the findings from a survey conducted among 196 young people between the ages of 11 and 16. On the basis of this survey the pollsters concluded that this group of 11–16 year olds had a well-developed sense of right and wrong. Their data indicated that 95 per cent said it is never right to steal other people's money and things; 88 per cent said that it is never right to cheat in school work; 55 per cent said that it is never right to call people names; 50 per cent said that it is never right to fight. Although the values debate was beginning to be informed by the voices of pupils themselves, the sample of pupils was small and the range of issues on which they were invited to comment was limited.

The National Forum for Values in Education and the Community produced and published in May 1997 'The Statement of Values', which attempted to present national consensus in four areas: the self, relationships, society and the environment. Taken in this order, the value statements are as follows:

- We value ourselves as unique human beings capable of spiritual, moral, intellectual and physical growth and development.
- We value others for themselves, not only for what they have or what they can do for us. We value relationships as fundamental to the development and fulfilment of ourselves and others, and to the good of the community.
- We value truth, freedom, justice, human rights, the rule of law and collective effort for the common good. In particular, we value families as sources of love and support for all their members, and as the basis for a society in which people care for others.
- We value the environment, both natural and shaped by humanity, as the basis of life and a source of wonder and inspiration.

Personal and social education

The curriculum document *Personal and Social Education Framework*, published by the Qualifications, Curriculum and Assessment Authority for Wales (2000), identifies the role of values within the context of personal and social education (PSE) and shapes this role within the perspective of the new National Assembly for Wales. The document argues as follows:

The National Assembly for Wales recognises the role of PSE in empowering pupils to be active, informed and responsible citizens aware of their rights and committed to the practice of participative democracy and the challenges of being a citizen of Wales and the world. In particular, PSE will help schools to promote:

- positive relationships and participation in communities and the democratic process;
- lifelong learning and effective contribution to adult and working life;
- better health;
- progress toward concern and action for equal opportunities, social justice and sustainable development at local to global scales.

The curriculum document proceeds to identify ten key aspects of personal and social education which it characterises as social, community, physical, sexual, emotional, spiritual, moral, vocational, learning and environmental. Each aspect is developed in turn.

Within the social aspect it is argued that pupils can be helped to enjoy successful relationships within their families, friendship groups and the wider community. This involves interpersonal skills, respect for differences, the ability to cope with peer and other influences, the ability to deal with changing relationships and conflict, communication and participation, team work, parenting skills and the acceptance of responsibility.

Within the community aspect it is argued that pupils can be encouraged to become active citizens in local to global contexts. This involves appreciation of conflicts and inequalities which affect the quality of life, exploration of rights and responsibilities in a democratic society, commitment to community life, service which promotes community well-being, and political literacy.

Within the physical aspect it is argued that pupils can be helped to maintain their physical health and well-being, sustain their growth and development and know how to keep themselves safe. This involves attention to proper nutrition, exercise, hygiene and health choices, awareness of safety in road, water, home and other environments and discussion regarding the use and misuse of substances.

Within the sexual aspect it is argued that as children and young people develop sexually they need to understand bodily changes, manage sexual feelings and enjoy safe, responsible and happy relationships. This involves features such as family life in all its different forms, marriage, sexual behaviours, parenthood, abortion, sexually transmitted infections, same-sex and opposite-sex relationships, personal responsibility and the ability to keep oneself and others safe.

Within the emotional aspect it is argued that pupils can be enabled to examine and explore their feelings, develop self-awareness and self-respect and improve their self-esteem. This involves the intelligent management of feelings and emotions, self-awareness and self-respect, sense of personal control, opportunities for achievement and affirming success, personal motivation and the ability to cope with conflict, stress and loss.

Within the spiritual aspect it is argued that pupils can be helped to develop their personal insights, beliefs and values and the ability to reflect upon their experiences and upon some of life's deeper qualities and issues. This involves developing the inner life and looking beyond ourselves, reflection on experiences, pondering the deeper questions of life, seeking for meaning and truth, promotion of imagination and creativity, recognising the human experience of transcendence, and the sense of awe and wonder evoked by the natural world, by the mysteries of life and death, by the limitations of human understanding and by response to a divine being.

Within the moral aspect it is argued that the school ethos can provide a stable and ordered environment in which values such as respect, honesty and responsibility can be presented. This involves developing a personal code of morality and the decision-making skills necessary to facilitate reasoned and responsible moral judgements.

Within the vocational aspect it is argued that pupils can be encouraged to develop insight into their potential and capabilities and into the changing demands of the world of work. This involves educational and occupational choices, making the best use of abilities and qualifications, decision making and action planning, developing responsibility as consumers and cultivating a financial literacy.

Within the learning aspect it is argued that pupils can be helped to improve their learning and performance and to develop a commitment to lifelong learning. This involves confidence in one's own potential, organisational and study skills, personal management, practical skills for living, insight into one's own learning processes, and identifying strengths and weaknesses and setting targets for improvement.

Within the environmental aspect it is argued that pupils need to be made aware that their responses to environmental issues will affect the future quality of life. This involves the principles of stewardship and sustainability, informed concern for the environment and responsible use of the environment.

Further clarification and definition regarding the relationship between personal and social education and values during the years of secondary education is provided by the learning outcomes specified for key stages three and four. These include:

- showing care and consideration for others and their property and being sensitive toward their feelings;
- having respect for themselves and for others;
- valuing cultural diversity and equal opportunities and respecting the dignity of all;
- valuing friends and families as a source of love and mutual support;
- having a responsible attitude toward keeping the body safe and healthy;
- valuing their own achievement and success and being committed to life-long learning in a changing world;
- considering the deeper questions in life and the search for meaning and purpose;
- being disciplined and taking responsibility for actions and decisions;

- being moved by injustice, exploitation and denial of human rights;
- being committed to practical involvement in the community;
- developing a sense of personal responsibility toward the environment and a concern for the quality of life both in the present and the future.

Citizenship education

Following proposals in the White Paper *Excellence in Schools*, the Secretary of State for Education and Employment pledged to 'strengthen education for citizenship', and set up an advisory group. The Advisory Group on Citizenship (1998) published its final report on 22 September 1998 under the title *Education for Citizenship and the Teaching of Democracy in Schools*.

The introduction of citizenship, from September 2002, as part of the statutory National Curriculum in England at key stages three and four provides a further enhancement for the discussion of values. According to the Qualifications and Curriculum Authority (1999) citizenship education is designed to promote pupils' spiritual, moral, social and cultural development, as well as promoting key skills and promoting other aspects of the curriculum. Citizenship education provides opportunities for:

- spiritual development, through fostering pupils' awareness and understanding of meaning and purpose in life and of differing values in human society;
- moral development, through helping pupils develop a critical appreciation of issues of right and wrong, justice, fairness, rights and obligations in society;
- social development, through helping pupils acquire the understanding and skills needed to become responsible and effective members of society;
- cultural development, through helping pupils understand the nature and role of the different groups to which they belong, and promoting respect for diversity and difference.

Elsewhere *Citizenship: The National Curriculum for England* underscores the importance of citizenship education in the following terms:

Citizenship gives pupils the knowledge, skills and understanding to play an effective role in society at local, national and international levels. It helps them to become informed, thoughtful and responsible citizens who are aware of their duties and rights. It promotes their spiritual, moral, social and cultural development, making them more self-confident and responsible both in and beyond the classroom. It encourages pupils to play a helpful part in the life of their schools, neighbourhoods, communities and the wider world. It also teaches them about our economy and democratic institutions and values; encourages respect for different national, religious and ethnic identities; and develops pupils' ability to reflect on issues and take part in discussions.

Further clarification and definition regarding the relationship between citizenship and values during the years of secondary education is provided by the objectives set for key stages three and four:

During key stage 3 pupils study, reflect upon and discuss topical political, spiritual, moral, social and cultural issues, problems and events. They learn to identify the role of the legal, political, religious, social and economic institutions and systems that influence their lives and communities. They continue to be actively involved in the life of their school, neighbourhood and wider communities and learn to become more effective in public life. They learn about fairness, social justice, respect for democracy and diversity at school, local, national and global level, and through taking part responsibly in community activities.

During key stage 4 pupils continue to study, think about and discuss topical political, spiritual, moral, social and cultural issues, problems and events. They study the legal, political, religious, social, constitutional and economic systems that influence their lives and communities, looking more closely at how they work and their effects. They continue to be actively involved in the life of their school, neighbourhood and wider communities, taking greater responsibilities. They develop a range of skills to help them do this, with a growing emphasis on critical awareness and evaluation. They develop knowledge, skills and understanding in these areas through, for example, learning more about fairness, social justice, respect for democracy and diversity at school, local, national and global levels, and through taking part in community activities.

Central initiatives

The question of values has remained at the centre of government initiatives to regenerate aspects of the educational system for the twenty-first century. Two high-profile examples are provided by the fields of drug education and sex education. The nature of the debate on these issues is well illustrated by two recent government press releases.

Speaking on the subject of the cross-governmental anti-drugs strategy launched on 3 December 1999 by Dr Mo Mowlam, the Minister for the Cabinet Office, and Keith Hellawell, the UK Anti-Drugs Co-ordinator, the Schools Minister Jacqui Smith issued the following statement:

It is vital that young people are educated about the dangers of drugs and schools need support to increase their pupils' knowledge about the risks and consequences of drug taking. This is vital in our efforts to reverse the terrible damage and waste caused by drug misuse. We want to encourage all schools to have policies on drug education.

We believe that schools which provide effective drug education, and have a protocol on responding to drug-related incidents, are demonstrating responsibility for the young people in their care.

Speaking in the context of the amendment to the Learning and Skills Bill tabled to the House of Lords and published on 16 March 2000, the Education and Employment Secretary, David Blunkett, issued the following statement:

I firmly believe the framework to our Amendment will enable young people to move from adolescence into adulthood with confidence. It will safeguard and protect young people and help reduce the unacceptably high level of teenage pregnancies. It reinforces the importance of marriage for family life and for the bringing up of children to ensure that love and stable relationships are seen as key building blocks for community and society.

The new guidance addresses a wide range of issues which previous guidance did not such as education, advice, sexual health, delaying sexual activity, teenage pregnancies and child protection.

We want schoolchildren to learn to understand human sexuality; learn the good reasons for postponing sexual activity and learn about obtaining appropriate advice on sexual health. Our Amendment and guidance also seek to promote the spiritual, moral, cultural, mental and physical development of the pupils and of society and prepare pupils for the opportunities, responsibilities and experiences of adult life.

MAPPING VALUES

During the late 1970s a Leverhulme-sponsored project coordinated by the London Central YMCA (Centymca) and the Department of Community

Medicine at the Westminster Medical School set out to provide a conceptual and empirical map of values relevant to that period of transition through adolescence into young adulthood. The map was developed as a consequence of four interrelated processes (see Francis, 1982a).

The first process involved a careful and exhaustive review of previous empirical research concerned with values and related constructs among school pupils, adolescents, students and young adults. The review embraced such classic studies as Reed (1950), McLeish (1970), Yankelovich (1974), Glock *et al.* (1975), Austin (1977), McCann-Erickson Advertising Agency (1977), Market and Opinion Research International (1979) and Kitwood (1980). What became quite clear from this review was that no current inventory of values assessed an appropriate range of issues and areas.

The second process involved consultation with a wide variety of people and organisations who were concerned with the development of values among young people during the final years of schooling and into work or higher education. Particular attention was given to schools and teachers, to work and employers, and to the voluntary sector. The London Central YMCA and the National Council of YMCAs were central to facilitating this network. These contributions helped to define the precise areas within which research would be useful.

The third process involved settling down alongside young people in schools, in the YMCA and elsewhere, to listen to the issues that they were discussing and to the matters that were important to them. In this way a conceptual map began to develop of values and attitudes which properly helped to define the young person's world-view. At the same time this map was able to reflect the language and ideas of young people themselves.

The fourth stage involved drawing up a series of pilot inventories and field testing the items. After considerable modification the first edition of the Centymca Attitude Inventory was ready to set to work. This first edition was employed in three studies: *Youth in Transit* (Francis, 1982a), *Experience of Adulthood* (Francis, 1982b) and *Young and Unemployed* (Francis, 1984a). Learning from the experience of these three studies some revision was undertaken for a fourth study reported by Francis (1984b) under the title *Teenagers and the Church*. This version was translated into Dutch and used by van Driel and Kole (1987). A second revision was undertaken to reflect the changing culture of the 1990s and used by Francis and Kay (1995) in their study *Teenage Religion and Values*. This version was translated into Czech and used by Quesnell (2000). The five studies conducted in England and Wales will be reviewed in turn.

Youth in Transit

Youth in Transit, the first study to employ the Centymca Attitude Inventory, reported by Francis (1982a), provides a profile of 16–25 year olds. Data were provided by 1,085 members of the London Central YMCA who fell within the age category and who completed a copy of the inventory sent to them by post. These 1,085 respondents constituted a response rate of 57 per cent.

Research among 16–25 year olds is notoriously difficult to conduct given the diverse and mobile nature of the population. There were many strengths associated with basing the study on membership of the London Central YMCA. The sample included a good mix of young men and young women from a wide variety of educational, social and geographical backgrounds. Students and young workers from the north of England, from the south of England, from Wales and from the rest of the world congregate in central London. At the same time, however, there are serious weaknesses in basing a study on such a population since there is no evidence that young people who move to central London are really representative of young people throughout England and Wales. For this reason Francis (1982a) expressed greater confidence in employing the data to report on the relationship between values and other factors than in using the data to generalise to the level of support given for specific value areas by young people in general.

In *Youth in Transit* nine main comparisons were made between different groups of young people. For example, the comparison between men and women identified a lower level of well-being and a greater anxiety over health-related issues among women. The women showed a greater interest in religion and a greater level of concern over social issues; they showed less ambition in their work and a lower level of interest in sport.

The comparison between 16–21 year olds and 22–25 year olds identified a significant growth in self-esteem and confidence between the two age groups. The older group took more interest in politics and less interest in having a good time, religion and their horoscope. They became more liberal in their moral values but stricter in their attitude to the law over issues like drinking and driving. They showed a greater level of social concern as well as greater satisfaction with their leisure activities.

The comparison between different social classes demonstrated that those in higher social-class employment enjoyed a higher level of psychological well-being and a more positive attitude toward work and toward politics.

The comparison between different educational levels showed a very clear correlation between higher educational attainment and psychological well-being, positive work-related attitudes and interest in politics. Higher levels of education were also associated with lower levels of religious belief, greater moral liberalism and greater concern about world development and environmental politics

Experience of Adulthood

Experience of Adulthood, the second study to employ the Centymca Attitude Inventory, reported by Francis (1982b), provided a profile of 26–39 year olds. This time data were provided by 2,074 members of the London Central YMCA who fell into the older age category. The strengths and weaknesses of basing a study of young adulthood on the membership of a voluntary association are similar to those discussed in respect of the 16–25-year-old cohort. Once again the main emphasis in the published analysis is on the comparison between different groups. The ten comparisons are between men and women, between those in their twenties and those in their thirties, between the married and the single, between different employment categories, between different social classes, between those born overseas and those born in Britain, between those living in different types of accommodation, between those living in different types of social groups, between different educational levels, and between different religious groups.

The comparison between different denominational groups showed that Anglicans enjoyed a higher level of well-being than either Roman Catholics or those who had no religious allegiance.

Anglicans were less likely to be worried over personal matters than Roman Catholics. In comparison with Roman Catholics, Anglicans placed less value on religion and less importance on moral issues. Anglicans were more tolerant of abortion, euthanasia and pornography; they were more right-wing in their politics.

The comparison between the married and the single demonstrated a higher level of well-being among the married, and overall a lower level of worry. The married were generally more conservative in their moral outlook. They were also more politically alert and more concerned about some of the social trends in society; they were more content and stable in their work.

The comparison between different age groups begun in *Youth in Transit* now enabled comparisons to be made between four groups: 16–21, 22–25, 26–29 and 30–39 year olds. Comparing the youngest and oldest of these two groups revealed a significant improvement in well-being, although some increase in age-related concerns. The older group demonstrated a much greater concern with politics and with moral issues. Religious belief and belief in horoscopes continued to decline across the age span. The older group showed more tolerance for soft drugs and less tolerance for hard drugs. The older group continued to display more law-abiding attitudes and to grow in concern for world development issues. The older group was beginning to show less contentment and less ambition at work.

Young and Unemployed

In *Young and Unemployed* Francis (1984a) returned to the database of 1,085 16–25 year olds used in *Youth in Transit* in order to shape an analysis specifically concerned with learning about the socio-psychological features associated with unemployment among this age group. Two main types of analysis were undertaken in the study.

The first type of analysis concentrated on identifying the characteristics of the young people most vulnerable to experiencing unemployment. Discriminant analysis profiled those most vulnerable to unemployment as the 16–19-year-old women who were born overseas and were relative newcomers to England, who left school at 16 without any academic qualifications, whose parents were divorced, who were living with their partners in bedsitters, and who were currently working in low-status and poorly paid employment.

The second type of analysis concentrated on identifying the value correlates of having experienced unemployment. Factor analysis identified two main factors which transcended the value areas. These factors can be described as social conservatism and personal well-being. Young people who had experienced unemployment were characterised by more radical social values and by less positive personal values and a lower sense of well-being.

Teenagers and the Church

In *Teenagers and the Church* Francis (1984b) employed a revised form of the Centymca Attitude Inventory with a view to profiling the values of young churchgoers between the ages of 13 and 20 years. The sample was defined as the young people between these ages who attended churches within carefully specified geographical areas on a given Sunday. A lot of care was taken in preparing the ground for churches to help identify these young churchgoers. By this method a total of 1,902 names and addresses were assembled. Questionnaires were distributed by post. The response rate of 70 per cent produced 1,328 questionnaires completely and thoroughly answered.

The key interest in the analysis of the data produced by this project concerned the similarities and differences between the young people shaped by three different denominational traditions: the Anglican Church, the Roman Catholic Church and the Free Churches. For example, in the area of sexual ethics, 15 per cent of the young Roman Catholics followed their church's teaching and agreed that contraception is wrong, compared with 7 per cent of the Free Church teenagers and 4 per cent of the Anglicans. Over half (55 per cent) of the Free Church members agreed that sex outside marriage is wrong, compared with 32 per cent of Roman Catholics and 28 per cent of Anglicans. On the subject of homosexuality, 55 per cent of the Free Church members said that it is wrong, compared with 40 per cent of the Anglicans and 40 per cent of the Roman Catholics. Similar striking differences occurred between the denominations over a wide range of value areas.

Teenage Religion and Values

In *Teenage Religion and Values* Francis and Kay (1995) employed a further revision of the Centymca Attitude Inventory with the view to profiling the values of young people between the ages of 13 and 15 years. The sample was derived from year-nine and year-ten pupils across a wide range of schools. Drawing on a database of just over 13,000 teenagers this book examined the relationship between values and three different conceptualisations of religion within a Christian context. Adherents of other world faiths were intentionally excluded from this analysis. The first conceptualisation of religion was based on reported frequency of church attendance, distinguishing between those who attended weekly, those who attended less often than weekly and those who never attended. The second conceptualisation of religion was based on levels of belief in God among those young people who never attended church, distinguishing between theists, agnostics and atheists. The third conceptualisation of religion was based on denominational affiliation among those young people who attended church weekly, distinguishing between Roman Catholics, Anglicans and members of the Free Churches. The relationship between religion and values can be illustrated by reference to three value areas, namely environmental concern, the use of substances and abortion.

Regarding environmental concern, all three indicators of religion proved significant. Thus, 74 per cent of weekly churchgoers reported concern about pollution, compared with 59 per cent of those who never attended church. Among the non-churchgoers, 66 per cent of the theists reported concern about pollution, compared with 55 per cent of the atheists. Among the weekly churchgoers, 77 per cent of the Free Church members reported concern about pollution, compared with 73 per cent of the Roman Catholics.

Regarding substances, 53 per cent of the weekly churchgoers

considered that it is wrong to smoke cigarettes, compared with 42 per cent of those who never attend church. Among the non-churchgoers, 45 per cent of the theists considered that it is wrong to smoke cigarettes, compared with 40 per cent of the atheists. Among the weekly churchgoers, 56 per cent of the Free Church members considered that it is wrong to smoke cigarettes, compared with 48 per cent of the Roman Catholics.

Regarding abortion, 50 per cent of the weekly churchgoers judged abortion to be wrong, compared with 35 per cent of those who never attend church. Among the non-churchgoers, 43 per cent of the theists judged abortion to be wrong, compared with 32 per cent of the atheists. Among the weekly churchgoers, 66 per cent of the Roman Catholics judged abortion to be wrong, compared with 38 per cent of the Anglicans.

THE SURVEY

Against this background a new survey was conceived which would be able to provide secure information about the values of year-nine and year-ten pupils during the final decade of the twentieth century as schools prepared to shape values education for the third millennium. The aim was the ambitious one of assembling a database of over 30,000 respondents. There were two reasons behind this ambition. First, a database of this size would allow analysis as presented in this book to claim authority. Second, a database of this size would allow secondary analyses to focus on properly defined minority subsets of young people, such as young Jehovah's Witnesses or young people who have suffered the death of a parent.

The instrument

The revision of the Centymca Attitude Inventory employed in this survey was designed to profile values over 15 areas defined as personal well-being, worries, counselling, school, work, religious beliefs, church and society, the supernatural, politics, social concerns, sexual morality, substance use, right and wrong, leisure and the local area. Each area comprised a set of short well-focused statements designed for Likert scaling (see Likert, 1932). Pupils were required to grade their agreement with each statement on a five-point scale anchored by 'agree strongly', 'agree', 'not certain', 'disagree' and 'disagree strongly'. A five-point scale was chosen for two reasons. First, the odd number of response categories allows a middle position of uncertain to be available. This is an important and legitimate option since the survey contains areas and issues on which some young people have not reached a clear decision. Second, a five-point scale permits a finer range of responses than is available through a more basic three-point scale.

Alongside the battery of Likert-type items the instrument included a number of forced-choice questions designed to profile the respondents' background, beginning with forced-choice questions on sex and age.

Before turning attention to the method of data collection, each of the 15 areas covered by the instrument will be introduced briefly in turn.

Personal well-being

Personal well-being is concerned with how young people feel about themselves. How much do they value themselves as individuals? To what extent do they feel that their life has a sense of purpose? Do they feel life is really worth living? On the other hand, how much are they aware of feelings of depression in their lives? How many of them have been driven to consider taking their own life?

Worries

The questions on worries bring together the issues which are known to trouble some young people. How many young people growing up in today's world are worried about getting AIDS? How many of them are worried about their relationships, how they get on with other people or how attractive they are to the opposite sex? Are they worried about their sex lives? To what extent are young people worried about going out at night in their area, or about being attacked by pupils from other schools?

Counselling

This section is concerned with the value that young people associate with their need to talk things through with others. How many young people long for someone to turn to for advice? How many of them find it helpful to talk about their problems with their father, with their mother or with close friends? How do young people perceive the caring professionals and how willing are they to discuss their problems with a schoolteacher, a youth leader, a doctor, a priest or minister or a social worker?

School

This section is concerned with school-related values. What do the pupils think of their school and how happy are they there? What do they think of the people with whom they go to school and how positive are they about teachers? How much do they worry about their school work and about exams at school? What proportion of young people are worried about being bullied at school these days?

Work

This section is concerned with work-related values. Would young people today rather be unemployed than be working in a job they do not like? Or are young people fearful of being unemployed? Do they think that a job brings with it a sense of purpose? Are they committed to working hard and ambitious to get to the top in their work when they get a job? Do they think that most unemployed people could really get a job if they tried?

Religious belief

This section is concerned with the value that young people place on religion. What proportion of young people believe in God? How many believe that Jesus really rose from the dead? Who believes in life after death? In what kind of God do young people believe? Do they believe that God punishes people who do wrong? Do they believe in a God who made the world in six days and rested on the seventh? Who thinks that Christianity is the only true religion?

Church and society

This section is concerned with the value young people place on the role of the church in society. How do they perceive the relevance of the church for life today, or the relevance of the Bible for life today? What proportion of young people still see a role for the church in major rites of passage like marriage or christenings? Indeed, how do young people perceive the church and the clergy? While still at school what view have they formed about the statutory value of religious education and the daily religious assembly?

The supernatural

This section is concerned with the value young people place on the supernatural as a whole. Do young people, in any numbers, believe in black magic or in the possibility of contacting the spirits of the dead? Do they believe in their horoscopes or in fortune-tellers? Would they be frightened of going into a church alone? Do they believe in the Devil?

Politics

This section is concerned with the political values of young people. Do young people have confidence in the main political parties? Are they sceptical about the whole political process and think that it does not really matter which party is in power? What do young people think about private schools and about private medical practice outside the National Health Service? How racist are young people today and what are their views on immigration policies?

Social concerns

This section is concerned with the social values of young people. To what extent do young people feel that they are empowered to help solve the world's problems and what do they consider those problems to be? How concerned are they about environmental pollution, about the poverty of the Third World or about the risks of nuclear war? What do young people feel about violence on television or about the availability of pornography?

Sexual morality

This section is concerned with the sexual values of young people. What view do young people take on issues like sexual intercourse outside marriage or sexual intercourse under the legal age? What view do young people take on homosexuality? How do young people feel about issues like contraception, abortion and divorce?

Substance use

This section examines young people's values on the use of substances. What view do young people take on the use of substances such as glue, marijuana, alcohol, butane gas, cigarettes and heroin? Which of these substances do pupils feel that it is most wrong to take? Is alcohol thought to be more socially acceptable than tobacco, or vice versa?

Right and wrong

This section examines young people's values on law and order. It is concerned with down-to-earth practical matters. How many young people think there is nothing wrong with shoplifting, or travelling on public transport without buying a ticket, or buying alcohol or cigarettes under the legal age? Is writing graffiti generally thought to be all right? Is playing truant actually wrong? What do they think about riding a bicycle at night without lights? What do young people feel about the police?

Leisure

This section is concerned with the value that young people place on their leisure. How satisfied are they with their leisure time? How many wish for more things to do with their leisure or feel that they just hang about with friends doing nothing in particular? How do they perceive their parents' attitude to what they do in their leisure time? Does this meet with parental approval or disapproval?

My area

The final section is concerned with the neighbourhood where the young people live. How content are young people in their neighbourhood? Do they feel that their area actually cares about them as young people? Looking around, how many of them perceive that there is in their area a growth in crime, vandalism or violence? Do they feel that drug-taking or alcohol abuse is on the increase? How do they perceive the employment prospects in their area?

DATA COLLECTION

The intention to build up a database of over 30,000 young people sets the present study apart from many comparable studies in two ways. First, the majority of studies have based their findings on a much smaller sample of young people. For example, in their study on health issues Shucksmith and Hendry (1998) interviewed 44 young people individually. The study on social attitudes among 12–19 year olds reported by Roberts and Sachdev (1996) employed a database of 580 interviews. The study of young people in the 1980s published by the Department of Education and Science (1983) was based on 635 14–19 year olds. In their study of the attitudes, values and beliefs of 15 year olds, Simmons and Wade (1984) drew information from 820 pupils. The study of young people's social attitudes reported by Furnham and Gunter (1989) employed data from over 2,000 young people. The study of young people's involvement in sport edited by Kremer, Trew and Ogle (1997) drew data from 2,400 children between the ages of 7 and 16 years. And Hendry *et al.* (1993) assembled 9,916 responses in their 1987 survey of young people's leisure and lifestyle.

Second, because a larger database has been generated, a larger period of time has been required to assemble, code, check and analyse these data. The project was set up in 1990 and has progressed at a consistent pace throughout the 1990s. What is offered, therefore, is a thorough profile of young people in the 1990s rather than a snapshot of a particular year.

Data were provided by 163 schools throughout England and Wales, from Pembrokeshire to Norfolk, and from Cornwall to Northumberland. A proper mix of rural and urban areas was included, as was a proper mix of independent and state-maintained schools. Within the state-maintained sector attention was given to the balance between Roman Catholic voluntary schools, Anglican voluntary schools and non-denominational schools.

Participating schools were asked to follow a standard procedure. The questionnaires were to be administered in normal class groups to all year-nine and year-ten pupils throughout the school. Pupils were asked not to write their name on the booklet and to complete the inventory under examination-like conditions. Although pupils were given the choice not to participate very few declined to do so. They were assured of confidentiality and anonymity. They were told that their responses would not be read by anyone in the school, and that the questionnaires would be despatched to the University of Wales for analysis.

Participating schools were also given assurance that their data would not be published independently. However, before data from each school were merged with the growing database, a confidential profile was made available to the school.

As a consequence of this process thoroughly completed questionnaires were processed for 33,982 pupils. Of these respondents, 51 per cent were male and 49 per cent were female; 53 per cent were in year nine and 47 per cent were in year ten. Of those educated within the state-maintained sector, 86 per cent were in non-denominational schools, 9 per cent in Roman Catholic schools and 5 per cent in Anglican schools. Of the total sample of pupils, 10% were being educated outside the state-maintained sector.

THE ANALYSIS

The aim of the present book is to profile the values of the 33,982 13–15 year olds from two perspectives. The first perspective is developed in Chapter 2 which sets out to describe and discuss the overview of young people's values in the 1990s. Each of the 15 value areas identified by the survey is taken in turn and full use is made of the range of information given in response to each individual question. In one sense this chapter is looking for a consensus in the values held by young people.

The second perspective is developed in Chapters 3 to 8. Each of these chapters takes one factor which may help to predict individual differences in the values held by different groups of young people. These chapters focus on differences which may be attributed to age, sex, social-class background, experience of parental separation or divorce, church attendance and excessive television watching. Behind each of these headings is a considerable amount of debate, controversy and evidence from previous research. In one sense these chapters are looking for a lack of consensus in the values held by young people.

Chapters 3 to 8 follow a consistent pattern. The first half of each of these chapters examines the wider research topic in which the theme of the chapter is located. Evidence from previous research is gathered and assessed. The second half of each chapter presents a clear cross-tabulation of the responses of the pupils according to the issue being examined. This method of working provides a clear and transparent statement of the correlation between values and each of the seven issues explored. It does not, however, prove causation or take into account the influence of contaminating variables which may enhance or suppress the observed patterns of correlations. The strengths and limitations of the method are emphasised at appropriate points within each chapter.

A database of 33,982 adolescents provides a valuable and almost inexhaustible resource which cannot be adequately exploited in a single volume. The range of themes displayed in Chapters 3 to 8 are but examples of how individual differences in adolescent values can be conceptualised and explored. Other analyses are already planned to examine such issues as the north–south divide, the impact of independent schooling, the consequences of growing up in a religious group like the Jehovah's Witnesses, and the values associated with growing up a Muslim, Sikh or Hindu in England and Wales today.

TECHNICAL NOTE

Chapters 3 through to 8 have been designed to interrogate the database to learn how far information about factors like age, sex, social class and church attendance can predict the values held by young people. Information is presented clearly in a sequence of tables. First, the tables present the percentage of each group (for example, male or female) who endorse the individual statements. Then the tables present the chi square test and the significant level (calculated on the raw data not on the percentages). The chi square test is designed to assess whether differences between groups could have occurred simply by chance or whether the differences are 'real'. A number of factors influence how large the difference between groups needs to be in order for the difference to be 'real' and not merely the consequence of chance. It is not possible to guess the significant of a difference simply by seeing how large the percentage gap is between groups. In the tables, the convention 'NS' is used to say that the difference between groups is not significant or could have happened merely by chance.

2

VALUES PROFILE

The aim of this chapter is to provide a straightforward overview of the responses of the 33,982 pupils who participated in the survey. The chapter profiles the views of the 13–15 year olds as a group, examining in turn the 15 value areas identified by the questionnaire, namely personal well-being, worries, counselling, school, work, religious beliefs, church and society, the supernatural, politics, social concerns, sexual morality, substance use, right and wrong, leisure and the local area.

When completing the questionnaire the pupils were required to rate their assessment of each question on a five-point scale anchored as 'agree strongly', 'agree', 'not certain', 'disagree' and 'disagree strongly'. In this chapter, for clarity of presentation, the 'agree strongly' and 'agree' responses are collapsed into one category expressed as 'yes'. The 'disagree strongly' and 'disagree' responses are also collapsed into one category expressed as 'no'. The 'not certain' responses are expressed as '?'.

PERSONAL WELL-BEING

The survey proposes five indicators of personal well-being. The first indicator is rooted in the theory of self-concept and self-esteem (Rosenberg, 1965; Coopersmith, 1967) and assessed by the statement 'I feel I am not worth much as a person.' One in every eight (13 per cent) of the young people hold themselves in sufficiently low self-esteem to recognise themselves in that sentence. Moreover, a further 22 per cent of the young people lack the self-confidence to reject that statement. Seen from another perspective, one in every three young people (35 per cent) lack the confidence to assert their self-worth, leaving just 65 per cent of the sample who have sufficiently high self-esteem to know that that is not the way in which they see themselves.

Table 2.1: Personal well-being

	yes (%)	? (%)	no (%)
I feel my life has a sense of purpose	56	34	10
I find life really worth living	69	21	9
I feel I am not worth much as a person	13	22	65
I often feel depressed	52	18	29
I have sometimes considered taking my own life	27	15	58

Note: 'yes' combines the 'agree strongly' and 'agree responses'
       '?' expresses the 'not certain' responses
       'no' combines the 'disagree strongly' and 'disagree' responses

The second indicator of personal well-being is rooted in the concept of purpose in life (Crumbaugh, 1968; Crumbaugh and Maholick, 1969), which provides a key to motivation and to meaning-making. Just over half of the young people (56 per cent) feel that their lives have a sense of purpose. This means that more than four out of every ten young people (44 per cent) are not clear that their lives have a sense of purpose. The data demonstrate that 10 per cent of the young people are completely without a sense of purpose and a further 34 per cent are drifting. It is such lack of purpose which may lead some young people into a range of problems and difficulties.

The third indicator of personal well-being is a direct question to do with general satisfaction in life (Diener et al., 1985). According to this marker a more promising picture emerges. Seven out of every ten young people (69 per cent) are able to say that they find life really worth living. On the other hand, one in every ten young people (9 per cent) clearly do not find life really worth living and a further two in every ten (21 per cent) are not really sure that they find life worth living.

In his classic analysis of the structure of psychological well-being, Bradburn (1969) drew attention to the complex relationship between positive affect and negative affect. The two constructs often function orthogonally. To be high on positive affect does not imply a low score on negative affect. Accordingly, Bradburn's model of balanced affect saw positive well-being to be the presence of positive affect and the absence of negative affect. In accordance with Bradburn's model the remaining two indicators of personal well-being access negative affect.

The fourth indicator of personal well-being invites the young person to respond to the direct statement 'I often feel depressed.' This item touches a range of mild affective disorders from relatively harmless neuroticism (Eysenck and Eysenck, 1975) to more serious depression (Beck et al., 1961). The data demonstrate that five out of every ten young people (52 per cent) recognise that they often feel depressed. A further two out of every ten (18 per cent) do not deny that this is true for them, leaving three out of every ten (29 per cent) who are clear that they do not often experience feelings of depression.

The fifth indicator of personal well-being targets suicidal ideation (Goldney et al., 1989; Metha and McWhirter, 1997). Suicidal ideation, suicidal behaviour and suicide are seen to constitute a growing problem among young people in many western societies (Diekstra, Kienhorst and de Wilde, 1995). Just over a quarter of the young people (27 per cent) report that they have sometimes considered taking their own life. A further 15 per cent are not confident that they could deny this idea. This leaves 58 per cent who have not considered taking their own life.

By way of summary, the data provide a profile of a generation of young people, the majority of whom find life worth living but who at the same time experience mood swings and feelings of depression. A significant minority, however, lack a sense of purpose in life, have a low self-esteem and entertain suicidal thoughts. Values education needs to take this significant minority seriously and address the issues of self-worth, purpose in life and enhanced self concept.

WORRIES

The survey focuses on three areas which generate worry and anxiety among young people: sex, relationships and personal safety.

In the area of sex-related anxiety a number of studies have concentrated on attitudes and beliefs concerning AIDS (Barling and Moore, 1990; Zimet et al., 1992). Greater concern about AIDS seems to lead to a greater commitment to practise safer sex. According to the present data three out of every five young people (62 per cent) register concern about getting AIDS, with only one in five (21 per cent) saying that they have no worries over this issue.

Table 2.2: Worries

	yes (%)	? (%)	no (%)
I am worried about my sex life	18	25	58
I am worried about my attractiveness to the opposite sex	35	23	42
I am worried about getting AIDS	62	17	21
I am worried about how I get on with other people	52	22	26
I am worried about being attacked by pupils from other schools	19	22	59
I am worried about going out alone at night in my area	31	15	53

More generally adolescence has been seen as a period of sexual unfolding (Sarrel and Sarrel, 1981) involving physical development, psychological challenge and sexual readiness. Such sexual awakening, it is argued, can be an anxious and confusing time (Heaven, 1996). In spite of this high level of anxiety over AIDS the majority of young people (58 per cent) claim to have no worries about their sex life. A further 25 per cent may experience some worry over this issue and 18 per cent are quite clearly worried.

In the area of anxiety concerning personal relationships the questionnaire targets two issues, worries about how the individual gets on with other people and worries about attractiveness to the opposite sex. The data demonstrate that this is an age group of considerable social uncertainty. Two in every four young people (52 per cent) confess to being worried about how they get on with other people, compared with one in every four (26 per cent) who confidently deny this proposition. The remaining one in four (22 per cent) are aware that this may constitute an area of anxiety for them.

The data also demonstrate that there is less anxiety over attractiveness to the opposite sex than over relationships in general. A higher proportion of young people (42 per cent) claim not to be worried about their attractiveness to the opposite sex than claim to be worried about this issue (35 per cent). This still leaves a further 23 per cent who are conscious that this may be an area of anxiety for them.

Issues regarding anxiety over personal safety have been raised in the contexts of both urban and rural studies (Francis, 1999). Some young people may become prisoners in their own homes if they envisage excessive dangers. Two questions explore this area of life. The data demonstrate that one young person in three (31 per cent) experience anxiety about going out alone at night in their area, while another 15 per cent may also sometimes share that anxiety. On the other hand, 53 per cent of young people are not worried about going out alone at night in their area.

One source of fear over personal safety comes from the rivalry that exists between different groups of young people. The data demonstrate that as many as 19 per cent of young people live under the fear of being attacked by pupils from other schools, while a further 22 per cent are not willing to discount this fear altogether. On the other hand, 59 per cent of the young people have no anxiety over being attacked by pupils from other schools.

By way of summary, the data provide a profile of a generation of young people who are accepting their developing sexual identity but who are anxious about growing up in a world in which AIDS is so well established. A large number of these young people, however, feel insecure in their personal relationships and a significant minority doubt their own attractiveness to the opposite sex. A significant minority are anxious about their personal safety. Values education needs to address enhanced confidence and skills in interpersonal relationships and to enable young people to confront anxieties over personal safety.

COUNSELLING

Adolescence is often seen as a time of development and turmoil during which growing young people need to test out their feelings, behaviours and ideas with others. After first examining the actual extent to which young people feel the need to turn to others for advice, this section of the survey assesses the value young people place on three potential key areas of support: parents, close friends and the caring professions.

The data make it clear that one young person in three (35 per cent) often find themselves longing for someone to turn to for advice, while a further one in four (26 per cent) suspect that this might be the case. This leaves just 39 per cent of young people who deny that they often find themselves longing for someone to turn to for advice.

The relationships between adolescents and their parents are often portrayed as conflictual. A considerable body of research evidence, however, suggests that relationships with parents continue to be important sources of support and closeness for many adolescents (Youniss and Smollar, 1985). In many cases harmony outweighs conflict (Steinberg, 1990). The data demonstrate that one in every two (50 per cent) of the young people find it helpful to talk about their problems with their mother, compared with one in three (31 per cent) who do not find that helpful. Moreover, the remaining 20 per cent do not dismiss out of hand the idea that it may be helpful to talk things over with their mother.

Table 2.3: Counselling

	yes (%)	? (%)	no (%)
I often long for someone to turn to for advice	35	26	39
I would be reluctant to discuss my problems with a schoolteacher	47	27	26
I would be reluctant to discuss my problems with a youth club/group leader	48	30	22
I would be reluctant to discuss my problems with a doctor	33	34	33
I would be reluctant to discuss my problems with a Christian minister/vicar/priest	41	33	27
I would be reluctant to discuss my problems with a social worker	39	36	25
I find it helpful to talk about my problems with my mother	50	20	31
I find it helpful to talk about my problems with my father	32	23	45
I find it helpful to talk about my problems with close friends	63	19	18

Fathers are generally seen as less supportive than mothers. While one in two (50 per cent) of the young people find it helpful to talk about their problems with their mother, the proportion falls to one in three (32 per cent) who find it helpful to talk about their problems with their father. Moreover, 45 per cent of the young people are quite clear that they do not find it helpful to talk about their problems with their fathers, while the remaining 23 per cent are not quite clear how they feel about this issue.

Adolescence also witnesses a growing importance attached to the peer group and to friends, and a number of studies have documented the role of friends in providing support and advice (Shucksmith and Hendry, 1998). According to the present data more young people find it helpful to talk about their problems with close friends (63 per cent) than with mothers (50 per cent) or with fathers (32 per cent). Looked at from the opposite perspective, only 18 per cent of the young people fail to derive help from talking with close friends, compared with 31 per cent who fail to derive help from talking with their mothers and 45 per cent who fail to derive help from talking with their fathers.

Young people's perceptions of the caring professions provide an indication of the extent to which they would be willing to turn to professional people for advice. Overall the data demonstrate considerable reluctance to turn to professionals. Thus, 48 per cent would be reluctant to discuss their problems with a youth leader and 47 per cent would be reluctant to discuss their problems with a teacher. There is a little less reluctance to discuss problems with a priest (41 per cent) or with a social worker (39 per cent). The lowest level of reluctance is expressed in relationship to doctors (33 per cent).

Closer inspection of the data demonstrates that even in relationship to doctors young people retain a reticence to discuss their problems. Only one in three (33 per cent) of the young people are clear that they would not be reluctant to talk with a doctor, while another one in every three (33 per cent) are reluctant and the remaining one in three (34 per cent) are far from confident that they would want to discuss their problems with a doctor.

By way of summary, the data provide a profile of a generation of young people who draw particularly heavily on their peer group for support and who are reluctant to seek advice and help from professionals. Values education needs to equip young people with the skills required to listen effectively to their friends and to offer good counsel and support. It is also necessary to help young people appreciate the resources available to them through the caring professions and perhaps in particular to build up greater trust and confidence in doctors.

SCHOOL

The title of Rutter's classic study on schooling, Fifteen Thousand Hours (Rutter et al., 1979), provided a salutary reminder of the significant part played by schools in the lives of young people. After first examining the young person's overall attitude to school, this section of the survey focuses on four specific issues: the positive value young people derive from school, the anxiety they experience at school, the problem of bullying, and their view of those who teach them.

Table 2.4: School

	yes (%)	? (%)	no (%)
School is boring	37	23	41
I am happy in my school	72	17	11
I like the people I go to school with	90	7	3
My school is helping to prepare me for life	68	20	12
I often worry about my school work	64	16	20
I am worried about my exams at school	74	13	14
I am worried about being bullied at school	28	22	50
Teachers do a good job	45	30	25

An overall indicator of attitude toward school is provided by the simple complaint 'School is boring.' Just over two-fifths (41 per cent) of the young people reject this criticism of school, while just under two-fifths (37 per cent) accept the criticism. The remaining 23 per cent do not feel strongly either way.

Three positive benefits of school include the social aspect of school life, the sense of personal happiness with the time spent there, and the sense that there is some purpose in education. On all three criteria the young people project a positive view of their schooling. Nine out of every ten (90 per cent) of the young people vote for the social benefit of school in the sense that they like the people they go to school with. By way of contrast, only 3 per cent of the young people claim that they do not like the people they go to school with. Seven out of every ten (72 per cent) of the young people vote for the personal benefit of school in the sense that they are happy in their school. Seven out of every ten (68 per cent) of the young people vote for the value of education in the sense that they feel that their school is helping to prepare them for life. Looked at from the opposite perspective, however, as many as 28 per cent of the young people cannot say that they are happy in their school and 32 per cent remain unconvinced that school is preparing them for life.

Two indicators of school-related anxiety are provided by worry over school work in general and over exams in particular. On both of these criteria the young people reveal themselves as concerned and anxious. Thus, two-thirds (64 per cent) of the young people claim that they often worry about their school work. The proportion rises to three-quarters (74 per cent) of the young people who claim that they are worried about their exams at school. Looked at from the opposite perspective, only 20 per cent of the young people deny that they often worry about their school work. The proportion drops even further to 14 per cent of the young people who deny that they are worried about exams at school.

The issue of bullying at school has been given considerable attention in recent years from the perspective of understanding bullies and victims (Smith *et al.*, 1999). Bullying is no longer dismissed as insignificant. Some young lives can be tormented or ruined by it. The data demonstrate that more than one young person in every four (28 per cent) live under the shadow of bullying in the sense that they are worried about being bullied at school, while almost another one in every four (22 per cent) are unable to dismiss confidently such fear.

Attitude toward teachers is assessed by the single item, 'Teachers do a good job.' Overall the balance of opinion on this item is in favour of teachers. Thus, 45 per cent of the young people support the view that teachers do a good job, compared with 25 per cent who flatly reject the view. For a large number of young people (30 per cent), however, the jury is still out on the worth of the teaching profession.

By way of summary, the data provide a profile of a generation of young people who remain basically well disposed toward their schooling. Many of them, however, are under considerable pressure to perform well. An unacceptably high number of them live under the fear of being bullied. Respect for the teaching profession is not high. Values education needs to take seriously the significant minority who are not convinced about the value of education and who are not convinced about the job done by teachers. Considerable attention needs to be given to the culture and climate of schools which can breed such fear of bullying.

WORK

Research concerned with the transition from school to work has recognised that work-related attitudes and values are shaped well before the school-leaving age (Hill and Scharff, 1976). Two specific areas of work-related attitudes are explored in the survey: commitment to work and attitudes toward unemployment. The problem of unemployment among young people has been seen by many commentators as one of the major shifts in living conditions in the late twentieth century (Smith, 1995a) and to be related to factors like adolescent crime (Sampson and Laub, 1993), substance abuse (Peck and Plant, 1986; Hammer, 1992) and suicide (Lester, 1992).

Table 2.5: Work

	yes (%)	? (%)	no (%)
A job gives you a sense of purpose	77	19	4
I think it is important to work hard when I get a job	95	3	2
I want to get to the top in my work when I get a job	87	10	3
I would not like to be unemployed	85	6	9
I would rather be unemployed on social security than get a job I don't like doing	18	25	57
Most unemployed people could have a job if they really wanted to	52	25	24

In contemporary society the work that people do still continues to define to some extent who they are and still continues to give some sort of shape to their lives. The data demonstrate that the young people continue to inhabit that sort of society. Three-quarters (77 per cent) of the young people agree that a job gives people a sense of purpose. By way of contrast only 4 per cent deny this view, while the remaining 19 per cent are undecided.

The majority of young people are committed to investing energy into the world of work and demonstrate signs of personal ambitions. Thus, 95 per cent agree that it is important to work hard when they get a job, compared with just 2 per cent who disagree with this perspective. Similarly, 87 per cent agree that they want to get to the top of their work when they get a job, compared with just 3 per cent who disagree with this view.

The work culture remains so important to these young people that the majority (85 per cent) clearly confirm that they would not like to be unemployed, compared with just 9 per cent who affirm that unemployment would not bother them and a further 6 per cent who have not yet decided how they feel on the issue.

There is some support from the survey for the view that today's young people are work-shy and look to the state to support them. The majority (57 per cent) are clear that they would rather be employed in a job which they dislike than be unemployed. Nonetheless, nearly one in five (18 per cent) take a different view and say that they would rather be unemployed than get a job which they do not like doing, and a further 25 per cent remain open to this possibility.

The final question in this section examines the young persons' views on the nature of unemployment by exploring their perception of the extent to which the unemployed are responsible for their own plight. The data demonstrate that twice as many young people (52 per cent) consider that most unemployed people could have a job if they really want to, compared with those who disagree with this view (24 per cent). A further 25 per cent do not know what to think on this matter.

By way of summary, the data provide a profile of a generation of young people who remain committed to a world of work, whose future identity hinges on appropriate employment and who may hold an unrealistic view regarding the availability of job opportunities. A significant minority, however, have set their sights on a jobless future and on being supported by the state. Values education needs to take seriously the shifting world of employment and prepare young people for a future which will not only require dedication to the employment market but also the ability to build self-identity independently of the work environment.

RELIGIOUS BELIEFS

Classically adolescence has been seen as a time for conversion and crisis in religious beliefs and convictions (Hall, 1904). In England cross-sectional surveys conducted since 1974 at four-yearly intervals have charted the decline in adolescent attitude toward Christianity and the persistent drift from the churches (Kay and Francis, 1996). Against this background the present survey concentrates on six specific issues. The first focuses on the overall level of belief in God. The second focuses on the key tenet of Christianity, namely the resurrection of Jesus. The third focuses on personal belief in life after death. The fourth issue focuses on the image of a threatening God. The fifth issue focuses on creationist beliefs. The sixth issue focuses on the exclusive claims of Christianity.

Table 2.6: Religious beliefs

	yes (%)	*?* (%)	*no* (%)
I believe in God	41	33	26
I believe that Jesus really rose from the dead	30	42	28
I believe in life after death	45	38	17
I believe God punishes people who do wrong	20	38	42
I think Christianity is the only true religion	16	37	47
I believe that God made the world in six days and rested on the seventh	20	40	40

First, the question regarding belief in God divides the sample of young people into three groups which may be conveniently defined as theists, agnostics and atheists. The theists comprise the largest group of young people, with two in every five (41 per cent) claiming to believe in God. The agnostics comprise the second largest group of young people, with one in three (33 per cent) claiming to be uncertain as to whether or not they believe in God. The atheists comprise the smallest group of young people, with one in four (26 per cent) claiming that they do not believe in God.

Second, the question regarding the resurrection of Jesus from the dead shows that today's young people are less clear about the truth of Christianity than they are about the existence of God. Regarding the resurrection of Jesus it is the uncertain respondents who comprise the largest group, with two in five (42 per cent) not having made up their minds. Those who clearly believe in the resurrection of Jesus and those who clearly reject the belief comprise quite evenly balanced groups, with 30 per cent believing that Jesus really rose from the dead and 28 per cent rejecting the idea.

Third, belief in life after death is espoused by a higher proportion of young people than those who believe in God. Moreover, belief in life after death is rejected by a lower proportion of young people than those who reject belief in

God. In other words, belief in life after death does not depend on belief in God. Overall, 45 per cent of the young people believe in life after death, 17 per cent reject the idea and 38 per cent remain unsure on the matter.

Fourth, while 41 per cent of the young people profess belief in God, the proportion who believe in a God who punishes wrongdoers falls to 20 per cent. Young believers appear, therefore, to be evenly divided between those whose God exercises a threatening moral control and those whose God does not.

Fifth, the data suggest that the young people who believe in God are equally divided between those whose view of God has been shaped by a literalist view of scripture and those whose view of God has not been shaped in this way. While 41 per cent of the young people profess belief in God, 20 per cent of them believe that God made the world in six days and rested on the seventh. The implications of holding to a literal and creationist view of God for other religious attitudes and for views on science have been modelled by Francis, Gibson and Fulljames (1990), Francis, Fulljames and Gibson (1992) and Francis and Greer (1999a).

Sixth, the exclusivist claims of Christianity are supported by half of the number of young people who profess belief in the resurrection of Jesus. While 30 per cent believe that Jesus really rose from the dead, the proportion falls to 16 per cent who think Christianity is the only true religion. By way of contrast, nearly one in every two young people (47 per cent) confidently reject the view that Christianity is the only true religion, while as many as 37 per cent have not formed a view on the issue.

By way of summary, the data provide a profile of a generation of young people who are divided between theists, agnostics and atheists. Large numbers have no real opinion to declare on issues like the resurrection of Jesus, life after death and the exclusivist claims of Christianity. The danger may be that young people who are not forming views on religious matters may become vulnerable to the persuasion of cults and quasi-religious systems. Values education needs to equip young people to think rationally and intelligently about contrasting and conflicting religious claims within a rapidly changing pluralist society.

CHURCH AND SOCIETY

Studies concerned with church leaving and religious disaffiliation have drawn a clear distinction between matters of religious faith and belief on the one hand and views concerning the institutional church on the other hand (Richter and Francis, 1998). The survey proposes six indicators of attitude toward the relationship between church and society: the relevance of the Bible and the church for life today, the relationship between Christianity and the church, the attractiveness of the church, the role of the church in rites of passage, the place of religion in school and attitude toward the clergy.

Table 2.7: Church and society

	yes (%)	? (%)	no (%)
I believe that I can be a Christian without going to church	51	32	18
The church seems irrelevant to life today	28	44	28
The Bible seems irrelevant to life today	31	41	28
I want my children to be baptised/christened in church	54	27	19
I want to get married in church	73	19	8
Religious education should be taught in school	38	34	28
Schools should hold a religious assembly every day	8	21	71
Church is boring	52	26	22
Christian ministers/vicars/priests do a good job	36	46	18

According to the first indicator, the data demonstrate that the majority of young people today feel neither passionately for the church and the Bible nor passionately against them. For example, 44 per cent of young people express no view on the contemporary relevance of the church to life today, compared with 28 per cent who reject the church as irrelevant and 28 per cent who defend it. Similarly, 41 per cent of young people express no view on the contemporary relevance of the Bible to life today, compared with 31 per cent who reject the Bible as irrelevant and 28 per cent who defend it.

As often maintained by Edward Bailey's analysis of implicit religion in English society (Bailey, 1986, 1997), the majority of young people have dissociated Christianity from church attendance. Half of the young people (51 per cent) believe that they can be a Christian without going to church and a further 32 per cent have an open mind on the issue. This leaves a small minority of 18 per cent who reject the notion that they can be a Christian without going to church.

The majority of young people hold a negative image of the church. More than twice as many young people consider the church to be boring as reject this image of the church (52 per cent compared with 22 per cent). The remaining 26 per cent may not have close enough familiarity with the church to form a view.

In spite of holding to this negative image of the church, the majority of young people still envisage the church as playing a major role in key rites of passage in their lives. As many as three out of every four (73 per cent) young people still consider that they want to get married in church. What may be even more remarkable is the finding that as many as 54 per cent of the young people want their children to be baptised or christened in church. Looked at from the opposite perspective, only a small proportion of young people have completely ruled out of order the role of the church at these key stages in life. Only 8 per cent are clear that they do not want to get married in church. Only 19 per cent are clear that they do not want their children to be baptised or christened in church. This raises all sorts of interesting questions concerning the ways in which churches deal with requests for infant baptism from young parents who themselves are reluctant to attend church or to profess belief in the resurrection of Jesus (Francis, Littler and Thomas, 2000).

The 1988 Education Reform Act reaffirmed the religious provision of the 1944 Education Act (Cox and Cairns, 1989; Department of Education and Science, 1989). According to this legal provision all state-maintained schools are required to provide religious education and a daily act of collective worship. Several studies have already drawn attention to a general lack of goodwill for this provision among secondary school pupils (Francis and Lewis, 1996). The present data demonstrate that nine times as many young people vote against schools holding a religious assembly every day as vote in favour of it (71 per cent compared with 8 per cent). The remaining 21 per cent are neither for nor against the provision. Voting regarding the place of religious education in school is more evenly balanced, with the largest group coming out in support of the subject. Thus, 38 per cent of the young people argue that religious education should be taught in schools, compared with 28 per cent who argue that religious education should not be taught in schools and 34 per cent who argue neither for nor against the subject.

The largest sector of the young people remain neutral toward the clergy. Almost half (46 per cent) of them express no view as to whether or not the clergy do a good job. Among those who have a view on the clergy, for every one young person who speaks against the clergy, two speak in their favour (18 per cent compared with 36 per cent).

By way of summary, the data provide a profile of a generation of young people who have separated their Christian heritage from the institution and practice of the church. Many want to retain the notion of being Christian, to have the church involved in their weddings and to bring their children for christening. Many feel neutral about the contribution made to life by the Bible, the church and the clergy. When it comes to school worship, however, their stance of neutrality passes over into active hostility. Values education needs to help young people think through the religious heritage of their culture, to appreciate more fully the positive role of religion within the lives of practising adherents, and to explore more positively the personal, social, cultural and spiritual dimensions of the school assembly.

THE SUPERNATURAL

As the traditional religious climate of a Christian culture has eroded, a more eclectic range of beliefs has attracted popular attention. Such beliefs range from New Age therapies (Heelas, 1996) to less healthy obsessions with the occult (Boyd, 1996). In order to examine the extent to which young people inhabit a world which allows for the supernatural, the following issues are included in the survey: horoscopes, ghosts, fortune-tellers and contact with the spirits of the dead. More sinister aspects are embraced by posing questions about black magic and about the Devil. A more general apprehension of the natural and supernatural world is accessed by a question on going into a church alone.

Table 2.8: The supernatural

	yes (%)	? (%)	no (%)
I believe in my horoscope	35	29	36
I believe in ghosts	40	29	31
I believe in the Devil	22	28	51
I believe in black magic	20	33	47
I believe that fortune-tellers can tell the future	20	30	50
I believe it is possible to contact the spirits of the dead	31	33	36
I am frightened of going into a church alone	12	22	66

The data demonstrate that the level of belief in horoscopes is almost on a par with belief in God. While 41 per cent of the young people express belief in God, 35 per cent express belief in their horoscope. The proportion of young people who accept belief in horoscopes is almost equally balanced by the proportion of young people who reject belief in horoscopes (35 per cent and 36 per cent respectively). This leaves three young people in every ten (29 per cent) who seem to remain open to persuasion either way.

Roughly the same proportion of young people believe in ghosts (40 per cent) as believe in God (41 per cent). The remaining three-fifths of the young people who do not believe in ghosts are almost equally divided between 31 per cent who clearly reject them and 29 per cent who remain agnostic on the issue.

The question concerning belief in the possibility of contacting the spirits of the dead divides the young people into three groups of roughly similar proportions: 31 per cent believe that it is possible to contact the spirits of the dead; 36 per cent reject the idea; 33 per cent remain agnostic on the issue.

Overall young people are less convinced about fortune-tellers than they are convinced about ghosts, horoscopes and contact with the spirits of the dead. Five in every ten young people (50 per cent) reject the view that fortune-tellers can tell the future, while a further three in every ten (30 per cent) remain unconvinced. This leaves two in every ten young people (20 per cent) who believe that fortune-tellers can tell the future.

The more sinister aspects of the supernatural included in the survey are acknowledged as real by around one young person in every five. Thus, 20 per cent believe in black magic and 22 per cent believe in the Devil. Viewed from the opposite perspective, 51 per cent of the young people reject belief in the Devil and 47 per cent reject belief in black magic. About a third (33 per cent) keep an open mind about black magic, while just over a quarter (28 per cent) remain agnostic about the Devil.

Only a small proportion of young people (12 per cent) say that they would be frightened of going into a church alone, although a further 22 per cent are not confident enough to reject this possibility outright. This leaves 66 per cent who have no fear of going into a church alone.

By way of summary, the data provide a profile of a generation of young people who have not rejected the world of the supernatural to inhabit a materialistic and mechanistic universe. Two out of every three leave the door open for horoscopes, ghosts and communication with the spirits of the dead. One out of every two leave the door open for fortune-telling and for black magic. Values education needs to leave space for a spirituality which embraces the transcendent and enables young people to make rational and informed choices regarding the ways in which they conceptualise the horizons of their universe.

POLITICS

By the age of 18 young people are taking a full part in the democratic process through their ability to vote. A long tradition of research, however, has consistently drawn attention to a lack of interest in, understanding of and knowledge about political issues during adolescence (Adelson and

O'Neil, 1966; Lonkey, Reihman and Serlin, 1981; Furnham and Gunter, 1983, 1987, 1989). The present survey includes four indicators of political values. The first indicator proposes a marker of political cynicism. The second assesses confidence in two long-established political parties. The third identifies two political issues concerned with education and with health care. The fourth indicator focuses on racial integration.

Table 2.9: Politics

	yes (%)	? (%)	no (%)
It makes no difference which political party is in power	23	33	44
I have confidence in the Conservative Party	15	37	48
I have confidence in the Labour Party	20	39	42
Private schools should be abolished	24	31	45
Private medicine should be abolished	16	44	41
There are too many black people living in this country	16	14	70
I think that immigration into Britain should be restricted	31	39	31

The first indicator confirms the view that many young people are cynical about the political institutions. Well under half (44 per cent) consider that it makes a real difference which political party is in power. One in four (23 per cent) take the view that it makes no difference which political party is in power, while a further one in three (33 per cent) remain unconvinced that any real difference is likely.

The second indicator confirms the view that only a minority of young people have real confidence in the long-established political parties. Thus, 20 per cent profess confidence in the Labour Party and 15 per cent profess confidence in the Conservative Party. Twice as many young people express no confidence in the Labour Party as express confidence in it (42 per cent and 20 per cent respectively). Three times as many young people express no confidence in the Conservative Party as express confidence in it (48 per cent and 15 per cent respectively). The high proportions of young people who do not know whether or not to have confidence in the Labour Party (39 per cent) and in the Conservative Party (37 per cent) is itself very telling. These are the floating voters who do not feel well informed about party politics.

The third indicator confirms the view that many young people have not formed political opinions on key issues concerning education and health care. More than four out of every ten young people (44 per cent) have not formed a view on private medicine outside the National Health Service. More than three out of every ten young people (31 per cent) have not formed a view on private schools outside the state-maintained educational system. Where they have formed a view the balance of opinion is clearly on the side of supporting private schools and private medicine. Thus, twice as many young people consider that private schools should be permitted as consider that they should be abolished (45 per cent and 24 per cent respectively). Two and a half times as many young people consider that private medicine should be permitted as consider that it should be abolished (41 per cent and 16 per cent respectively).

The fourth indicator does not confirm the view suggested by the findings of Bagley and Verma (1975) and Furnham and Gunter (1989) that considerable racial prejudice exists among English teenagers. Seven out of every ten (70 per cent) of the young people reject the view that there are too many black people living in this country, compared with 16 per cent who support the view. On this issue a comparatively small proportion of young people (14 per cent) have failed to form a view. The question of immigration policies, however, is much less well thought through. On this issue 39 per cent of the young people have formed no real opinion. Among those who have formed an opinion, the vote is evenly balanced between 31 per cent who consider that immigration into Britain should be restricted and 31 per cent who consider that immigration into Britain should not be restricted.

By way of summary, the data provide a profile of a generation of young people who are cynical about political institutions, who have comparatively little confidence in the long-established political parties and whose political views are often unformed. They are not, however, generally racist in their attitudes. Values education needs to help equip young people for a more active and better informed part in the democratic process which is the responsibility of all citizens.

SOCIAL CONCERNS

Benny Henriksson's classic study of young people in society concluded that young people have little interest in social matters (Henriksson, 1983). The present survey tests this conclusion by exploring the young person's response to three kinds of issues: domestic issues, world issues and a personal sense of being able to make a difference to matters of social concern.

Table 2.10: Social concerns

	yes (%)	? (%)	no (%)
There is too much violence on television	20	22	58
Pornography is too readily available	33	35	31
I am concerned about the risk of pollution to the environment	66	24	10
I am concerned about the poverty of the Third World	61	26	13
I am concerned about the risk of nuclear war	55	26	19
There is nothing I can do to help solve the world's problems	25	30	45

The first domestic issue explored by the survey concerns violence on television. According to Cumberbatch *et al.* (1987), 56 per cent of broadcast programmes in the UK contained violence. The proportion was even higher in the USA (80 per cent). According to Wober (1988) young people in Britain between the ages of 10 and 15 were more drawn to programmes that contained violence than to programmes that did not. The data demonstrate that the majority of young people register no concern over the level of violence screened on television. Three times as many young people reject the view that there is too much violence on television as support that view (58 per cent and 20 per cent respectively).

The second domestic issue explored by the survey concerns the availability of pornography. Comparatively little reliable information is available on teenage access to and consumption of pornography (Moore and Rosenthal, 1993). The data demonstrate that there is a greater concern among the young people over pornography than over violence on television. While 58 per cent deny that there is too much violence on television, the proportion falls to 31 per cent who deny that pornography is too readily available. While 20 per cent positively agree that there is too much violence on television, the proportion rises to 33 per cent who positively agree that pornography is too readily available. Another point of comparison worth noting is that teenagers as a whole are less clear about pornography than about violence. While 22 per cent have not formed a view about violence on television, the proportion rises to 35 per cent who have not formed a firm view about pornography.

The first issue of global concern explored by the survey concerns pollution to the environment. Furnham and Gunter (1989) predicted that this issue would hold particular saliency among young people 'because they have longer to live in this increasingly polluted and physically damaged world'. The data support this prediction. Two-thirds (66 per cent) of the young people express concern about the risk of pollution to the environment, compared with just 10 per cent who deny sharing this concern. Nonetheless, as many as one in four (24 per cent) of the young people have failed to come to an opinion on this issue.

The second issue of global concern explored by the survey concerns the poverty of the Third World. Attitude surveys in this area have been of particular concern to world aid agencies (Spencer and Snape, 1994). The data indicate that nearly five times as many young people express concern about the poverty of the Third World as deny such concern (61 per cent and 13 per cent respectively). Nonetheless, as many as one in four (26 per cent) of the young people have failed to come to an opinion on this issue.

The final issue of global concern explored by the survey concerns the risk of nuclear war. The study of the attitudes, values and beliefs of young people in 1981 conducted by Simmons and Wade (1984) found a considerable level of concern about the consequences of nuclear war. Changes in the climate of world politics may have lessened this concern somewhat. The data support this view in the sense that concern about the risk of nuclear war clearly takes second place to concern about environmental pollution. It is still the case, however, that three times as many young people express concern about the risk of nuclear war as deny such concern (55 per cent and 19 per cent respectively). Once again, as many as one in four (26 per cent) of the young people have failed to come to an opinion on this issue.

The final indicator in this section demonstrates considerable hope among young people that they could make a positive impact on the world in which they live. While one in four (25 per cent) succumb to the view that there is nothing they can do to help solve the world's problems, the other three in every four take a less pessimistic view: 45 per cent deny the proposition outright and 30 per cent remain reluctant to agree.

By way of summary, the data provide a profile of a generation of young people who are quite concerned about world issues such as pollution and poverty, but who are much less concerned about domestic issues such as pornography and violence on television. On balance they remain hopeful that it is within their power to improve the world in which they live. Values education needs to build on the commitment of these young people toward responsible global citizenship and to address seriously the significant minority who are still making up their minds where they stand on such issues.

SEXUAL MORALITY

Changing attitudes toward sex and sexual behaviour during adolescence are comparatively well-charted territory (Goldman and Goldman, 1982, 1988; Moore and Rosenthal, 1993). The present survey includes six indicators of sexual morality: sexual intercourse outside marriage, sexual intercourse under the legal age, homosexuality, contraception, abortion and divorce.

Table 2.11: Sexual morality

	yes (%)	? (%)	no (%)
It is wrong to have sexual intercourse outside marriage	14	15	71
It is wrong to have sexual intercourse under the legal age (16 years)	24	22	55
Homosexuality is wrong	37	24	39
Contraception is wrong	5	21	73
Abortion is wrong	36	30	34
Divorce is wrong	19	26	56

Social trends throughout western Europe have shown a decline in marriage and an increase in cohabitation (Kiernan and Eastaugh, 1993; Hess, 1995). The data demonstrate that the majority of young people (71 per cent) have come to the clear view that it is not wrong to have sexual intercourse outside marriage. This leaves 14 per cent who maintain the traditional ethic of believing that it is wrong to have sexual intercourse outside marriage and 15 per cent who have not yet formed their view on this aspect of sexual morality.

In England and Wales the minimum legal age of consent for heterosexual intercourse remains 16 years. International studies suggest that adolescents are, however, engaging in intercourse much younger than this. For example, a study among Danish teenagers aged 16–20 years by Wielandt and Boldsen (1989) found that about one-third had experienced intercourse by the time they were 16 years. An Australian survey by Zubrick *et al.* (1995) found that 21 per cent of teenagers reported having had sexual intercourse at 13 years of age or younger. The proportion rose to 43 per cent by 16 years of age. The data demonstrate that the majority of young people (55 per cent) have come to the view that it is not wrong to have sexual intercourse under the legal age. This leaves 24 per cent who maintain the traditional ethic of believing that it is wrong to have sexual intercourse under the legal age and 22 per cent who have not yet found their view on this aspect of sexual morality.

During the past couple of decades a new research tradition has developed with a specific focus on gay and lesbian identities during adolescence (Troiden, 1989; Remafedi *et al.*, 1992; Goggin, 1993). At the same time homophobia remains a significant influence (Herek and Birrell, 1992). The data demonstrate that the young people remain more conservative in their attitude toward homosexuality than in their attitude toward extramarital sex. Here the vote is fairly equally divided between two-fifths (37 per cent) who judge homosexuality to be wrong and two-fifths (39 per cent) who do not judge homosexuality to be wrong. At the same time, one in four young people (24 per cent) have not yet formed their view on this aspect of sexual morality.

Although contraceptive use is generally accepted in contemporary society, research suggests that contraceptive use by sexually active teenagers is irregular or non-existent (Meikle, Peitchinis and Pearce, 1985; McCabe and Collins, 1990; Rosenthal, Moore and Brumen, 1990). Some religious traditions continue to teach that contraception itself is morally wrong. The data demonstrate that just 5 per cent of the young people agree with the view that contraception is wrong, although a further 21 per cent have not formed a view on the issue. This leaves slightly less than three quarters of the young people (73 per cent) who are clear that contraception is morally acceptable.

The legalisation of abortion in many parts of the world has brought with it a substantial increase in the number of terminations of teenage pregnancies (Phoenix, 1991; Hudson and Ineichen, 1991). Attitudes toward abortion continue to vary across different parts of Europe (Harding, Phillips and Fogarty, 1986). The data demonstrate the pro-abortionists and anti-abortionists are equally represented among the young people with one-third (36 per cent) agreeing that abortion is wrong and another third (34 per cent) disagreeing that abortion is wrong. This leaves slightly less than one-third (30 per cent) of the young people who have not yet formed their view on this aspect of sexual morality.

The growth in divorce rates throughout western Europe since the 1960s has been charted by Hess (1995). In Britain a sharp increase in the number of divorces followed the implementation in 1971 of the 1969 Divorce Reform Act which established the irretrievable breakdown of marriage as the sole ground for divorce. The data demonstrate that the majority of young people now accept divorce as quite acceptable. Only 19 per cent of the young people judge divorce to be wrong compared with three times that number (56 per cent) who do not. This leaves around a quarter (26 per cent) of other young people who have not yet formed their view on this aspect of sexual morality.

By way of summary, the data provide a profile of a generation of young people who have adopted a liberal stance on sex outside marriage and divorce. They remain more conservative in their attitude toward homosexuality. Nearly a third have not made up their minds about abortion. Values education needs to steer a careful path between discussing traditional family values and respecting the range of alternative lifestyles represented within the pupils' own immediate and wider home environment.

SUBSTANCE USE

Considerable attention has been given in recent years to the use and abuse of substances by teenagers and to the wider health implications (Woodroffe *et al.*, 1993; Heaven, 1996). The six substances explored in the present survey are tobacco, alcohol, marijuana, heroin, glue and butane gas.

Table 2.12: Substance use

	yes (%)	? (%)	no (%)
It is wrong to smoke cigarettes	42	18	40
It is wrong to become drunk	19	17	64
It is wrong to use marijuana (hash or pot)	51	22	27
It is wrong to use heroin	74	13	14
It is wrong to sniff glue	78	9	14
It is wrong to sniff butane gas	73	14	13

According to Lader and Matheson (1991) a quarter of 15 year olds regularly smoked at least one cigarette a week. The average for boys who smoked was 56 cigarettes a week and for girls 49. Only a third of 15 year olds had never smoked. Moreover, the general decline in smoking among the population as a whole has been less pronounced among young people, while smoking even seems to be on the increase among young women. According to Balding (1993) 34 per cent of year-ten girls had never smoked compared with 42 per cent of year-ten boys. The data demonstrate an even balance among the young people between those who support smoking and those who do not. Two-fifths (42 per cent) agree that it is wrong to smoke cigarettes and another two-fifths (40 per cent) disagree that it is wrong to smoke cigarettes. The remaining one-fifth (18 per cent) have not made up their minds.

According to Lader and Matheson (1991) over 40 per cent of young people in England and Wales reported having one or more alcoholic drinks in the previous week. According to Goddard (1991) around 10 per cent of the 16–17 year olds who drank at all were classified as heavy drinkers by the standards established for adults. Balding (1993) found that around 5 per cent of year-ten pupils had consumed in the past week more units of alcohol than the recommended maximum levels for adults. The present data confirm that the majority of young people find inebriation acceptable. Two out of every three (64 per cent) maintain that there is nothing wrong in becoming drunk, compared with only 19 per cent who consider it wrong to become drunk. The remaining 17 per cent have not made up their minds.

A large survey among Australian teenagers by Zubrick *et al.* (1995) found that 7 per cent reported having smoked marijuana by the age of 13, rising to 34 per cent among 15–16 year olds. The data demonstrate that the young people have a less permissive attitude toward marijuana than toward tobacco and alcohol. Two in four (51 per cent) consider that it is wrong to use marijuana, compared with one in four (27 per cent) who do not consider it to be wrong. The remaining 22 per cent have not made up their minds.

Heaven (1996) considers the use of heroin to be very low among adolescents. Balding (1993) found that 1 per cent of year-ten pupils reported having taken heroin at least once. The same level of usage was reported by Smith and Nutbeam (1992) among 15–16 year olds. The data demonstrate that the young people have a less permissive attitude toward heroin than toward marijuana. Three out of every four young people (74 per cent) take the view that it is wrong to use heroin. The other one in four are divided between those who consider it not wrong (14 per cent) and those who have not made up their minds on the issue (13 per cent).

In their survey of drug abuse among people between 1969 and 1979, Wright and Pearl (1981) found that solvent abuse was mentioned for the first time in 1979. By 1983 Desforges (1983) identified this as a growing problem. By 1990 Smith and Nutbeam (1992) found that 12 per cent of 15–16 year olds had used glue or solvents at least once, while Balding (1993) found that around 7 per cent of year-ten pupils had experimented with solvents. The data demonstrate that the majority of young people recognise the dangers in solvent abuse. Around three-quarters agree that glue-sniffing is wrong (78 per cent) and that sniffing butane gas is wrong (73 per cent). Between one in seven and one in eight deny that it is wrong to sniff glue (14 per cent) or butane gas (13 per cent). Only 9 per cent have not made up their minds on glue and 14 per cent on gas.

By way of summary, the data provide a profile of a generation of young people who are very tolerant about alcohol and quite tolerant about tobacco. They are less tolerant about marijuana and generally quite intolerant about heroin and solvents. Values education needs to help young people make mature decisions about the use of alcohol and tobacco and about the attendant risks of these substances. Moreover, it is clear from the data that drugs-related education needs to remain vigilant in respect of hard drugs and solvents.

RIGHT AND WRONG

Smith (1995b) argues that the most important single fact about crime is that it is committed mainly by teenagers and young adults. Constructing longitudinal data from the official statistics for England and Wales, Farrington (1990) found the offending rate peaking between 15 and 19 years. As indicators of attitudes toward law-abiding behaviour the present survey includes seven specific issues: shoplifting, travelling without a ticket, cycling after dark without lights, playing truant, buying cigarettes under the legal age, buying alcohol under the legal age and writing graffiti. The section concludes with a question concerning attitudes toward the police.

Table 2.13: Right and wrong

	yes (%)	? (%)	no (%)
There is nothing wrong in shoplifting	7	8	85
There is nothing wrong in travelling without a ticket	20	26	54
There is nothing wrong in cycling after dark without lights	17	11	72
There is nothing wrong in playing truant (wagging) from school	17	19	64
There is nothing wrong in buying cigarettes under the legal age (16 years)	30	17	53
There is nothing wrong in buying alcoholic drinks under the legal age (18 years)	42	20	38
There is nothing wrong in writing graffiti (tagging) wherever you like	15	20	66
The police do a good job	54	22	24

Although it is illegal to sell alcohol to young people under the age of 18, Balding (1993) found that around one in four year-ten pupils had bought alcohol during the past week. The present data demonstrate that this is the law young people see as the least binding. Thus, 42 per cent of the young people agree that there is nothing wrong in buying alcohol under the legal age, compared with 38 per cent who judge this to be wrong. The remaining 20 per cent have not yet made up their minds.

Young people are less inclined to condone buying cigarettes under the legal age than they are to condone buying alcohol under the legal age. While 38 per cent judge buying alcohol under the legal age to be wrong, the proportion rises to 53 per cent who judge buying cigarettes under the legal age to be wrong. This leaves 30 per cent who find nothing wrong in buying cigarettes under the legal age and 17 per cent who have not yet made up their minds.

Young people are more inclined to condone travelling without a ticket than they are to condone shoplifting. Just over half the young people (54 per cent) consider that it is wrong to travel without a ticket, but the proportion rises to 85 per cent who consider that it is wrong to engage in shoplifting. Looked at from the opposite perspective, 20 per cent agree that there is nothing wrong in travelling without a ticket, compared with 7 per cent who agree that there is nothing wrong in shoplifting.

The majority of young people are law-abiding when it comes to issues like cycling after dark without lights or writing graffiti. Just 15 per cent feel that there is nothing wrong in writing graffiti wherever you like. Just 17 per cent feel that there is nothing wrong in cycling after dark without lights. Looked at from the opposite perspective, 66 per cent refuse to condone graffiti and 72 per cent refuse to condone cycling after dark without lights.

The problem of truancy has been analysed from both sociological (Budgell, 1983) and psychological perspectives (Jones and Francis, 1995). The proportion of pupils absenting themselves from schools increases nearer the school-leaving age. The data demonstrate that nearly four times as many young people judge truancy to be wrong as argue that there is nothing wrong in playing truant (64 per cent and 17 per cent respectively).

Just over half the young people (54 per cent) judge the police as doing a good job. One in four (24 per cent) disagree with the view that the police do a good job and 22 per cent prefer not to voice an opinion.

By way of summary, the data provide a profile of a generation of young people who are largely law-abiding in respect of issues which they feel really matter. When, however, the law restricts their freedom to express the maturity they feel they have properly attained, then they are more inclined to flout such laws. Overall their attitude toward the police is not entirely positive. Values education needs to develop proper respect for the law as befits good citizenship and to work on the basic goodwill for the law which many young people display.

LEISURE

Young people's leisure has been the subject of several recent studies (Hendry, 1983; Hendry *et al.*, 1993). The present survey concentrates on three specific aspects of leisure: overall contentment with leisure provision, time spent 'doing nothing in particular', and parental reaction to the way in which leisure is used.

Table 2.14: Leisure

	yes (%)	? (%)	no (%)
I often hang about with my friends doing nothing in particular	68	10	22
I wish I had more things to do with my leisure time	27	15	58
My youth centre is boring	35	43	22
My parents prefer me to stay in as much as possible	20	18	62
My parents allow me to do what I like in my leisure time	49	17	35
My parents do not agree with most of the things that I do in my leisure time	29	19	52

In his analysis of teenage culture, Henricksson (1983) spoke of 'a vacuum of leisure'. His view was that adolescents are cut off from productive paid work. In an extended hiatus between childhood and adulthood they are left to their own devices. The data demonstrate that twice as many young people are content with their leisure time as those who are not. Just over a quarter (27 per cent) wish that they had more things to do with their leisure time, compared with 58 per cent for whom this is not the case.

Hendry (1983) identified six main factors in the ways in which adolescents use their leisure time, characterised as attending a club or group, sport, visiting friends, discos, pubs and hanging around with friends. It was this latter category which scored highest among young people under the age of 17. The data confirm the view that two-thirds (68 per cent) of the young people often hang about with their friends doing nothing in particular, while only 22 per cent deny that this is the case for them. Hendry's analysis also demonstrated that youth clubs and groups were waning in popularity by the age of 16. The data confirm the view that only one young person in five (22 per cent) defend the local youth centre against the damming assertion of being boring.

Fisher and Holder's (1981) study illustrated the lengths to which some teenagers would go to disguise their leisure activities from parental scrutiny. The assumption was that parents disapproved of their adolescent offsprings' activities. The data no longer really support this view. A higher proportion of the young people report that their parents allow them to do what they like in their leisure time than deny that this is so (49 per cent and 35 per cent respectively). Similarly, a higher proportion of the young people report that their parents agree with most of the things that they do in their leisure time than feel that their parents disagree with these activities (52 per cent and 29 per cent respectively).

Around one young person in five (20 per cent) report that their parents prefer them to stay in as much as possible. Three times this number (62 per cent) do not feel that their parents constrain them in this way.

By way of summary, the data provide a profile of a generation of young people who spend a great deal of time hanging about with friends doing nothing in particular. The majority of them are content with how they spend their leisure time; and the majority of them do not experience conflict with their parents over how they choose to spend their leisure time. Values education needs to help young people to assess creatively their use of leisure and to develop their sense of using leisure time for the benefit of themselves and for the benefit of others as growing and responsible citizens.

MY AREA

The local area provides the immediate experiences from which young people grow and develop. The survey provides three indicators of attitude toward the local area. The first indicator prepares a global index of the extent to which young people like living in their local area. The second explores their perception of the extent to which they matter as young people in their local area. The third indicator explores their perceptions of the problems facing their local area.

Table 2.15: My area

	yes (%)	? (%)	no (%)
Crime is a growing problem in my area	42	31	27
Vandalism is a growing problem in my area	45	28	27
Drug-taking is a growing problem in my area	32	36	32
Violence is a growing problem in my area	32	32	36
Drunks are a growing problem in my area	25	38	37
Unemployment is a growing problem in my area	36	45	20
I like living in my area	74	12	14
My area cares about its young people	21	41	38

The first indicator reveals that the majority of young people hold a positive attitude toward their local area. Five times as many young people say that they like living in their area as say that they dislike living in their area (74 per cent and 14 per cent respectively). A further 12 per cent feel ambivalent about their area.

The second indicator reveals that the majority of young people are not convinced that they really matter to their local area. Only one in five (21 per cent) of the young people really feel that their local area cares about its young people. Two in five (38 per cent) are quite clear that their local area does not care about its young people. Another two in five (41 per cent) remain to be convinced.

The third indicator divides the young people into three roughly equal groups. When their responses to six questions are averaged it emerges that 35 per cent feel that problems are growing in their local area; 30 per cent feel that problems are not growing in the local area; and the remaining 35 per cent are not sure one way or another. Looking at the six questions separately, vandalism and crime are the two biggest problems which young people perceive in their area. Thus, 45 per cent consider that vandalism is a growing problem and 42 per cent consider that crime is a growing problem. Third in line after vandalism and crime comes unemployment, with 36 per cent considering that unemployment is a growing problem in their area. Fourth and fifth in line come drug-taking (32 per cent) and violence (32 per cent). In sixth place come drunks (25 per cent).

By way of summary, the data provide a profile of a generation of young people who hold a basically positive attitude toward their local area, although they feel that their area does not really care about its young people. At the same time, a number of them perceive the social conditions of their local area to be worsening. Values education needs to help young people integrate more positively and successfully within their local community and make an active contribution to community life. In this way young citizens may make a more effective contribution to their local area and also derive a more affirming sense of mattering to that community.

CONCLUSION

This chapter has provided a general overview of the values of year-nine and year-ten pupils. The overview, established on the responses of 33,982 young people, provides a reliable benchmark against which variations and individual differences can be assessed. The intention of the following chapters is to delve further beneath the surface and to explore just how much this consensus overview disguises very real differences between identifiable groups of young people. The further analysis begins with the two clear demographic variables of age and sex.

3

AGE

Age is an important predictor of individual differences throughout the lifespan. The question posed by this chapter, however, is much more specific and much more restricted. The question is whether real and consistent differences can be detected between 13–14 year olds in year-nine classes and 14–15 year olds in year-ten classes. Comparatively little previous research has focused the question as tightly as this. A broader context will be provided, therefore, by reviewing studies which have employed a wider age range.

In this chapter detailed attention will be given to five specific sources of information. The first is the survey reported by the Department of Education and Science (1983), *Young People in the '80s*. The second is the survey reported in *The Anatomy of Adolescence* by Furnham and Gunter (1989). The third is the survey reported in *Young People's Social Attitudes* by Roberts and Sachdev (1996). The fourth is the series of studies reported by the Schools Health Education Unit (Balding, 1993, 1997, 1998, 1999). Finally, attention will be drawn to a series of independent studies concerned with changing views on science and religion.

Young People in the '80s

The report *Young People in the '80s* (Department of Education and Science, 1983) was based on a sample of 635 young people between the ages of 14 and 19. Age comparisons were published between the 14–16 year olds and the 17–19 year olds in respect of issues such as drinking alcohol, drug-related experiences, gender roles, youth clubs, parental constraints, personal expenditure and leisure activities.

Reasons for drinking alcohol changed with age. The 17–19 year olds were more likely than the 14–16 year olds to perceive drinking alcohol as being sociable (55 per cent and 36 per cent) and as being part of discos and clubs (45 per cent and 25 per cent). The older age group was more likely than the younger age group to be drinking alcohol in a pub (78 per cent and 31 per cent) and less likely than the younger age group to be drinking alcohol at home with parents (46 per cent and 67 per cent).

Familiarity with drugs increased with age. While 45 per cent of the 14–16 year olds claimed to know someone taking drugs, the proportion rose to 59 per cent among the 17–19 year olds. With familiarity came greater acceptance. Three-quarters (75 per cent) of the 14–16 year olds rejected drug use completely, but this fell to 58 per cent among 17–19 year olds.

Gender-role stereotypes continued to erode with age. While 41 per cent of 14–16 year olds favoured the traditional model of husbands as earners and women as mothers, the proportion fell to 34 per cent among 17–19 year olds.

Participation in youth clubs declined quickly with age. Among 14–16 year olds two in five (38 per cent) claimed attendance at youth clubs. By the 17–19 age group only one in five (19 per cent) claimed such attendance.

The older age group reported considerably less parental constraint than the younger age group. Thus, 63 per cent of the 17–19 year olds reported that there were no time constraints on them as long as their parents knew where they had been, compared with 38 per cent of the 14–16 year olds. The proportion of young people who felt that their parents preferred them to stay in fell from 29 per cent among the 14–16 year olds to 20 per cent among the 17–19 year olds.

Considerable variations took place in the financial spending priorities of the two age groups. The younger group were more likely to spend money on comics and magazines and on crisps and sweets. The older group were more likely to spend money on clothes, toiletries, alcohol and cigarettes. For example, 23 per cent of 17–19 year olds spent money on sweets and crisps, compared with 38 per cent of 14–16 year olds. On the other hand, 27 per cent of 17–19 year olds spent money on toiletries, compared with 12 per cent of 14–16 year olds.

Preferred leisure activities underwent significant changes between the two age groups. For example, 17–19 year olds were less likely than 14–16 year olds to watch television regularly (47 per cent and 56 per cent). On the other hand, 17–19 year olds were more likely than 14–16 year olds to listen to music regularly (63 per cent and 53 per cent). A smaller proportion of 17–19 year olds compared with 14–16 year olds claimed that they often hung about with their friends doing nothing in particular (24 per cent compared with 35 per cent).

The Anatomy of Adolescence

The report *The Anatomy of Adolescence* (Furnham and Gunter, 1989) was based on a sample of over 2,000 young people between the ages of 10 and 22 recruited through the National Association of Youth Clubs. Age comparisons were published between the 10–14 year olds, the 15–16 year olds and the 17–21 year olds in respect of issues such as the problems facing Britain, predicted developments in the next decade, gender roles, sexual relationships, beliefs about racial minorities (West Indians, Asians and Irish), the paranormal, environmental pollution, work-related attitudes, unemployment and school-related attitudes. The following discussion highlights the comparison between the 10–14 year olds and the 15–16 year olds.

Regarding the importance attributed to the problems facing Britain, little difference was found between the responses of the 10–14 year olds and the 15–16 year olds. Similar proportions of both groups considered it important to reduce the differences between the regions by helping the less developed or those in most need (70 per cent and 69 per cent). Similar proportions of both groups considered it important to reduce the numbers both of very rich and very poor people (58 per cent and 60 per cent). Similar proportions of both groups considered it important to protect nature and fight pollution (80 per cent and 81 per cent).

On the other hand, the older group showed less concern over some issues. For example, while 84 per cent of the 10–14 year olds considered it important to ensure non-nuclear energy supplies, the proportion fell a little to 78 per cent among the 15–16 year olds. While 86 per cent of the 10–14 year olds considered it important to help poor countries in Africa, Asia and South America, the proportion fell to 79 per cent among the 15–16 year olds.

Regarding predicted developments in the next decade, overall the 15–16 year olds were a little less optimistic than the 10–14 year olds about the way things will develop in the world. The proportion of young people in these two groups who considered that international tensions will have lessened dropped from 45 per cent to 39 per cent. The proportion who considered that progress in science and technology will have allowed us to improve the situation of the poorest countries dropped from 79 per cent to 74 per cent.

Regarding gender roles, the 15–16 year olds were somewhat less inclined than the 10–14 year olds to support the traditional stereotypes. Thus, 37 per cent of the 15–16 year olds agreed that women should worry less about being equal with men and more about becoming good wives and mothers, compared with 47 per cent of the 10–14 year olds. Similarly, 20 per cent of the 15–16 year olds agreed that women should not be bosses in important jobs in business and industry, compared with 28 per cent of the 10–14 year olds.

The older group also supported more equal distribution of household chores. Thus, 50 per cent of the 15–16 year olds considered that men and women should be equally involved in doing the cleaning, compared with 38 per cent of the 10–14 year olds. Two-fifths (39 per cent) of the 15–16 year olds considered that men and women should be equally involved in repairing electrical equipment, compared with 22 per cent of the 10–14 year olds. Similarly, 36 per cent of the 15–16 year olds considered that men and women should be equally involved in doing the washing and ironing, compared with 26 per cent of the 10–14 year olds.

Regarding sexual relationships, the 15–16 year olds displayed a more liberal attitude than the 10–14 year olds. While premarital sex was approved by 64 per cent of the 10–14 year olds, the proportion rose to 77 per cent among the 15–16 year olds. While 44 per cent of the 10–14 year olds agreed that society should be permissive of all types of sexual relationships, the proportion rose to 53 per cent among the 15–16 year olds.

Regarding beliefs about racial minorities, a very slight reduction in prejudice occurred between the 10–14 year olds and the 15–16 year olds. For example, 25 per cent of the younger group considered that West Indians generally do not show much inclination to work, and so did 22 per cent of the older group; 25 per cent of the younger group considered that the Irish generally do not show much inclination to work, and so did 22 per cent of the older group; 31 per cent of the younger group considered that Asian people generally do not show much inclination to work, and so did 29 per cent of the older group.

On the other hand, some of the racial stereotypes were more likely to be questioned by the older group. For example, while 44 per cent of the 10–14 year olds agreed that drunkenness is one of the greatest problems with Irish people, the proportion fell to 35 per cent among the 15–16 year olds. While 62 per cent of the 10–14 year olds agreed that given the chance the Irish will work as hard as other people, the proportion rose to 71 per cent among the 15-16 year olds.

Regarding the paranormal, a general decline in belief occurred between the 10–14 year olds and the 15–16 year olds. For example, 16 per cent of the older group said that they had encountered something they thought was a ghost, compared with 27 per cent of the younger group. Belief in telepathy declined from 30 per cent to 25 per cent; belief in clairvoyance declined from 38 per cent to 29 per cent; belief in spiritualism declined from 29 per cent to 26 per cent.

Regarding beliefs about environmental pollution, comparatively little change occurred between the 10–14 year olds and the 15–16 year olds. Industrial waste was rated as a serious problem by 83 per cent of the younger group and 86 per cent of the older group. Waste from nuclear power stations was rated as a serious problem by 86 per cent of the younger group and 84 per cent of the older group. On the other hand, the older group was less inclined to rate noise from aircraft as a serious problem (29 per cent compared with 41 per cent).

Regarding work-related attitudes, considerable changes were found between the 10–14 year olds and the 15–16 year olds. As the reality of a working future drew nearer, so the 'uncertain' responses to work-related questions declined. Three-fifths (61 per cent) of the 15–16 year olds took the view that hard work makes someone a better person, compared with 53 per cent of the 10–14 year olds. Three-fifths (59 per cent) of the 15-16 year olds took the view that the principal purpose of a person's job is to provide a means for enjoying free time, compared with 41 per cent of the 10–14 year olds.

Views on what are the most important things to look for in a job also developed between these two age groups. For example, 76 per cent of the 15–16 year olds rated security for the future as very important, compared with 64 per cent of the 10–14 year olds. Two-thirds (64 per cent) of the 15–16 year olds rated satisfying work as very important, compared with 46 per cent of the 10–14 year olds. Similarly, 57 per cent of the 15–16 year olds rated opportunities for career development as very important, compared with 42 per cent of the 10–14 year olds.

Regarding views on unemployment, the findings demonstrated considerable shifts between 10–14 year olds and 15–16 year olds. The shifts do not lead, however, to a coherent view of unemployment. One view sees unemployment as the responsibility of young people themselves. While 57 per cent of the 10–14 year olds agreed that most young people get jobs if they look hard, are confident and have a lot to offer, the proportion rose to 70 per cent among the 15–16 year olds. A second view blames the government for youth unemployment. While 49 per cent of the 10–14 year olds argued that the government is to blame for young people being out of work, the proportion rose to 60 per cent among the 15–16 year olds. A third view is that unemployment is a kind of lottery.

While 35 per cent of the 10–14 year olds felt that getting a job is mainly a matter of being in the right place at the right time, the proportion rose to 55 per cent among the 15–16 year olds.

Regarding school-related attitudes, the findings demonstrated two somewhat conflicting trends. On the one hand, overall attitude toward school deteriorated between the two age groups. For example, while 41 per cent of the 10–14 year olds agreed that they got bored and fed up with school and did not really enjoy anything connected with it, the proportion rose to 47 per cent among the 15–16 year olds. While 59 per cent of the 10–14 year olds said that most of the subjects they took were interesting, the proportion fell to 52 per cent among the 15–16 year olds. While 40 per cent of the 10–14 year olds considered that teachers were good at getting their ideas across in the classroom, the proportion fell to 30 per cent of the 15–16 year olds.

On the other hand, the older age group had come to recognise a greater relevance of education for employment prospects. For example, 54 per cent of the 15–16 year olds considered that a lot of schooling is necessary to avoid a dead-end job, compared with 46 per cent of the 10–14 year olds. Three-quarters (75 per cent) of the 15–16 year olds had come to the view that employers pay a lot of attention to school reports and examination results, compared with 59 per cent of the 10–14 year olds.

Young People's Social Attitudes

The report *Young People's Social Attitudes* (Roberts and Sachdev, 1996) was based on a sample of 580 young people between the ages of 12 and 19. Age comparisons were published between three groups: 12–15 year olds, 16–17 year olds and 18–19 year olds. The following discussion draws attention particularly to the differences between the youngest and the oldest of these three groups. Seven chapters explored different themes within the survey, although only five of them included age trends in their analysis.

In the first chapter, Newman (1996) concentrated on the way in which perceptions of the adult world changed through the three age groups. The pattern identified by the data was quite clear. The younger group wanted adult responsibilities at a younger age. While 38 per cent of the 12–15 year olds considered that 16 year olds should be allowed to vote, the proportion fell to 9 per cent among the 18–19 year olds. While 32 per cent of the 12–15 year olds considered that 16 year olds should be allowed to buy alcohol, the proportion fell to 12 per cent among the 18–19 year olds. While 49 per cent of the 12–15 year olds considered that 16 year olds should be allowed to leave home, the proportion fell to 34 per cent among the 18–19 year olds.

In the second chapter, Sachdev (1996) focused on racial discrimination and racial prejudice. The data demonstrated a growing awareness of racial prejudice with age. While 46 per cent of the 12–15 year olds perceived there to be a lot of prejudice in Britain against Asian people, the proportion rose to 66 per cent among the 18–19 year olds. While 38 per cent of the 12–15 year olds perceived there to be a lot of prejudice in Britain against black people, the proportion rose to 43 per cent among the 18–19 year olds.

In the third chapter, McNeish (1996) focused on crime, justice and punishment. The data demonstrated a growing toughness on crime with age. Asked the best way of dealing with a first-time burglar under 16 years of age, 31 per cent of the 12–15 year olds resisted custodial sentences and community service in favour of a strong warning. The proportion of 18–19 year olds taking this lenient view dropped to 23 per cent. Asked whether British courts should be able to sentence murderers to death, 30 per cent of the 12–15 year olds suggested definite approval. The proportion of 18–19 year olds taking this tough view rose to 52 per cent.

The fourth chapter, Hughes and Lloyd (1996) focused on perceptions of the educational system. The data revealed changing perceptions of what is good and bad in the educational system with age. The older age group was more inclined to see value in published league tables of school performance. Thus, 35 per cent of the 18–19 year olds regarded the publication of secondary school results as very useful, compared with 28 per cent of the 12–15 year olds. The younger age group was more inclined to see bullying as widespread in schools. Thus, 88 per cent of the 12–15 year olds believed that bullying happens at least a little in schools, compared with 73 per cent of the 18–19 year olds.

In the fifth chapter, Roberts (1996) focused on religion and morality. The data demonstrated a clear decline in religious affiliation, practice and belief with age. While 48 per cent of the 12–15 year olds claimed religious affiliation, the proportion fell to 37 per cent among the 16–17 year olds. While 28 per cent of the 12–15 year olds attended religious meetings or ceremonies at least once a year, the proportion fell to 21 per cent among the 16–17 year olds. While 62 per cent of the 12–15 year olds believed in God, the proportion fell to 52 per cent among the 16–17 year olds. In terms of honesty, however, little variation emerged between the age groups.

Schools Health Education Unit

The Schools Health Education Unit based in the University of Exeter has published a long-established series of reports on young people's health-related attitudes which allows close attention to be given to age trends. For example, the 1992 report (Balding, 1993), based on the responses of 20,218 pupils between the ages of 11 and 15, enables close comparison to be made between the views of year-nine and year-ten pupils on eight themes defined as diet, doctor and dentist, health and safety, activities after school, drugs, money, sport, and social and personal issues.

Regarding attitudes toward diet and food, the data demonstrated two somewhat opposing trends between year-nine and year-ten pupils. On the one hand, there was a slight increase in the proportion of young people who said that they never considered their health when choosing what to eat, from 10 per cent in year-nine to 14 per cent in year-ten. On the other hand, there was a slight increase in the proportion of young people who had elected never to eat meat or to eat meat only occasionally, from 13 per cent in year-nine to 16 per cent in year-ten.

Regarding attitudes toward doctors and dentists, there was a slight increase in self-confidence between year-nine and year-ten. While 55 per cent of year-nine pupils felt at ease with the doctor on their most recent visit, the proportion grew slightly to 58 per cent among year-ten pupils.

Regarding attitudes and practices related to health and safety, the data showed a slight decrease in remedies and medication taken between year-nine and year-ten. Among year nine pupils 53 per cent had taken remedies within the past week for asthma, colds, diabetes, allergies and skin problems. The proportion fell slightly to 50 per cent among year-ten pupils. Among year-nine pupils 73 per cent had taken within the past week iron tablets, vitamins, antibiotics, painkillers or other remedies or medicines. The proportion fell slightly to 70 per cent among year-ten pupils.

Regarding time spent on activities after school, there were some considerable differences between year-nine and year-ten pupils. Over this period time spent listening to music and being with friends increased, while time spent doing homework or reading decreased. Thus, the proportion of pupils who had listened to music the previous day increased from 60 per cent to 69 per cent and the proportion who had met with friends increased from 42 per cent to 51 per cent. The proportion of pupils who had spent time on homework the previous day decreased from 76 per cent to 70 per cent and the proportion who had read a book decreased from 37 per cent to 28 per cent.

Regarding drugs and substances, the proportion of pupils who could claim that they had never smoked fell from 48 per cent in year-nine to 38 per cent in year-ten. The proportion of pupils who had consumed alcohol within the past week grew from 43 per cent in year nine to 56 per cent in year-ten. The proportion of pupils who had purchased alcohol for themselves within the past week grew from 12 per cent in year nine to 24 per cent in year-ten.

Regarding money, the proportion of pupils engaged in regular paid work during term time grew from 34 per cent in year nine to 42 per cent in year ten. Moreover, among those engaged in regular paid employment the average weekly pay increased by around 25 per cent between year nine and year ten.

Regarding sport and fitness, little change took place in basic attitudes between year nine and year ten. For example, 32 per cent of pupils in year nine regarded themselves as active or very active, and so did 31 per cent in year ten. Similarly, 27 per cent of pupils in year nine regarded themselves as fit or very fit, and so did 26 per cent in year ten.

Regarding social and personal attitudes, the following main developments occurred between year nine and year ten. The proportion of pupils who nominated both parents as the adults with whom they got on best fell from 43 per cent to 33 per cent. The proportion of pupils who felt at ease when meeting people of their own age and opposite sex for the first time rose from 35 per cent to 38 per cent. The proportion of pupils who felt that they were in charge of their health rose from 55 per cent to 61 per cent.

The 1996 report from the Schools Health Education Unit (Balding, 1997) and the 1997 report (Balding, 1998) also allow comparisons to be made between pupils in year nine and pupils in year ten: the 1998 report presented comprehensive information only for year eight and year ten (Balding, 1999). The 1996 report, based on the responses of 22,067 pupils between the ages of 12 and 15, enabled comparisons to be made between pupils in year nine and pupils in year ten on the following issues: cycling and safety helmets, favourite television programmes, engagement with the national lottery, and aerobic exercises.

The section on health and safety included several questions on cycling. The data demonstrated a decrease in the proportions of pupils who used a cycle from 80 per cent in year nine to 73 per cent in year ten. Among those who used a cycle there was an increase in the proportion who never or hardly ever used a safety helmet, from 63 per cent in year nine to 72 per cent in year ten.

The section on home included a question about favourite television programmes. The data demonstrated shifts in the proportion of pupils claiming to be regular viewers of specific soaps. Regular viewers of *Neighbours* dropped from 38 per cent in year nine to 33 per cent in year ten. On the other hand, regular viewers of *EastEnders* rose from 27 per cent in year nine to 33 per cent in year ten.

The section on money included questions on the national lottery. The data demonstrated a slight increase over the two age groups. While 11 per cent of the year-nine pupils had bought a national lottery draw ticket during the previous seven days, the proportion rose to 13 per cent among year-ten pupils. While 10 per cent of the year-nine pupils had bought an instant scratch card during the previous seven days, the proportion rose to 11 per cent among year-ten pupils.

The section on sport included a question about aerobic exercise. The data demonstrated a slight decrease in the proportion of pupils who had exercised and had to breathe harder three times or more during the previous seven days from 34 per cent in year nine to 31 per cent in year ten.

The 1997 report, based on the responses of 37,538 pupils between the ages of 9 and 16, enabled comparison to be made between pupils in year nine and pupils in year ten on a number of themes not included in the 1992 report, including bullying, computer games, cigarette advertising, savings, enjoyment of physical activities and availability of contraceptives.

The section on health and safety included a question on bullying. The data demonstrated that there was a slight decline in the proportion of pupils who felt afraid of going to school because of bullying from 29 per cent in year nine to 24 per cent in year ten.

The section on family and home included a question on playing computer games after school. The data demonstrated that there was a slight decline in the proportion of pupils who had engaged in this activity during the previous day from 37 per cent in year nine to 34 per cent in year ten.

The section on drugs included a question regarding the influence of cigarette advertising. The data demonstrated that there was a slight decline in the proportion of pupils who considered that cigarette advertising had a lot or quite a lot of influence on young people starting smoking from 49 per cent in year nine to 41 per cent in year ten.

The section on money included a question on saving. The data demonstrated that there was a slight increase in the proportion of pupils who had put some of their own money into a savings scheme within the previous seven days from 32 per cent in year nine to 35 per cent in year ten.

The section on sport included a question about enjoyment of physical activities. The data demonstrated that there was a slight decrease in the proportion of pupils who said that they enjoyed physical activities a lot from 46 per cent in year nine to 44 per cent in year ten.

The section on social and personal attitudes included a question on the availability of contraceptives. The data demonstrated that there was an increase in the proportion of pupils who claimed to know that there was a special birth-control service available for young people locally from 14 per cent in year nine to 33 per cent in year ten.

Science and religion

During the 1980s and 1990s, a series of independent studies monitored age trends among secondary pupils' attitudes toward science and religion. The studies were based on the different cultures of England, Northern Ireland and Scotland.

Gibson (1989) investigated attitudes toward religion and science among 6,653 secondary school pupils in a Scottish city. He found that between the ages of 13 and 15 interest in both science and religion declined and that the perceived conflict between science and religion was sharpened. For example, while 48 per cent of 13 year olds claimed that studying science gave them much pleasure, the proportion fell to 37 per cent among 15 year olds. While 21 per cent of 13 year olds considered that science has disproved the Bible, the proportion rose to 28 per cent among 15 year olds. Such shifts were accompanied by a more mechanistic view of human life. The proportion of young people who agreed that human beings are just complex chemical machines grew from 16 per cent to 22 per cent between the ages of 13 and 15.

Francis (1989) investigated attitudes toward Christianity among 400 year-nine pupils and 400 year-ten pupils in England. He found a significant deterioration over this period in attitude toward God, Jesus, the Bible, prayer and the church. For example, the proportion of pupils who said that they found it hard to believe in God increased from 41 per cent to 49 per cent. The proportion of pupils who believed that Jesus helped them declined from 30 per cent to 23 per cent. Those who dismissed the Bible as boring rose from 37 per cent to 49 per cent. Those who found help from saying their prayers dropped from 28 per cent to 19 per cent. Those who regarded the church as important to them dropped from 19 per cent to 12 per cent.

Francis, Gibson and Fulljames (1990) compared the attitudes of 1,478 13 year olds and 1,354 15 year olds to scientism and creationism in Scotland. They found a small decrease in scientism and a small decrease in believing that Christians were committed to creationism between these two age groups. For example, while 30 per cent of 13 year olds agreed that nothing should be believed unless it can be proved scientifically, the proportion fell to 25 per cent among 15 year olds. While 35 per cent of 13 year olds believed that all church leaders teach that there are no errors in the Bible, the proportion fell to 29 per cent among 15 year olds.

Francis (1992a) compared the responses of 766 12 year olds and 955 15 year olds in England concerning their attitudes toward God, Jesus, prayer, the church, Christians and religious education. Over all these areas the data demonstrated loss of religious faith. For example, 53 per cent of 15 year olds professed belief in God, compared with 62 per cent of 12 year olds. Among 15 year olds 37 per cent believed that Jesus really rose from the dead, compared with 44 per cent of 12 year olds. Among 15 year olds 13 per cent considered that most of their best friends believe in prayer, compared with 21 per cent of 12 year olds. Among 15 year olds 15 per cent considered that most of their best friends go to church, compared with 23 per cent of 12 year olds. The proportion who considered that people who believe in God are more honest declined from 44 per cent among 12 year olds to 25 per cent among 15 year olds. The proportion who liked religious education lessons fell from 42 per cent among 12 year olds to 29 per cent among 15 year olds.

Francis and Greer (1999a) compared the responses to creationism and evolutionary theory of 1,047 third- and fourth-formers with 1,082 fifth- and sixth-formers attending Catholic and Protestant schools in Northern Ireland. They found a movement away from creationist belief as pupils grew older. For example, the proportion who believed that God created the world as described in the Bible declined from 56 per cent to 40 per cent. The proportion who accepted the idea of evolution creating everything over millions of years rose from 44 per cent to 54 per cent.

Evaluation

The foregoing review has confirmed that age is a significant factor in mapping individual differences in the values of young people. While the majority of studies have employed broader age categories than single school years, those studies which have focused specifically on the comparison between year-nine and year-ten pupils have demonstrated that significant differences occur between these two groups on a range of issues.

EXPLORING THE DATA

Aim

The aim of the present analysis is to divide the database into two distinct groups in order to compare young people in year-nine classes who are generally between 13 and 14 years of age with young people in year-ten classes who are generally between 14 and 15 years of age. The comparisons are based on 17,889 year-nine pupils and 16,041 year-ten pupils.

The main body of the present analysis maps the relationship between age and the 15 areas explored by the survey, namely personal well-being, worries, counselling, school, work, religious beliefs, church and society, the supernatural, politics, social concerns, sexual morality, substance use, right and wrong, leisure and the local area. First, however, attention is given to the demographic characteristics distinguishing the year-nine and year-ten pupils.

Demographic characteristics

SEX

Similar proportions of male and female pupils are found in the year-nine and in the year-ten classes. In year nine males account for 50.9 per cent of the respondents and in year ten for 51.1 per cent of the respondents.

SOCIAL CLASS

Social class is calculated on the classification system proposed by the Office of Population Censuses and Surveys (1980). The data demonstrate that the year-ten pupils are slightly more likely to locate their fathers within non-manual employment. Thus, 53.8 per cent of the fathers of pupils in year ten are located in non-manual employment, compared with 52.5 per cent of fathers of pupils in year nine.

RELIGION

Religious affiliation remains basically constant over the two year groups. Thus, 49.6 per cent of pupils in year nine claim no religious affiliation and so do 49.0 per cent in year ten.

Personal well-being

According to Table 3.1 levels of personal well-being remain basically stable across year nine and year ten. The same proportion of pupils in both year groups claim similar levels of positive affect in the sense of finding life really worth living and in the sense of feeling that their lives have purpose. The same proportion of pupils in both year groups claim similar levels of negative affect in the sense of often feeling depressed and in the sense of sometimes considering taking their own life. Only one of the five indicators in this section shows a *significant difference* between the two age groups, indicating a slightly higher sense of self-worth among the year-ten pupils.

Table 3.1: Personal well-being: by age

	year nine (%)	year ten (%)	χ^2	P<
I feel my life has a sense of purpose	56	56	0.9	NS
I find life really worth living	69	70	3.5	NS
I feel I am not worth much as a person	14	13	8.5	.01
I often feel depressed	52	52	0.0	NS
I have sometimes considered taking my own life	27	27	1.1	NS

Worries

Year-nine and year-ten pupils display basically the same levels of anxiety over interpersonal matters. Table 3.2 demonstrates that the same proportion of pupils in both year groups are worried about their sex life, their attractiveness to the opposite sex, how they get on with other people and getting AIDS. On the other hand, there is a significant decline in the level of anxiety displayed by the older age group in respect of personal safety: year-ten pupils are less anxious than year-nine pupils about going out alone at night in their area or about being attacked by pupils from other schools.

Table 3.2: Worries: by age

	year nine (%)	year ten (%)	χ^2	P<
I am worried about my sex life	18	18	0.5	NS
I am worried about my attractiveness to the opposite sex	35	35	2.4	NS
I am worried about getting AIDS	61	62	4.6	NS
I am worried about how I get on with other people	52	52	0.9	NS
I am worried about being attacked by pupils from other schools	21	18	42.0	.001
I am worried about going out alone at night in my area	33	30	50.7	.001

Counselling

The data presented in Table 3.3 demonstrate that the same proportion of young people in year nine and year ten often long for someone to turn to for advice. A significant shift takes place, however, between these two age groups in respect of to whom it is that they turn for this advice. Pupils in year ten are less likely than pupils in year nine to say that they find it helpful to talk about their problems with their mother or with their father. In place of this parental support, pupils in year ten are more likely than pupils in year nine to say that they find it helpful to talk about their problems with their close friends.

Table 3.3: Counselling: by age

	year nine *(%)*	*year ten* *(%)*	χ^2	*P<*
I often long for someone to turn to for advice	35	35	0.1	NS
I would be reluctant to discuss my problems with a schoolteacher	45	49	47.5	.001
I would be reluctant to discuss my problems with a youth club/group leader	46	49	35.5	.001
I would be reluctant to discuss my problems with a doctor	33	33	0.0	NS
I would be reluctant to discuss my problems with a Christian minister/vicar/priest	39	43	39.0	.001
I would be reluctant to discuss my problems with a social worker	39	40	13.1	.001
I find it helpful to talk about my problems with my mother	52	48	49.0	.001
I find it helpful to talk about my problems with my father	33	32	9.7	.01
I find it helpful to talk about my problems with close friends	62	65	38.0	.001

The second development that takes place between year nine and year ten concerns a growing reluctance to discuss problems with professional people, including schoolteachers, youth leaders, clergy and social workers. This trend does not, however, extend to doctors. The proportion of young people who are reluctant to discuss their problems with a doctor remains stable over the two year groups.

School

Three significant changes take place in the young person's attitude toward school between year nine and year ten. Two of these changes are negative in character and one is positive. The positive change is a reduction in the proportion of pupils who are worried about being bullied at school. The first negative change concerns a growing alienation from school: more pupils in year ten than in year nine describe school as boring and fewer pupils in year ten than in year nine describe themselves as happy in their school. The second negative change concerns a growing sense of school-related anxiety: more pupils in year ten than in year nine often worry about their school work and their exams at school. On the other hand, attitudes toward fellow pupils and toward teachers remain stable over the two year groups. The same proportion of pupils in year nine and in year ten like the people with whom they go to school. The same proportion of pupils in year nine and in year ten feel that teachers do a good job.

Table 3.4: School: by age

	year nine (%)	year ten (%)	χ^2	$P<$
School is boring	35	38	20.1	.001
I am happy in my school	73	70	18.5	.001
I like the people I go to school with	90	90	0.0	NS
My school is helping to prepare me for life	69	67	24.0	.001
I often worry about my school work	62	66	54.8	.001
I am worried about my exams at school	73	75	16.0	.001
I am worried about being bullied at school	30	26	95.7	.001
Teachers do a good job	45	44	1.9	NS

Work

Table 3.5 demonstrates two distinct patterns in work-related attitudes
between year nine and year ten. First, attitudes toward work itself remain
stable over this period. The same proportion of pupils in year nine and in
year ten consider that a job gives you a sense of purpose; the same
proportion of pupils in year nine and in year ten want to get to the top in
their work and think it is important to work hard when they get a job.
Second, there is a significant shift in attitude toward unemployment over
the two year groups. Pupils in year ten are less likely than pupils in year
nine to consider that they would rather be unemployed than get a job they
do not like doing. Pupils in year ten are more likely than pupils in year
nine to say that they would not like to be unemployed. At the same time
pupils in year ten are less likely than pupils in year nine to believe that
most unemployed people could have a job if they really wanted to be
employed.

Table 3.5: Work: by age

	year nine (%)	year ten (%)	χ^2	P<
A job gives you a sense of purpose	77	77	2.0	NS
I think it is important to work hard when I get a job	95	95	3.9	NS
I want to get to the top in my work when I get a job	87	87	1.5	NS
I would not like to be unemployed	85	86	14.3	.001
I would rather be unemployed on social security than get a job I don't like doing	19	17	13.8	.001
Most unemployed people could have a job if they really wanted to	53	50	19.7	.001

Religious beliefs

According to Table 3.6 there is a general decline in religious beliefs
between year nine and year ten. In comparison with pupils in year nine,
fewer pupils in year ten believe in God or believe that Jesus really rose
from the dead. Fewer pupils in year ten believe that God punishes people

who do wrong or that God made the world in six days and rested on the seventh. Fewer pupils in year ten take the view that Christianity is the only true religion. The only area of religious belief included in the survey which does not show decline over this period concerns belief in life after death: no significant difference emerges between the proportion of pupils in year nine and in year ten who believe in life after death.

Table 3.6: Religious beliefs: by age

	year nine (%)	year ten (%)	χ^2	P<
I believe in God	43	40	30.2	.001
I believe that Jesus really rose from the dead	32	28	42.9	.001
I believe in life after death	45	46	2.8	NS
I believe God punishes people who do wrong	21	19	12.2	.001
I think Christianity is the only true religion	17	16	18.0	.001
I believe that God made the world in six days and rested on the seventh	21	19	15.7	.001

Church and society

Table 3.7 demonstrates a significant deterioration in attitudes toward the place of the church in society between year nine and year ten. Compared with pupils in year nine, a higher proportion of pupils in year ten take the view that the church and that the Bible are irrelevant for life today. Compared with pupils in year nine, pupils in year ten are more inclined to dismiss the church as boring and less inclined to consider that the clergy do a good job. Year ten pupils are less inclined than year nine pupils to envisage that they will want to get married in church or have their children christened in church. Year ten pupils are much less likely than year nine pupils to consider that religious education should be taught in schools. Just two items in this section show no significant change between year nine and year ten. The proportion of pupils who consider that schools should hold a religious assembly every day is already so small that no further deterioration takes place in year ten. The same proportion of pupils in year nine and year ten believe that they can be a Christian without going to church.

Table 3.7: Church and society: by age

	year nine (%)	year ten (%)	χ^2	P<
I believe that I can be a Christian without going to church	51	50	3.0	NS
The church seems irrelevant to life today	26	29	33.6	.001
The Bible seems irrelevant to life today	29	32	39.1	.001
I want my children to be baptised/christened in church	56	53	32.1	.001
I want to get married in church	75	72	42.6	.001
Religious education should be taught in school	41	34	139.0	.001
Schools should hold a religious assembly every day	8	8	1.0	NS
Church is boring	50	53	31.1	.001
Christian ministers/vicars/ priests do a good job	37	34	39.9	.001

The supernatural

Although four of the seven items listed in Table 3.8 show a statistically significant shift between year nine and year ten, none of the figures vary by more than one or two percentage points. There is a very slight increase in the proportion of pupils in year ten compared with year nine who believe in the Devil or who believe in black magic. At the same time, there is a very slight decrease in the proportion of pupils in year ten compared with year nine who believe in ghosts. Increased self-confidence is shown in year ten by a slight decrease in the proportion of pupils who are frightened of going into a church alone. No differences occur between the two age groups in the proportion of pupils who believe in their horoscope, who believe that fortune-tellers can tell the future, or who believe that it is possible to contact the spirits of the dead.

Table 3.8: The supernatural: by age

	year nine (%)	year ten (%)	χ^2	P<
I believe in my horoscope	34	35	2.0	NS
I believe in ghosts	41	40	8.8	.01
I believe in the Devil	21	23	9.9	.01
I believe in black magic	20	21	8.1	.01
I believe that fortune-tellers can tell the future	20	20	0.2	NS
I believe it is possible to contact the spirits of the dead	31	32	4.7	NS
I am frightened of going into a church alone	12	11	16.6	.001

Politics

According to the data presented in Table 3.9 three main trends occur in political attitudes between year nine and year ten. First, attitudes toward the established political parties remain stable over this period. The same proportion of pupils in year nine and in year ten express confidence in the policies of the Conservative Party or in the policies of the Labour Party; the same proportion of pupils in year nine and in year ten take the view that it makes no difference which political party is in power. Second, there is a slight movement away from left-wing attitudes regarding education and health care: slightly fewer pupils in year ten than in year nine agree that private schools should be abolished or agree that private medicine should be abolished. Third, there is a slight movement toward right-wing racist views: slightly more pupils in year ten than in year nine say that there are too many black people living in this country or think that immigration into Britain should be restricted.

Social concerns

Pupils in year ten have a slightly greater sense than pupils in year nine of their capability of influencing the world in which they live. They are a little less likely to feel that there is nothing they can do to help solve the world's problems. The level of concern registered for world problems, however, remains basically stable over the two age groups. Roughly the same proportion of pupils in year nine and in year ten express concern about the risk of pollution to the environment. Roughly the same proportion of pupils in year nine and in year ten express concern about the poverty of the Third World. On the other hand, year-ten pupils express slightly less concern than year nine pupils about the risk of nuclear war. The level of concern registered for domestic issues does show a significant change between year nine and year ten. The older pupils express more concern than the younger pupils in respect of the availability of pornography. The younger pupils express more concern than the older pupils in respect of violence on television.

Table 3.9: Politics: by age

	year nine (%)	year ten (%)	χ^2	P<
It makes no difference which political party is in power	23	22	0.8	NS
I have confidence in the Conservative Party	15	16	0.2	NS
I have confidence in the Labour Party	20	19	6.1	NS
Private schools should be abolished	25	22	53.1	.001
Private medicine should be abolished	16	15	7.0	.01
There are too many black people living in this country	15	17	28.1	.001
I think that immigration into Britain should be restricted	28	34	144.8	.001

Table 3.10: Social concerns: by age

	year nine (%)	year ten (%)	χ^2	P<
There is too much violence on television	21	19	14.7	.001
Pornography is too readily available	32	35	22.9	.001
I am concerned about the risk of pollution to the environment	66	66	0.2	NS
I am concerned about the poverty of the Third World	60	61	4.0	NS
I am concerned about the risk of nuclear war	57	54	28.1	.001
There is nothing I can do to help solve the world's problems	26	24	8.6	.01

Sexual morality

According to Table 3.11 there is a progressive liberalisation of attitudes toward heterosexual practices and family life between year nine and year ten. Pupils in year ten are more likely than pupils in year nine to condone sexual intercourse outside marriage or to condone sexual intercourse under the legal age. Pupils in year ten are less likely than pupils in year nine to agree that contraception is wrong, to agree that abortion is wrong, or to agree that divorce is wrong. This liberalisation of attitudes toward heterosexual practices is not, however, extended to homosexual practices. The same proportion of pupils in year ten judge homosexuality to be wrong as is the case among year-nine pupils.

Table 3.11: Sexual morality: by age

	year nine (%)	year ten (%)	χ^2	$P<$
It is wrong to have sexual intercourse outside marriage	15	12	62.1	.001
It is wrong to have sexual intercourse under the legal age (16 years)	26	21	134.7	.001
Homosexuality is wrong	37	38	1.8	NS
Contraception is wrong	6	4	71.9	.001
Abortion is wrong	38	33	87.1	.001
Divorce is wrong	20	18	34.1	.001

Substance use

Table 3.12 demonstrates that there is a liberalisation in attitudes toward substance use across all substances listed in this survey between year nine and year ten. There is quite a large shift in attitudes toward tobacco and alcohol, with year-ten pupils being less likely than year-nine pupils to consider it wrong to smoke cigarettes or to become drunk. There is a smaller shift in attitudes toward marijuana, with year-ten pupils being less likely than year-nine pupils to consider it wrong to use marijuana. There is a small shift in attitudes toward hard drugs and solvents, with year-ten pupils being slightly less likely than year-nine pupils to consider it wrong to use heroin, sniff glue or sniff butane gas.

Table 3.12: Substance use: by age

	year nine (%)	year ten (%)	χ^2	P<
It is wrong to smoke cigarettes	46	39	174.5	.001
It is wrong to become drunk	22	16	198.8	.001
It is wrong to use marijuana (hash or pot)	53	49	53.0	.001
It is wrong to use heroin	74	73	10.7	.01
It is wrong to sniff glue	79	77	11.9	.001
It is wrong to sniff butane gas	74	72	13.8	.001

Right and wrong

Overall Table 3.13 demonstrates that there is a slight growth in disregard for the law between year nine and year ten. In comparison with pupils in year nine, pupils in year ten are much more likely to condone buying alcoholic drinks or cigarettes under the legal age. In comparison with pupils in year nine, pupils in year ten are also slightly more likely to condone travelling without a ticket, cycling after dark without lights, or playing truant from school. On the other hand, there are no significant differences in the proportion of the two age groups who condone shoplifting or writing graffiti. Table 3.13 also shows a significant deterioration in attitudes toward the police between the two age groups. Pupils in year ten are less likely than pupils in year nine to agree that the police do a good job.

Leisure

Only small changes take place in leisure-related attitudes between year nine and year ten. These small changes suggest three trends. First, there is a slight increase in satisfaction with the way in which leisure time is spent. This is illustrated by the fact that significantly fewer pupils in year ten than in year nine complain that they wish they had more things to do with their leisure time. Nonetheless, the same proportion of both groups say that they often hang about with their friends doing nothing in particular. Second, there is a slight hardening of attitudes toward the youth centre. This is illustrated by the fact that significantly more pupils in year ten than in year nine write off their youth centre as boring. Third, there are changing relationships with parents over the use of leisure time. This is illustrated by three different perceived responses on the part of the parents. Year-ten pupils are more likely than year-nine pupils to feel that their parents do not agree with most of the things that they do in their leisure time, that their parents prefer them to stay in as much as possible and that their parents allow them to do what they like in their leisure time.

Table 3.13: Right and wrong: by age

	year nine (%)	year ten (%)	χ^2	P<
There is nothing wrong in shoplifting	7	8	3.8	NS
There is nothing wrong in travelling without a ticket	19	22	37.5	.001
There is nothing wrong in cycling after dark without lights	16	18	36.7	.001
There is nothing wrong in playing truant (wagging) from school	16	18	30.1	.001
There is nothing wrong in buying cigarettes under the legal age (16 years)	25	34	296.8	.001
There is nothing wrong in buying alcoholic drinks under the legal age (18 years)	37	47	372.8	.001
There is nothing wrong in writing graffiti (tagging) wherever you like	14	15	2.7	NS
The police do a good job	56	52	46.9	.001

My area

The data presented in Table 3.15 demonstrate a deterioration in attitudes toward the local area between year nine and year ten. Compared with pupils in year-nine, year-ten pupils are less likely to report that they like living in their area and less likely to consider that their area cares about its young people. Compared with pupils in year nine, year ten pupils are more likely to feel that a range of problems are getting worse in their area, including crime, vandalism, violence and, above all, drug-taking. On the other hand, year-nine pupils and year-ten pupils share similar perceptions about the problem of drunks and about the problem of unemployment.

Table 3.14: Leisure: by age

	year nine (%)	year ten (%)	χ^2	P<
I often hang about with my friends doing nothing in particular	69	68	2.1	NS
I wish I had more things to do with my leisure time	59	57	9.6	.01
My youth centre is boring	34	37	21.1	.001
My parents prefer me to stay in as much as possible	20	21	8.3	.01
My parents allow me to do what I like in my leisure time	48	50	12.5	.001
My parents do not agree with most of the things that I do in my leisure time	28	30	10.3	.01

Table 3.15: My area: by age

	year nine (%)	year ten (%)	χ^2	P<
Crime is a growing problem in my area	40	44	39.6	.001
Vandalism is a growing problem in my area	44	46	15.3	.001
Drug-taking is a growing problem in my area	28	36	262.6	.001
Violence is a growing problem in my area	30	33	33.0	.001
Drunks are a growing problem in my area	24	25	2.1	NS
Unemployment is a growing problem in my area	35	36	5.9	NS
I like living in my area	76	72	75.8	.001
My area cares about its young people	24	18	142.3	.001

CONCLUSION

This chapter has compared the values of pupils in year nine with the values of pupils in year ten. The data make it clear that there are some significant detectable differences in values across this very narrow age range.

In comparison with pupils in year nine, year-ten pupils have grown in self-confidence; derive more support from close friends and less support from parents; have become more reluctant to discuss their problems with many professionals, hold a less positive attitude toward school but worry more about their school work, show a greater abhorrence of unemployment; are less likely to believe in God; feel less positive about the role of the church in society; display more racist attitudes; feel more positive about their effect on the world's future, hold more permissive attitudes toward sex outside marriage, abortion and divorce; hold more liberal attitudes toward substance use across a range of substances; see the police in a less positive light; experience more conflict with their parents over their use of leisure time; and feel less positive about the area in which they live. These findings are consistent with the wider field of research which demonstrates that age is a significant predictor of individual differences in values held by young people.

A clear weakness with the present analysis concerns the way in which the database only permits comparison to be made over a very narrow age range. It is not possible on the basis of comparing year-nine and year-ten pupils to model the kind of changes which may take place over the wider span of secondary schooling. That task remains for a comparable study which properly samples pupils from year seven, year eight and year eleven, as well as from year nine and year ten.

SEX

SETTING THE SCENE

In his classic review of sex as a key variable in social investigation, Morgan (1986) described this variable as 'both ubiquitous and hidden'. It is ubiquitous in the sense that it is one of the most common variables to be included in social surveys, almost as a matter of routine. It is hidden in the sense that the full potential of this variable is often ignored in the analysis and interpretation of data. It is also difficult to identify reviews which properly and exhaustively synthesise and explicate the findings from studies which may have included sex as an incidental rather than as a primary variable.

When, however, sex is identified as a key variable in the analysis of social attitudes, broadly conceived, this generally emerges as a highly fruitful and valuable exercise. Considering religiosity as a particular example of social attitudes, Francis (1997d) unearthed widespread cross-cultural contemporary support for the conclusion advanced earlier by Argyle and Beit-Hallahmi (1975). Argyle and Beit-Hallahmi had argued that it is in fact sex differences which constitute one of the most widely supported empirical findings within the psychology of religion.

In research of this nature the distinction between sex and gender is important. The distinction between sex and gender was defined by Oakley (1981, p. 41) in the following terms:

> sex refers to biological division into female and male; gender to the parallel and socially unequal division into femininity and masculinity.

A similar distinction was made by Matthews (1982, p. 31) as follows:

Sex is defined as the biological dichotomy between female and male, chromosomally determined and, for the most part, unalterable, while gender is that which is recognised as masculine and feminine by a social world.

In social research sex is accessed by reporting the biological dichotomy between female and male; gender or gender orientation tends to be accessed by a family of personality inventories designed to quantify masculinity and femininity within both men and women, as exampled by the Bem Sex Role Inventory (Bem, 1981).

It is not the concern of this chapter that sex differences can sometimes disintegrate under the closer inspection afforded by gender-orientation theory (Thompson, 1991; Francis and Wilcox, 1996, 1998). The concern is simply to establish what can be predicted about the world of values and attitudes from the simple knowledge that the respondent is male or female. In other words, the chapter sets out to establish the extent to which females and males inhabit the same or different universes of values.

The British Social Attitudes Survey has provided an annual report since 1984 covering a wide range of issues (see Jowell and Airey, 1984). Many of the chapters in the early editions of these annual reports published cross-tabulations by sex, although by no means all of these cross-tabulations were included in the commentary. In more recent years, as the wealth of time-trend data has increased, so less attention seems to have been given by these reports to publishing basic information on sex differences. This chapter begins, therefore, by distilling what can be gleaned from the published reports on the British Social Attitudes Survey about sex differences in values in Britain. This information has been organised within three main themes: political and social attitudes, sexual behaviour and family life, and personal matters.

After reviewing the findings of the British Social Attitudes Surveys conducted among adults, this chapter turns attention to the related survey of young people's social attitudes reported by Roberts and Sachdev (1996). The seven contributors to this report focused on the following topics: rights, rites and responsibilities; gender matters; prejudice and racial discrimination; crime, justice and punishment; educational issues; politics and the media; and religion and morality.

Political and social attitudes

The British and Social Attitudes Surveys have published data on sex differences in attitudes toward the welfare state, the monarchy, nuclear issues, environmental issues, educational issues and racial prejudice.

WELFARE STATE

Bosanquet (1984) identified differences between the attitudes of women and men toward aspects of social policy and the welfare state. Women were more inclined than men to support the view that taxes should be increased to increase social spending (34 per cent compared with 30 per cent). Women were more inclined than men to rank health care as their number one priority for extra government spending (39 per cent compared with 34 per cent). Women were more inclined than men to feel at least quite satisfied with the National Health Service (56 per cent compared with 52 per cent). This basic pattern was confirmed by Bosanquet (1994).

Bosanquet (1986) found that men and women had slightly different perceptions of the benefits afforded by the welfare state. Men were more inclined than women to feel that the welfare state encourages people to stop helping each other (35 per cent compared with 30 per cent).

MONARCHY

According to Topf, Mohler and Heath (1989) women showed a greater pride in the monarchy in comparison with men. For example, 46 per cent of women named the monarchy as the first source of their national pride, compared with 29 per cent of men.

NUCLEAR ISSUES

On the issue of nuclear weapons Young (1984) found both similarities and dissimilarities between the views of women and men. On the one hand, a smaller proportion of women (33 per cent) took the view that the siting of American nuclear missiles in Britain made Britain a safer place, compared with 45 per cent of men. On the other hand, a slightly higher proportion of women (79 per cent) than men (76 per cent) argued that Britain should keep its nuclear weapons until other nations also agreed to reduce theirs. A similar pattern of responses was identified by Whiteley (1985) and Young (1986, 1987a, 1990).

Young (1985b) found significant differences between the attitudes of women and men toward nuclear power. For example, 41 per cent of women considered that there were very serious risks from nuclear power stations, compared with 34 per cent of men. While 22 per cent of men argued for more nuclear power stations as a solution to Britain's energy needs, the proportion fell to 10 per cent among women. A similar picture was provided by Young (1987a, 1990).

Young (1990) found that a higher proportion of women than men considered that nuclear war was quite or very likely (8 per cent compared with 4 per cent).

ENVIRONMENTAL ISSUES

Young (1986) reported some significant differences between the attitudes of women and men toward the countryside and toward the farming community. Men were more likely than women to consider urban growth and housing development to pose a major threat to the countryside (26 per cent compared with 23 per cent). Women were more likely than men to consider litter to pose a major threat to the countryside (31 per cent compared with 20 per cent). While 71 per cent of men considered that farmers do a good job looking after the countryside, the proportion rose to 79 per cent among women. Similar findings were reported by Young (1987b, 1988).

Young (1991) found a higher level of environmental concern among women than among men across a range of issues. For example, 74 per cent of women expressed concern about the disposal of sewage compared with 64 per cent of men; 62 per cent of women expressed concern about insecticides, fertilisers and chemical sprays, compared with 51 per cent of men; 56 per cent of women expressed concern about the quality of drinking water, compared with 45 per cent of men. More women than men rated the following issues as very serious: cutting down tropical rainforests (69 per cent compared with 67 per cent), industrial fumes in the air (60 per cent compared with 54 per cent) and aerosol chemicals in the air (55 per cent compared with 47 per cent).

EDUCATIONAL ISSUES

Goldstein (1984) identified some key differences in the educational priorities of women and men. Women were more likely than men to identify the highest priority for extra government spending on education as provision for less able children with special needs (37 per cent compared with 27 per cent) and as nursery and pre-school children (13 per cent compared with 7 per cent). Men were more likely than women to identify the highest priority as secondary school children (33 per cent compared with 25 per cent) and as students at colleges or universities (12 per cent compared with 7 per cent). A similar pattern of responses was reported by Goldstein (1986) and Halsey (1991).

According to Goldstein (1984) women tended to show greater sensitivity than men for educational provision to acknowledge cultural diversity. For example, 46 per cent of women argued that schools should allow traditional dress for those to whom this is an important matter, compared with 40 per cent of men. Similarly, 35 per cent of women supported the provision of separate religious instruction if requested by parents, compared with 29 per cent of men.

Goldstein (1986) demonstrated slightly less support for private schools among men than among women. While 14 per cent of women proposed that private schools should be abolished, the proportion rose to 18 per cent among men.

RACIAL PREJUDICE

According to Airey (1984) women were slightly less inclined than men to see themselves as racially prejudiced. Thus, 33 per cent of women said that they were at least a little prejudiced against people of other races, compared with 39 per cent of men. On the other hand, when pressed women actually appeared more prejudiced in some ways. For example, 54 per cent of women said that they would mind if one of their close relatives were to marry a person of Asian origin, compared with 49 per cent of men. Similarly, 60 per cent of women said that they would mind if one of their close relatives were to marry a person of West Indian origin, compared with 55 per cent of men.

Sexual behaviour and family life

The British Social Attitudes Surveys have published data on sex differences in attitudes toward sexual behaviour, AIDS, divorce, child support, single-parent families, abortion, surrogacy, pornography and gender roles.

SEXUAL BEHAVIOUR

On the issue of sex before marriage, Airey (1984) found a less permissive view among women. While 22 per cent of men considered that sex before marriage was always or mostly wrong, the proportion rose to 33 per cent among women. A similar pattern was found by Wellings and Wadsworth (1990).

On the issue of sexual relations between two adults of the same sex, Airey (1984) found a more permissive view among women. While 67 per cent of men considered this to be wrong, the proportion fell to 57 per cent among women. A similar pattern was found by Wellings and Wadsworth (1990).

Airey and Brook (1986) found women to be more tolerant than men toward homosexuals. For example, 39 per cent of women agreed that it was acceptable for a homosexual person to be a teacher in a school, compared with 33 per cent of men; 54 per cent of women agreed that it was acceptable for a homosexual person to hold a responsible position, compared with 46 per cent of men.

According to Harding (1988), men were more likely than women to agree that doctors should be allowed to give contraceptive advice and supplies to young people under 16 without having to inform parents (35 per cent compared with 27 per cent).

AIDS

According to Brook (1988), men displayed a less sympathetic attitude toward those suffering from AIDS. For example, 42 per cent of men supported the view that employers should have the legal right to dismiss people who have AIDS, compared with 34 per cent of women. According to Wellings and Wadsworth (1990), women were less likely to argue that AIDS sufferers have only themselves to blame (52 per cent compared with 59 per cent).

DIVORCE

Ashford (1987) found that women were more likely than men to agree that divorce in Britain should be made more difficult to obtain (46 per cent compared with 31 per cent). At the same time, women were more likely than men to argue that as a society we ought to do more to safeguard the institution of marriage (75 per cent compared with 67 per cent). On the other hand, according to Scott (1990) women may have lower expectations of marriage. Thus, 31 per cent of women agreed that married people are generally happier than unmarried people, compared with 36 per cent of men.

The analysis afforded by Scott, Braun and Alwin (1993) demonstrated that women were more likely than men to consider that divorce is better than staying together in an unhappy marriage. Women were more likely than men to think that ending an unhappy marriage is better for the children (66 per cent compared with 52 per cent) and better for the wife (72 per cent compared with 59 per cent) and better for the husband (71 per cent compared with 59 per cent).

CHILD SUPPORT

Kiernan (1992a) found that men and women held different views on some aspects of child support after divorce. While 32 per cent of men agreed that on a mother's remarriage child maintenance from the father should continue irrespective of the new husband's income, the proportion rose to 51 per cent among the women.

SINGLE-PARENT FAMILIES

Scott (1990) found significant differences between the views of men and women on single-parent families. For example, 35 per cent of women argued that a single mother can bring up her child as well as a married couple, compared with 25 per cent of men; 28 per cent of women argued that a single father can bring up his child as well as a married couple, compared with 19 per cent of men.

ABORTION

Some significant differences in attitudes toward abortion have been found among women and men. For example, according to Airey and Brook (1986) women were less likely than men to believe that the law should allow an abortion when the couple agree they do not wish to have the child (50 per cent compared with 60 per cent).

SURROGACY

Airey and Brook (1986) found significant differences in attitude toward surrogacy among men and women. While 52 per cent of men agreed that the law should permit surrogate mothers without payment, the proportion fell to 42 per cent among women. While 32 per cent of men agreed that the law should permit surrogate mothers with payment, the proportion fell to 23 per cent among women.

PORNOGRAPHY

On the issue of the availability of pornographic magazines and films, Airey (1984) found a less permissive view among women. While 23 per cent of men considered that pornographic magazines and films should be banned altogether, the proportion rose to 37 per cent among women. A similar pattern was reported by Harding (1988).

GENDER ROLES

Scott (1990) found significant differences in the attitude of men and women toward gender roles. Women were more likely than men to agree that a working mother can establish as warm and secure a relationship with her children as a mother who does not work (63 per cent compared with 51 per cent). Women were more likely than men to agree that a woman and her family will all be happier if she goes out to work (22 per cent compared with 14 per cent). Looking at the issue from the opposite perspective, women were more likely than men to disagree that a husband's job is to earn money while a wife's job is to look after the home and family (57 per cent compared with 47 per cent). A similar pattern was reported by Scott, Braun and Alwin (1993).

Airey (1984) found a greater tendency for women to maintain a traditional division of family jobs. Women were more likely than men to consider that women should mainly be responsible for doing the household cleaning (74 per cent compared with 69 per cent) and for doing the evening dishes (44 per cent compared with 37 per cent).

Looking at the issue from a different angle, Witherspoon (1985) found that men and women had somewhat different perspectives on the actual division of labour which took place within their own home. While 34 per cent of men considered that the evening dishes were done mainly by the women in their home, 41 per cent of women took this view. While 87 per cent of men considered that the repairs to household equipment were done mainly by men in their home, the proportion fell to 79 per cent among women. Similar findings were reported by Witherspoon (1988).

Personal matters

The British Social Attitudes Surveys have published data on sex differences in attitudes toward religion, smoking, diet, honesty, work, fear and optimism.

RELIGION

Greeley (1992) reported significant differences in the proportions of men and women who expressed religious belief, experience, practice and affiliation. On all criteria women were more religious than men. While 76 per cent of women believed in God, the proportion dropped to 60 per cent of the men. While 61 per cent of women believed in life after death, the proportion fell to 47 per cent among men. While 50 per cent of the women believed in religious miracles, the proportion fell to 40 per cent among the men. Seven out of ten (69 per cent) women were affiliated to a religious group, compared with 58 per cent of men. One in three (33 per cent) women prayed weekly, compared with 21 per cent of men. One in five (19 per cent) women attended religious services at least twice a month, compared with 12 per cent of men. One in two (52 per cent) women said that they felt close to God, compared with 38 per cent of men.

Greeley's analysis also demonstrated that women held a more positive attitude than men toward the church and toward the place of religion in school. For example, 62 per cent of the women reported that they had confidence in the churches, compared with 53 per cent of the men. Looked at from a different perspective, 24 per cent of women criticised the churches for having too much power, compared with 33 per cent of men.

On the subject of religion in school, 74 per cent of women favoured school prayers, compared with 66 per cent of men.

SMOKING

Ben-Shlomo, Sheiham and Marmot (1991) found that in the population as a whole there was a higher proportion of smokers among men than among women, but within the general population there were significant age differences. Thus, among 18–34 year olds 31 per cent of men and 33 per cent of women smoked; among 35–54 year olds 34 per cent of men and 25 per cent of women smoked; among those aged 55 and over 19 per cent of men and 18 per cent of women smoked. This analysis also found a more negative attitude toward passive smoking among women across the age groups. Thus, 80 per cent of women regarded passive smoking as at least a fairly serious health risk, compared with 66 per cent of men.

DIET

Sheiham et al. (1987) classified more than half of women as healthy eaters, compared with less than two-fifths of men. Fewer women than men agreed that as long as you take enough exercise you can eat whatever foods you want (25 per cent compared with 37 per cent). More women than men reported that they had changed their diet to healthier eating. Thus, 38 per cent of women were drinking less full cream milk than two or three years previously, compared with 27 per cent of men.

HONESTY

Johnson (1988) reported the responses of men and women to a series of questions about their willingness to keep extra change given to them in a shop, to pocket money found in the street, and to overclaim on insurance. He found that men were more likely than women to say that they would keep extra change given in the corner shop to make £5 (13 per cent compared with 8 per cent), to keep extra change given in a large store to make £5 (28 per cent compared with 20 per cent) and to over claim on insurance to make £100 (33 per cent compared with 21 per cent). Men were also more likely than women to say that they would pocket money found lying on the pavement. Thus, 76 per cent of men and 63 per cent of women would pocket £5; 59 per cent of men and 38 per cent of women would pocket £20; 29 per cent of men and 15 per cent of women would pocket £100. Young (1985b) found that men were more likely than women to consider that they would break a law to which they were strongly opposed (37 per cent compared with 22 per cent).

WORK

Mann (1986) found a slightly lower level of commitment to work among women than among men. For example, in response to a question which hypothesised that the respondent could maintain a reasonable standard of living without having to work, 75 per cent of men said that they would still prefer to have a paid job. The proportion fell to 68 per cent among women.

In an analysis of reasons for working, Witherspoon (1985) found that women were more likely to highlight the social dimension. Thus, 36 per cent of women gave company of other people as a reason for working, compared with 16 per cent of men. A similar pattern was reported by Kiernan (1992a).

FEAR

Dowds and Ahrendt (1995) found significant differences in the levels of crime-related fear displayed by women and men. For example, 43 per cent of women said that they avoid going out at certain times, compared with 15 per cent of men; 44 per cent of women said that they avoid going to certain places, compared with 35 per cent of men. While 3 per cent of men claimed that they do not go out alone, the proportion rose to 17 per cent among women. While 3 per cent of men made the point that they avoid public transport, the proportion rose to 7 per cent among women. Similarly, 8 per cent of women carry a personal alarm or weapon, compared with 2 per cent of men.

OPTIMISM

Several studies suggest that women tend to take a more pessimistic view of the future in comparison with men. For example, Harrison (1984) found that 28 per cent of women expected inflation to have gone up a lot within the next year, compared with 20 per cent of men. Goodhardt (1985) found that 37 per cent of women expected prices to have gone up a lot within the next year, compared with 25 per cent of men.

Young people's social attitudes

In his analysis of rights, rites and responsibilities, Newman (1996) concluded that sex was not overall a very significant factor in shaping the age at which young people thought it appropriate to accept adult responsibilities. There were, however, some interesting sex differences. A higher proportion of young men (27 per cent) than young women (20 per cent) wished to lower the age for driving cars to 16 years. A higher proportion of young men (24 per cent) than young women (19 per cent) considered that the legal age for marriage should be 16 years, while 41 per cent of young men and 46 per cent of young women considered that the legal age for marriage should be 18 years.

Young men were rather more confident than young women at being left alone for the evening: 22 per cent of young men felt that this was appropriate between the ages of 8 and 12, compared with 17 per cent of young women. Young men were less willing than young women to be involved in household chores at an early age. For example, 25 per cent of young men considered that children under the age of 10 should help with the washing up, compared with 37 per cent of young women. Similarly, 42 per cent of young men considered that children under the age of 10 should make their own beds, compared with 56 per cent of young women.

In her analysis of gender matters, Oakley (1996) found young men revealing themselves as more conventional and pro-marriage than young women. For example, 66 per cent of young women maintained that one parent can bring up a child as well as two parents, compared with 45 per cent of young men. While 22 per cent of young men took the view that, when there are children in the family, parents should stay together even if they do not get along, the proportion fell further to 14 per cent among young women. Just 3 per cent of young women believed that it is better to have a bad marriage than no marriage at all, compared with 11 per cent of young men.

According to these data young men held more traditional views of gender roles. While 75 per cent of young women believed that a working mother can establish just as warm and secure a relationship with her child as a mother who does not work, the proportion fell to 63 per cent among young men. While 18 per cent of young men argued that it is not good if the man stays at home and cares for the children and the woman goes out to work, the proportion of women taking this view was only 10 per cent. Twice as many young men (14 per cent) as young women (7 per cent) said that a man's job is to earn money while a woman's job is to look after the home and family.

The view that housework should be shared equally by women and men was given greater support by young women. For example, young women were more likely than the young men to argue that the following tasks should be equally shared: making the evening meal (88 per cent compared with 74 per cent), grocery shopping (84 per cent compared with 75 per cent), washing and ironing (82 per cent compared with 73 per cent), looking after sick members of the family (83 per cent compared with 69 per cent) and household repairs (55 per cent compared with 35 per cent).

Young men were more likely than young women to regard certain jobs as better suited for one sex than for the other. For example, young men were less likely than young women to consider the following work equally suitable for men and women: general medical practitioner (89 per cent compared with 97 per cent), nurse (74 per cent compared with 87 per cent), police officer (79 per cent compared with 89 per cent), airline pilot (66 per cent compared with 71 per cent), car mechanic (45 per cent compared with 69 per cent) and secretary (49 per cent compared with 60 per cent).

When asked to rate their main ambition in life, young women and young men revealed some differences. Both placed being happy at the top of the list, but then young women did so a little more emphatically than young men (47 per cent compared with 40 per cent). More young men than young women gave emphasis to being well off (14 per cent compared with 3 per cent).

In her analysis of racial prejudice and racial discrimination, Sachdev (1996) found that young women perceived a greater level of prejudice in comparison with young men. Thus, 57 per cent of young women considered that there was a lot of prejudice against Asian people, compared with 45 per cent of young men; 44 per cent of young women considered that there was a lot of prejudice against black people, compared with 36 per cent of young men. At the same time, young women were less likely than young men to adopt racist attitudes themselves.

In her analysis of crime, justice and punishment, McNeish (1996) found that young women displayed more fear of crime in comparison with young men. For example, 67 per cent of young women said that they worry about the possibility that they or others living with them might become the victim of crime, compared with 56 per cent of young men. Only 5 per cent of young women said that they feel very safe walking alone after dark in their area, compared with 22 per cent of young men.

As a consequence of this greater fear, young women were more likely than young men to take precautions to avoid crime. For example, 30 per cent of young women did not go out alone, compared with 12 per cent of young men. Similarly, 16 per cent of young women said that they never answered the door, compared with 7 per cent of young men.

These data also pointed to some differences in perceptions of the justice system among young women and young men. Young women were slightly more likely to see the justice system as unfair on grounds of race: 47 per cent of young women thought a black person was more likely to be found guilty, compared with 41 per cent of young men. Young men were slightly more likely to see the justice system as unfair on the grounds of poverty: 67 per cent of young men thought a poor person more likely to be found guilty, compared with 62 per cent of young women.

While young women and young men generally shared similar views on the effectiveness of various means of crime prevention, there was one issue over which their views differed significantly. Young women were more inclined than young men to believe that reducing crime and violence on television would be effective: 60 per cent of young women thought reducing crime on television would be very or quite effective, compared with 44 per cent of young men.

Young women and young men adopted a slightly different perspective on the best way of dealing with a first-time under-16-year-old burglar. Young men were slightly more likely than young women to let such culprits off with a strong warning in preference to community service or sending them to an institution (31 per cent compared with 24 per cent). On the issue of capital punishment, however, young men took a tougher stance than young women. While 21 per cent of young women were firmly against the view that British courts should be able to sentence murderers to death, the proportion fell to 14 per cent among young men.

In their analysis of views on education, Hughes and Lloyd (1996) found that a higher proportion of young men than young women rated having a good education as essential for doing well in life (29 per cent compared with 22 per cent). Young women were more likely than young men to feel that a lot of bullying occurred in their present or most recent school (30 per cent compared with 25 per cent). Young women and young men had somewhat different emphases on how the problem of bullying could be tackled. Young men (29 per cent) were more likely than young women (23 per cent) to favour temporary suspension from school, while young women (33 per cent) were more likely than young men (28 per cent) to recommend expulsion. Young women were also more likely than young men to recommend the expulsion of pupils who threatened a teacher (61 per cent compared with 46 per cent).

In his analysis of views on politics and the media, Walker (1996) drew attention to the somewhat lower interest shown in politics by young women in comparison with young men: 64 per cent of young women said that they either had no interest or not very much interest in politics, compared with 52 per cent of young men. These data also demonstrated that young women were less likely than young men to read a newspaper at least three times a week (41 per cent compared with 50 per cent).

In her analysis of religion and morality, Roberts (1996) highlighted sex differences in religiosity. Young women were more likely than young men to regard themselves as belonging to a particular religious group (52 per cent compared with 39 per cent) and to believe in God (61 per cent compared with 56 per cent).

Young women demonstrated a higher level of law-abiding tendencies. When asked if they would pocket money found in an empty street, young men were more likely to do so irrespective of the value specified. Thus, 81 per cent of young men would keep £5, compared with 73 per cent of young women; 61 per cent of young men would keep £20, compared with 49 per cent of young women; 27 per cent of young men would keep £100, compared with 22 per cent of young women.

Evaluation

The foregoing analysis of what is known about sex differences in British social attitudes, both among adults and among young people, leads to two key conclusions. First, the evidence confirms Morgan's (1986) assertion that sex, although present in the database, often remains an unexplored and unexploited variable. In this sense sex differences remain hidden. Second, the evidence highlights the power of sex to predict individual differences across a wide range of attitudes and values. In this sense, once uncovered the hidden variable of sex asserts itself as of considerable importance in understanding contemporary society and the values by which that society is shaped.

EXPLORING THE DATA

Aim

The aim of the present analysis is to divide the database into two distinct groups in order to compare the responses of females and males. This analysis is based on 16,632 females and 17,340 males.

The main body of the analysis maps the relationship between sex and the 15 areas explored by the values survey, namely personal well-being, worries, counselling, school, work, religious beliefs, church and society, the supernatural, politics, social concerns, sexual morality, substance use, right and wrong, leisure and the local area. First, however, attention is given to the demographic characteristics of the two groups.

Demographic characteristics

AGE

The data confirm that the same balance between females and males occurs in year nine and year ten. Young women account for 49.1 per cent of the pupils in year nine and 48.9 per cent of the pupils in year ten.

SOCIAL CLASS

Social class is calculated on the classification system proposed by the Office of Population Censuses and Surveys (1980). The data demonstrate that similar proportions of young women (52.8 per cent) and young men (53.3 per cent) report that their fathers are engaged in non-manual occupations. This finding is consistent with the view that the sex of the child is irrelevant to the nature of paternal employment.

RELIGION

Sex remains an important predictor of differences in religiosity. The data demonstrate that young women are much more likely than young men to claim religious affiliation. Thus, while 53.2 per cent of young men report that they are affiliated to no religious group, the proportion falls to 45.1 per cent among young women.

Consequently many of the major Christian denominations are found to have more female members than male members. For example, among the Anglicans 53.6 per cent of members are female, among the Baptists 56.1 per cent, among the Methodists 57.6 per cent, among the Pentecostals 54.9 per cent and among the Presbyterian 55.2 per cent. The balance of membership among the Roman Catholics, however, more closely reflects the balance between females and males in the sample as a whole. Among Roman Catholics 49.8 per cent of members are female.

Among non-Christian faith groups the following pattern emerges. The Jewish and Hindu traditions attract a higher proportion of females: among self identified Jews 53.8 per cent are female and among the self-identified Hindus 54.1 per cent are female. The Sikh tradition attracts a balance between males and females: among the self-identified Sikhs 50.2 per cent are female. The Islamic tradition attracts a higher proportion of males: among the self-identified Muslims 47.8 per cent are female.

Personal well-being

Table 4.1 demonstrates that on many criteria young women report a lower level of personal well-being in comparison with the young men. Young women are less likely than young men to find life really worth living. Young women are more likely than young men to feel that they are not worth much as a person. Young women are more likely than young men to feel depressed and to consider taking their own life.

Worries

According to Table 4.2 young women are generally more anxious about life in comparison with young men. The largest difference is in respect of personal safety. Young women are much more anxious than young men about going out alone at night in their home area. The second largest differences are found in respect of relationships: young women worry more than young men about how they get on with other people and about their attractiveness to the opposite sex. The third area of difference is found in respect of sex. Young women worry slightly more than young men about their sex lives. On the other hand, there are no significant differences between young women and young men in respect of worry about being attacked by pupils from other schools or in respect of worrying about getting AIDS.

Table 4.1: Personal well-being: by sex

	male (%)	female (%)	χ^2	P<
I feel my life has a sense of purpose	56	56	1.5	NS
I find life really worth living	73	65	279.9	.001
I feel I am not worth much as a person	12	15	42.9	.001
I often feel depressed	45	60	685.4	.001
I have sometimes considered taking my own life	24	30	144.1	.001

Table 4.2: Worries: by sex

	male (%)	female (%)	χ^2	P<
I am worried about my sex life	16	19	37.4	.001
I am worried about my attractiveness to the opposite sex	30	41	449.6	.001
I am worried about getting AIDS	61	62	2.8	NS
I am worried about how I get on with other people	48	56	201.9	.001
I am worried about being attacked by pupils from other schools	20	19	4.9	NS
I am worried about going out alone at night in my area	19	45	2561.1	.001

Counselling

Young women are much more likely than young men to say that they often long for someone to turn to for advice. Young women also derive much more help than young men from talking about their problems with close friends. Table 4.3 also highlights the way in which young men and young women perceive their parents in different ways. Father is a greater source of help to his sons than to his daughters. Mother is a greater source of help to her daughters than to her sons. A higher proportion of young women say that they find it helpful to talk about their problems with their mother than is the case for young men. At the same time, a higher proportion of young men say that they find it helpful to talk about their problems with their father than is the case for young women.

Table 4.3: Counselling: by sex

	male (%)	female (%)	χ^2	P<
I often long for someone to turn to for advice	29	41	479.4	.001
I would be reluctant to discuss my problems with a schoolteacher	47	46	2.7	NS
I would be reluctant to discuss my problems with a youth club/group leader	49	46	16.1	.001
I would be reluctant to discuss my problems with a doctor	32	35	30.4	.001
I would be reluctant to discuss my problems with a Christian minister/vicar/priest	41	41	2.4	NS
I would be reluctant to discuss my problems with a social worker	43	36	178.4	.001
I find it helpful to talk about my problems with my mother	43	57	694.5	.001
I find it helpful to talk about my problems with my father	40	25	846.2	.001
I find it helpful to talk about my problems with close friends	48	79	3338.7	.001

There are both similarities and differences between the sexes in the ways in which they perceive the caring professions. First, young women and young men are equally reluctant to discuss their problems with a schoolteacher or a Christian minister. Second, young women are slightly less reluctant than young men to discuss their problems with a youth leader and considerably less reluctant than young men to discuss their problems with a social worker. Third, young women are slightly more reluctant than young men to discuss their problems with a doctor.

School

Four main patterns emerge from the comparison between the responses of young women and young men toward school. First, young women project a more positive attitude than young men toward school overall: they are more likely than young men to say that they are happy in their school and that they like the people with whom they attend school and they are less likely than young men to dismiss school as boring. Second, although young women project an overall more positive attitude, they are less convinced about the practical benefit of schooling: they are slightly less likely than the young men to feel that school is helping to prepare them for life. Third, young women generally display a higher level of school-related anxiety than young men: they are more likely than young men to worry about their school work and their exams. Young women are also more worried about being bullied at school. Fourth, there is no significant difference between the perceptions of young women and young men regarding the job done by teachers. Similar proportions of both sexes feel that teachers do a good job.

Table 4.4: School: by sex

	male (%)	*female* (%)	χ^2	*P*<
School is boring	40	33	152.5	.001
I am happy in my school	70	73	28.7	.001
I like the people I go to school with	88	91	85.5	.001
My school is helping to prepare me for life	70	66	49.2	.001
I often worry about my school work	60	68	222.0	.001
I am worried about my exams at school	68	81	699.3	.001
I am worried about being bullied at school	25	31	153.5	.001
Teachers do a good job	44	45	5.3	NS

Work

The section on work reveals two main differences between the attitudes of the sexes. First, young women are slightly less likely than young men to rate highly the importance of work to their lives. This is illustrated by the way in which young women are less likely than young men to feel that a job gives people a sense of purpose in life, and by the way in which they are less likely to want to get to the top in their work when they get a job. On the other hand, young women are even more likely than young men to feel that it is important to work hard when they get a job. Second, young women display a slightly higher level of distaste than young men for the prospect of unemployment. This is illustrated by the way in which young women are more likely than young men to say that they would not like to be unemployed and by the way in which young women are less likely than young men to say that they would rather be unemployed than get a job they do not like doing. On the other hand, young women are less likely than young men to consider that most unemployed people could have a job if they really wanted to be employed.

Table 4.5: Work: by sex

	male (%)	*female* (%)	χ^2	*P<*
A job gives you a sense of purpose	79	75	98.0	.001
I think it is important to work hard when I get a job	94	96	71.4	.001
I want to get to the top in my work when I get a job	89	84	183.8	.001
I would not like to be unemployed	84	87	46.7	.001
I would rather be unemployed on social security than get a job I don't like doing	20	17	65.4	.001
Most unemployed people could have a job if they really wanted to	56	47	223.0	.001

Religious beliefs

Table 4.6 demonstrates that young women hold a higher level of religious belief in comparison with young men. Young women are more likely than young men to believe in God, to believe that Jesus really rose from the dead and to believe in life after death. Young women are also more inclined than young men to hold the creationist view that God made the world in six days and rested on the seventh. They are, however, less committed to the view that Christianity is the only true religion. Just one item in this section fails to distinguish between the sexes. Young women and young men are equally likely to hold the view that God punishes people who do wrong.

Table 4.6: Religious beliefs: by sex

	male (%)	*female (%)*	χ^2	*P<*
I believe in God	38	45	156.0	.001
I believe that Jesus really rose from the dead	29	32	36.9	.001
I believe in life after death	44	46	15.7	.001
I believe God punishes people who do wrong	20	21	2.0	NS
I think Christianity is the only true religion	18	14	99.9	.001
I believe that God made the world in six days and rested on the seventh	19	21	23.5	.001

Church and society

It is clear from Table 4.7 that young women hold a more positive view than young men concerning the role of church in society. This is highlighted by five comparisons. First, young women are more likely than young men to feel that both the Bible and the church hold relevance for life today. They are less likely to dismiss the church as boring. Second, young women are more likely than young men to envisage the church playing a role in the major rites of passage within their own lives: a higher proportion of young women than young men say that they want to get married in church and have their children christened in church. Third, young women are more likely than young men to support the place of religion in school. A higher proportion of young women than young men argue that religious education should be taught in school and that schools should hold a religious assembly every day. Fourth, the more positive attitude which young women show toward the role of the church in society may be based more on a commitment to Christianity as an ethical system than to radical commitment to church attendance: in comparison with young men, a higher proportion of young women maintain that they can be a Christian without going to church. Finally, there is no significant difference between the perceptions of young women and young men regarding the job done by the clergy: similar proportions of both sexes feel that Christian ministers do a good job.

Table 4.7: Church and society: by sex

	male (%)	female (%)	χ^2	P<
I believe that I can be a Christian without going to church	48	54	111.7	.001
The church seems irrelevant to life today	33	22	553.2	.001
The Bible seems irrelevant to life today	36	26	391.4	.001
I want my children to be baptised/christened in church	49	60	424.5	.001
I want to get married in church	68	79	479.8	.001
Religious education should be taught in school	33	42	308.5	.001
Schools should hold a religious assembly every day	8	9	8.9	.001
Church is boring	56	46	340.1	.001
Christian ministers/vicars/ priests do a good job	36	35	5.6	NS

The supernatural

One way of classifying the range of items included in this section distinguishes between positive or potentially life-enhancing supernatural beliefs and negative or potentially life-threatening supernatural beliefs. According to this classification an important difference emerges between the sexes. Table 4.8 shows that young women are more likely than young men to espouse potentially positive aspects of the supernatural: they are more likely to believe in their horoscope, to believe that fortune-tellers can tell the future and to believe that it is possible to contact the spirits of the dead. Table 4.8 shows that young men are more likely than young women to espouse the potentially negative aspects of the supernatural: they are more likely to believe in black magic and to believe in the Devil. On this distinction between potentially positive and potentially negative aspects of the supernatural, belief in ghosts might hold an ambivalent position. Some ghosts may be life-threatening while other ghosts may be life-enhancing. Significantly, belief in this item does not distinguish between the sexes. Finally, there is no significant difference between the proportions of young men and young women who are frightened of going into a church alone.

Table 4.8: The supernatural: by sex

	male (%)	female (%)	χ^2	P<
I believe in my horoscope	23	47	2000.7	.001
I believe in ghosts	40	40	0.0	NS
I believe in the Devil	24	20	87.6	.001
I believe in black magic	23	18	127.6	.001
I believe that fortune-tellers can tell the future	14	25	677.5	.001
I believe it is possible to contact the spirits of the dead	29	33	70.0	.001
I am frightened of going into a church alone	11	12	2.9	NS

Politics

The data presented in Table 4.9 demonstrate that young women show a considerably lower level of commitment to politics than young men. This is illustrated by the fact that young women are less likely than young men to express confidence in the policies of either the Labour Party or the Conservative Party. On the other hand, very little real difference emerges between the proportions of young women and young men who consider that it makes no difference which political party is in power. Young women are less likely than young men to show commitment to ideological reforms, like the abolition of private medicine or the abolition of private schools. Finally, this section shows young women to be considerably less racist in their attitudes in comparison with young men: they are much less likely than young men to maintain that there are too many black people living in their country or that immigration into Britain should be restricted.

Social concerns

The data presented in Table 4.10 demonstrate that young women display a significantly higher level of concern than young men in respect of both domestic and world issues. In comparison with young men, a higher proportion of young women feel that there is too much violence on television and that pornography is too readily available. And a higher proportion of young women are concerned about the poverty of the Third World, about the risk of pollution to the environment and about the risk of nuclear war. At the same time, young women are less likely than young men to take a pessimistic or cynical view about their influence on such matters. Thus, significantly fewer young women than young men express the view that there is nothing that they can do to help solve the world's problems.

Table 4.9: Politics: by sex

	male (%)	female (%)	χ^2	P<
It makes no difference which political party is in power	23	22	12.9	.001
I have confidence in the Conservative Party	18	12	234.4	.001
I have confidence in the Labour Party	22	17	127.9	.001
Private schools should be abolished	28	20	288.7	.001
Private medicine should be abolished	17	14	54.0	.001
There are too many black people living in this country	23	9	1032.7	.001
I think that immigration into Britain should be restricted	40	21	1337.6	.001

Table 4.10: Social concerns: by sex

	male (%)	female (%)	χ^2	P<
There is too much violence on television	16	25	381.0	.001
Pornography is too readily available	26	41	813.9	.001
I am concerned about the risk of pollution to the environment	65	67	10.7	.01
I am concerned about the poverty of the Third World	55	67	526.0	.001
I am concerned about the risk of nuclear war	54	57	27.0	.001
There is nothing I can do to help solve the world's problems	30	20	458.9	.001

Sexual morality

According to Table 4.11 there are five key significant differences between
the values of young women and young men in the area of sexual morality
and family life. First, the largest difference is to be found in the area of
homosexuality: young women are much less likely than young men to
judge homosexuality to be wrong. Second, the next largest difference is to
be found in the area of sexual intercourse under the legal age. Young
women are more likely than young men to judge sexual intercourse under
the legal age to be wrong. Third, young women take a more conservative
view than young men on the subject of abortion, with a higher proportion
of young women judging abortion to be wrong. Fourth, young men take a
more conservative view than young women on the subject of divorce, with
more young men judging it to be wrong. Fifth, a slightly higher proportion
of young men than young women judge contraception to be wrong. On the
other hand, there is no significant difference between the views of young
women and young men on the issue of sexual intercourse outside marriage.

Table 4.11: Sexual morality: by sex

	male (%)	female (%)	χ^2	P<
It is wrong to have sexual intercourse outside marriage	14	14	5.2	NS
It is wrong to have sexual intercourse under the legal age (16 years)	19	29	472.7	.001
Homosexuality is wrong	53	21	3535.9	.001
Contraception is wrong	7	3	269.1	.001
Abortion is wrong	32	39	180.8	.001
Divorce is wrong	23	15	283.3	.001

Substance use

According to Table 4.12 young women hold a less permissive attitude than
young men toward a range of substances. Young women are less likely
than young men to condone the use of marijuana, heroin, glue or butane
gas. On the other hand, young women hold a more permissive attitude than
young men toward tobacco: they are less likely than young men to judge
smoking cigarettes to be wrong. Finally, there is no significant difference
between the proportions of young women and young men who judge it
wrong to become drunk.

Table 4.12: Substance use: by sex

	male (%)	female (%)	χ^2	P<
It is wrong to smoke cigarettes	47	39	262.3	.001
It is wrong to become drunk	20	19	1.8	NS
It is wrong to use marijuana (hash or pot)	49	53	51.3	.001
It is wrong to use heroin	71	76	111.2	.001
It is wrong to sniff glue	76	80	94.0	.001
It is wrong to sniff butane gas	70	76	97.6	.001

Right and wrong

Three main conclusions emerge from the pattern of responses in this section. First, over many issues young women display a more law-abiding attitude than young men. Young women are less likely than young men to condone shoplifting, travelling without a ticket, cycling after dark without lights, writing graffiti, playing truant from school or buying alcoholic drinks under the legal age. Second, the more permissive attitude toward smoking among young women identified in the previous section is reflected in their greater willingness to break the law in support of this habit: although young women are more reluctant than young men to condone buying alcoholic drinks under the legal age, they are less reluctant than young men to condone buying cigarettes under the legal age. Third, young women hold a more positive attitude than young men toward the police, with a higher proportion of young women agreeing that the police do a good job.

Leisure

Two main differences between the sexes emerge in this section. First, young women generally report a slightly lower level of satisfaction with their leisure time: and they are more likely than young men to wish that they had more things to do with their leisure time. Young women are more likely than young men to report that they hang about with their friends doing nothing in particular. Young women are slightly less likely than young men to say that their youth centre is boring. Second, young women show a slightly greater sense of parental control over their leisure time. Thus, young women are more likely than young men to report that their parents prefer them to stay in as much as possible. Looked at from another perspective, young women are less likely than young men to feel that their parents allow them to do what they like in their leisure time. Consistent with this image of greater parental control over their leisure time, young women are slightly less likely than young men to feel that their parents do not agree with most of the things that they do in their leisure time.

Table 4.13: Right and wrong: by sex

	male (%)	female (%)	χ^2	P<
There is nothing wrong in shoplifting	10	5	268.7	.001
There is nothing wrong in travelling without a ticket	25	15	569.4	.001
There is nothing wrong in cycling after dark without lights	25	8	1678.4	.001
There is nothing wrong in playing truant (wagging) from school	19	15	78.7	.001
There is nothing wrong in buying cigarettes under the legal age (16 years)	29	30	11.1	.001
There is nothing wrong in buying alcoholic drinks under the legal age (18 years)	45	38	160.0	.001
There is nothing wrong in writing graffiti (tagging) wherever you like	17	12	168.5	.001
The police do a good job	52	57	66.5	.001

Table 4.14: Leisure: by sex

	male (%)	female (%)	χ^2	P<
I often hang about with my friends doing nothing in particular	64	72	262.1	.001
I wish I had more things to do with my leisure time	56	60	55.8	.001
My youth centre is boring	36	34	15.0	.001
My parents prefer me to stay in as much as possible	19	22	56.8	.001
My parents allow me to do what I like in my leisure time	51	46	80.7	.001
My parents do not agree with most of the things that I do in my leisure time	30	28	17.3	.001

THE VALUES DEBATE

My area

In one sense, young women hold a less positive attitude toward their local area in comparison with young men. This is illustrated by the way in which a lower proportion of young women than young men report that they like living in their area and by the way in which young women are less likely to feel that their area cares about its young people. In another sense, young women hold a less pessimistic view of their local area in comparison with young men. This is illustrated by the way in which young women are less likely than young men to consider that problems such as crime, violence and drunks are on the increase in their area. On the other hand, there are no significant differences between the proportions of young women and young men who consider problems such as vandalism, drug-taking or unemployment are on the increase in their area.

Table 4.15: My area: by sex

	male (%)	female (%)	χ^2	P<
Crime is a growing problem in my area	44	40	72.9	.001
Vandalism is a growing problem in my area	45	44	3.9	NS
Drug-taking is a growing problem in my area	32	31	2.2	NS
Violence is a growing problem in my area	33	31	12.9	.001
Drunks are a growing problem in my area	26	23	50.2	.001
Unemployment is a growing problem in my area	35	36	4.1	NS
I like living in my area	76	73	44.7	.001
My area cares about its young people	23	19	67.4	.001

CONCLUSION

This analysis has profiled the relationship between sex and adolescent values over 15 specific areas. The data make it clear that there are significant differences across all 15 areas. Young women and young men not only inhabit different bodies, they also inhabit and shape quite different world-views. Sex is an important predictor of individual differences in values among young people.

As a consequence of this careful analysis it becomes possible to offer a profile of young women in terms of the characteristics which distinguish them from young men of comparable age. As a group young women experience a lower level of personal well-being; are more inclined to worry about personal safety and relationships; are more likely to long for someone to turn to for advice and derive a lot of support from talking problems through with close friends; derive more support from mother and less support from father; project a more positive attitude toward school but experience higher levels of school-related anxiety; show a slightly lower sense of purpose and ambition in work but a greater dislike for unemployment; are more likely to believe in God; hold a more positive attitude toward the role of the church in society; are more likely to believe in potentially positive aspects of the supernatural although less likely to believe in the potentially negative aspects; show a lower level of interest in party politics; are less racist in their attitudes; are more concerned about world issues; are more accepting of homosexuality and divorce but less accepting of under-age sex and abortion; are less permissive about most substances but more accepting of tobacco; generally hold more law-abiding attitudes; generally experience less satisfaction with their leisure time but more parental control over what they do; and are generally less content with the area where they live.

This profile of young women can be inverted in order to generate a profile of young men in terms of the characteristics which distinguish them from young women of comparable age. As a group young men enjoy a higher level of personal well-being; are less inclined to worry about personal safety and relationships; are less likely to long for someone to turn to for advice and derive less support from close friends; derive more support from father and less support from mother; experience lower levels of school-related anxiety but project an overall less positive attitude toward school; show a slightly higher sense of purpose and ambition in work but a greater acceptance of unemployment, are less likely to believe in God; hold a less positive attitude toward the role of the church in society; are more likely to believe in potentially negative aspects of the supernatural although less likely to believe in the potentially positive aspects; show a higher level of interest in party politics; are more racist in their attitudes; are less concerned about world issues; are more accepting of under-age sex and abortion but less accepting of divorce and homosexuality; are less accepting of tobacco but more permissive about many other substances; generally hold less law-abiding attitudes; generally experience more satisfaction with their leisure time and less parental control over what they do; and are generally more content with the area where they live.

On the basis of the present database it is not possible to assess the extent to which the observed differences between young men and young women are in fact a function of sex or gender. Further research is needed which includes adequate measures of the psychological constructs of masculinity and femininity in order to tease out the relative explanatory power of the two concepts of sex and gender. However, what remains irrefutable on the basis of the present study is the conclusion that simple knowledge about sex is a powerful predictor of individual differences.

5

SOCIAL CLASS

Recent reviews of the empirical evidence and speculative theories regarding social class in Britain make it clear that, in spite of the many problems of conceptualisation and operationalising, social class remains a key predictor of individual differences across a very wide range of issues (Argyle, 1994; Reid, 1998).

In order to chart a path through current research concerned with the potential impact of social class on young people's attitudes and values, this chapter distinguishes between two main groups of studies: those which have specifically explored social-class differences among adults from data provided by the British Social Attitudes Survey, and more wide-ranging studies conducted specifically among children and adolescents.

British Social Attitudes Survey

The British Social Attitudes Survey has provided an annual report since 1984 covering a wide range of issues (see Jowell and Airey, 1984). The survey underpinning these reports includes information on social class. The original classification was based on the Office of Population Censuses and Surveys (1980) classification of occupations. In the 1992 report onwards the revised schema produced by the Office of Population Censuses and Surveys (1991) was used. Additionally the schema produced by Goldthorpe and Heath (1992) has been incorporated to provide an alternative conceptualisation of social class. In particular the earlier volumes in the British Social Attitudes series made good use of cross-tabulations by social class. Detailed inspection of these reports provides insight into a wide range of social-class differences in British society toward the end of the twentieth century.

In the 1984 report Young (1984) traced a clear relationship between social class and identification with the major political parties. Conservative identifiers accounted for 54 per cent of classes one and two, 43 per cent of class three non-manual, 34 per cent of class three manual, and 24 per cent of classes four and five. Labour identifiers accounted for 17 per cent of classes one and two, 26 per cent of class three non-manual, 38 per cent of class three manual and 50 per cent of classes four and five. This analysis also pointed to a relationship between social class and political tolerance. The view that revolutionaries should be allowed to hold public meetings to express their views was endorsed by 66 per cent of those in classes one or two, compared with 48 per cent of those in classes four or five. The view that racists should be allowed to hold public meetings to express their views was endorsed by 69 per cent of those in classes one or two, compared with 52 per cent of those in classes four or five.

Harrison (1984) found a clear link between social class and views on economic policy. The view that the government has not done enough to create jobs was rated as very important by 53 per cent of those in classes four and five, compared with 35 per cent of those in classes one and two. While 74 per cent of those in classes four and five suggested control of prices by legislation, the proportion fell to 57 per cent of those in classes one and two.

Bosanquet (1984) reported a link between social class and views on social policy and the welfare state. The view that benefits are too high and discourage job search was endorsed by 29 per cent of those in classes four and five, compared with 44 per cent of those in classes one and two. The view that the government should increase taxes and increase social spending was endorsed by 33 per cent of those in classes four and five, compared with 28 per cent of those in classes one and two.

Airey (1984) reported a link between social class and social moral values. Support for legislation against racial discrimination was offered by 76 per cent of those in classes one and two, compared with 61 per cent of those in classes four and five. The view that sexual relationships before marriage are always or mostly wrong was supported by 32 per cent of those in classes four and five, compared with 26 per cent of those in classes one and two. The view that same-sex sexual relationships are always or mostly wrong was supported by 70 per cent of those in classes four and five, compared with 52 per cent of those in classes one and two.

In the 1985 report Goodhardt (1985) commented on the relationship between social class and perceptions of prices, incomes and consumer issues. This analysis found that 64 per cent of those in classes four and five considered that the prices of 12 general expenditures had increased 'more than average', compared with 52 per cent in classes one and two. Satisfaction with the BBC was expressed by 74 per cent of those in classes one and two, compared with 56 per cent of those in classes four and five.

Whiteley (1985) found a clear link between social class and attitudes to defence and international affairs. Support for Britain remaining a member of the then EEC was given by 69 per cent of those in classes one and two, compared with 33 per cent of those in classes four and five. Support for Britain remaining a member of NATO, however, was given by 88 per cent of those in classes one and two, compared with 66 per cent of those in classes four and five. The view that siting American nuclear missiles in Britain makes Britain a safer place was endorsed by 41 per cent of those in classes one and two, compared with 30 per cent of those in classes four and five.

Johnson and Wood (1985) found some links between social class and judgements about right and wrong in public and private life. If a policeman stops a driver for speeding and the driver offers money to forget the incident, 60 per cent of those in classes one and two judged this to be 'seriously wrong', compared with 54 per cent in classes four and five. If a council tenant applies for a transfer to a better house and the official asks for money to put the applicant near the front of the queue, 80 per cent of those in classes one and two judged this to be 'seriously wrong', compared with 69 per cent in classes four and five.

Young (1985a) found a link between some environmental attitudes and social class. Thus, 26 per cent of manual workers considered that industry should keep prices down even if this causes some environmental damage, compared with 14 per cent of non-manual workers.

In the 1986 report Mann (1986) found clear links between social class and work-related attitudes. For example, 63 per cent of those in classes four and five agreed that management always try to get the better of employees, compared with 35 per cent of those in classes one and two. For 87 per cent of those in classes one and two work is more than just earning a living, compared with 54 per cent of those in classes four and five.

Curtice (1986) explored the relationship between social class and views on wealth. He found that 52 per cent of those in classes four and five agreed that income and wealth should be redistributed toward ordinary working people, compared with 32 per cent of those in classes one and two. Similarly 50 per cent of those in classes four and five agreed that the government should spend more on unemployment benefit, compared with 26 per cent of those in classes one and two.

Young (1986) found links between social class and views on the countryside. While 40 per cent of those in classes one and two were very concerned about things that may happen to the countryside, the proportion fell to 24 per cent among those in classes four and five. While 57 per cent of those in classes one and two agreed that the government should withhold some subsidies from farmers and use them to protect the countryside, the proportion fell to 40 per cent among those in classes four and five.

Bosanquet (1986) found a link between social class and attitudes to the welfare state. For example, 80 per cent of those in classes four and five considered that the government should provide a job for everyone that wants one, compared with 53 per cent of those in classes one and two. Half (49 per cent) of those in classes one and two considered that the welfare state makes people less willing to look after themselves, compared with 38 per cent of those in classes four and five.

Airey and Brook (1986) charted the link between social class and discrimination against homosexuals. They found that 62 per cent of manual workers considered it unacceptable for a homosexual to be a teacher in a school, compared with 28 per cent of non-manual workers; 57 per cent of manual workers found it unacceptable for a homosexual to be a teacher in a college or university, compared with 39 per cent of non-manual workers.

In the 1987 report, Taylor-Gooby (1987) charted a link between social class and attitude toward private medicine. While 50 per cent of the salaried class considered that private medical treatment should be allowed in both private and NHS hospitals, the proportion fell to 35 per cent among the working class. While 63 per cent of the salaried class considered that GPs should be allowed to take on private patients, the proportion fell to 53 per cent among the working class.

Young (1987a) found a link between social class and views on nuclear disarmament, showing that 73 per cent of those in classes one and two argued that Britain should keep its nuclear weapons until we persuade other nations to reduce theirs, compared with 66 per cent of those in classes four and five.

Sheiham et al. (1987) employed the data to distinguish between healthy eaters, intermediate eaters and unhealthy eaters. They found a strong link with social class, showing that 60 per cent of those in classes one and two were categorised as healthy eaters compared with 39 per cent of those in classes four and five.

Ashford (1987) found significant social-class differences in the qualities which parents desired in their children. While 52 per cent of those in classes four and five rated cleanness and neatness among the five top qualities, the proportion fell to 26 per cent of those in classes one and two. While determination and perseverance were rated in the top five qualities by 11 per cent of those in classes four and five, the proportion rose to 35 per cent of those in classes one and two.

Young (1987b) found a clear link between social class and policy preferences for the countryside. For example, while 53 per cent of those in classes one and two considered that building new houses in country areas should be discouraged, the proportion fell to 27 per cent of those in classes four and five.

In the 1988 report Harding (1988) found a link between social class and trends in permissiveness. For example, 42 per cent of those in classes four and five considered that pornographic magazines and films should be banned altogether, compared with 31 per cent of those in classes one and two. While 38 per cent of those in classes one and two considered that doctors should be allowed to give contraceptive supplies to young people under 16 without informing parents, the proportion fell to 30 per cent among those in classes four and five.

Heath and Evans (1988) confirmed the link between social class and right-wing views. While 66 per cent of the salaried class supported the death penalty for some crimes, the proportion rose to 79 per cent among the working class. While 72 per cent of the salaried class supported the right of people to organise meetings to protest against the government, the proportion fell to 59 per cent among the working class.

Brook (1988) found a link between social class and attitudes toward AIDS. For example, 42 per cent of those in classes four and five took the view that employers should have the legal right to dismiss people who have AIDS, compared with 31 per cent of those in classes one and two.

Bosanquet (1988) charted a link between social class and attitudes toward the National Health Service. While 43 per cent of those in classes four and five expressed satisfaction with the NHS, the proportion fell to 33 per cent of those in classes one and two. While private health insurance had been taken by 23 per cent of those in classes one and two, the proportion fell to 7 per cent among those in classes four and five.

In the 1990 report Sheiham et al. (1990) documented a link between social class and attitudes toward food. For example, 69 per cent of those in classes four and five agreed that a proper meal should include meat and vegetables, compared with 46 per cent of those in classes one and two. In classes four and five 58 per cent agreed that food that is really good for you is usually more expensive, compared with 39 per cent in classes one and two.

In the 1991 report Ben-Shlomo, Sheiham and Marmot (1991) traced a link between social class and smoking. They found that 37 per cent of those in classes four and five were current smokers, compared with 20 per cent of those in classes one and two. Among current smokers 71 per cent of those in classes one and two considered that they were likely to try to give up smoking in the near future, compared with 49 per cent of those in classes four and five.

In the 1992 report Barnett and Saxon-Harrold (1992) mapped a relationship between social class and charitable giving. For example, 67 per cent of semi-skilled manual workers considered that we should support more charities which benefit people in Britain, rather than people overseas, compared with 42 per cent of intermediate non-manual workers.

In the 1999 report Ford and Burrows (1999) examined the relationship between social class and attitudes toward home-ownership. Using the 1986 data they found that 85 per cent of professional class one individuals considered that a young couple should buy 'as soon as possible', compared with 74 per cent of class three skilled manual workers and 56 per cent of class five unskilled manual workers. By 1998 fewer people within each social class were inclined to adopt this view. In 1998 support for buying 'as soon as possible' was given by 76 per cent in class one, 57 per cent in class three manual and 43 per cent in class five.

Stratford, Marteau and Bobrow (1999) mapped the relationship between social class and attitudes toward genetic manipulation, employing a scale which distinguished between three attitudinal positions characterised as enthusiastic, cautious and restrictive. They found that non-manual classes were much less likely to fall into the enthusiastic category in comparison with the manual classes. For example, 14 per cent of non-manual class three employees were classified as enthusiastic in respect of genetic manipulation, compared with 25 per cent of class three manual employees.

Children and adolescents

A series of studies has employed the social-class categorisation to map individual differences during childhood and adolescence. Francis and Gibson (1993) examined the relationship between social class and television viewing time and programme preferences among a sample of 5,532 pupils between the ages of 11 and 15 years in Dundee. They found that children from lower social-class backgrounds spent more time watching television than children from higher social-class backgrounds. This is consistent with the earlier finding of Murdock and Phelps (1973), although Hendry and Patrick (1977) failed to find a correlation between social class and levels of television-watching among 15–16 year olds in

Scotland. Francis and Gibson (1993) also found that social class emerged as an important predictor of adolescent television viewing preferences. Children from lower social-class backgrounds reported more frequent viewing of soaps, sport and light entertainment programmes. On the other hand, children from lower social-class backgrounds reported watching current awareness programmes less frequently than children from higher social-class backgrounds.

Two studies reported by Francis and Pearson (1989) and Pearson, Lankshear and Francis (1989) examined the relationship between social class and neuroticism among samples of 708 16 year olds and 326 11 year olds. No significant relationship was found between social class and neuroticism in either of these studies. Earlier studies among adults had reported mixed findings. Eysenck (1958, 1959, 1960) and Eysenck and Eysenck (1964, 1969) reported that the lower classes recorded a higher neuroticism score than the middle classes, while no such relationship was found by Child (1969) and Eysenck and Eysenck (1975).

Green et al. (1991) examined the relationship between social class and the smoking and drinking behaviour of adolescents and their parents in the west of Scotland. Both social class and parental smoking behaviour were independently associated with young people's smoking. Adolescents from lower social-class backgrounds whose parents smoked were the most likely to smoke themselves. Social class and sex were independently associated with young people's drinking. Male adolescents from non-manual backgrounds were the most likely to drink. Using data from another study based in Scotland, however, Glendinning, Shucksmith and Hendry (1994) found little relationship between the social class of the family and smoking in middle and later adolescence.

Lawrence and Bennett (1992) examined the relationship between social class and shyness among a sample of 650 11–18 year olds, using two self-report questionnaires which covered the spectrum of inherent, emotional and situational shyness. They found a significant correlation between shyness and social class with a higher percentage of shyness occurring among adolescents from lower social-class backgrounds.

Francis (1992b) examined the relationship between social class and attitudes toward school among a sample of 3,762 11 year old pupils in England who completed seven semantic differential grids of attitudes toward school, English lessons, maths lessons, music lessons, games lessons, religious education lessons and school assemblies. He found that, although children from higher social-class backgrounds reported more favourable attitudes toward school, they did not differ from other children in attitudes toward any of the curriculum subjects included in the survey.

This is consistent with the mixed message from earlier studies. For example, whereas Fitt (1956) found that New Zealand children from higher social-class backgrounds held a more positive attitude toward school, Richmond (1985) found a positive correlation at one age and a negative correlation at another age among Australian students, and Barker-Lunn (1972) found a relationship between social class and school-related attitudes for boys but not for girls among British students.

Two studies reported by Gibson, Francis and Pearson (1990) and Francis, Pearson and Lankshear (1990) explored the relationship between social class, church attendance and attitudes toward Christianity among samples of 2,717 14–15 year olds and 5,288 10–11 year olds respectively. Both studies confirmed the generally well-established finding that higher levels of church attendance both for the children and for their parents are associated with higher social classes. This is consistent with the findings of earlier studies reported, for example, by Francis (1979, 1986, 1987). At the same time, after controlling for church attendance, children from lower social-class backgrounds were found to hold a significantly more positive attitude toward Christianity than children from higher social class backgrounds. This is consistent with studies which find non-economic conservative social attitudes positively related to lower social class, as exampled within Eysenck's model of social attitudes (Eysenck, 1951, 1954, 1971).

In their analysis of the Young People's Leisure and Lifestyle Project, Hendry et al. (1993) gave particular attention to the role of social class in shaping a wide range of individual differences. For example, young people from non-manual social-class backgrounds displayed a more positive attitude toward school, less conflict with teachers and less inclination to contemplate truancy. Young people from manual social-class backgrounds were more likely to regard it as important to start work as soon as possible and much less likely to contemplate going on to college or university, although at the same time they were less confident about their ability to get a job. There was a significant link between those claiming a close friend as a drug user and social class, with 32 per cent of young people from professional or intermediate social-class backgrounds making the claim, compared with 23 per cent of those from semi-skilled or unskilled social classes. Young people from working-class backgrounds were more likely to feel it is important to be like their friends, conforming in appearance and fashion. Young people from working-class backgrounds were more likely to spend a lot of time at an earlier age with a close friend of the opposite sex. On the other hand, this study found no relationship between social-class background and self-reported physical health, mental health or sports involvement.

Francis and Jones (1996) examined the relationship between social class and self-esteem among a sample of 711 16 year olds. They found that adolescents from higher social-class backgrounds recorded higher levels of self-esteem on both the Coopersmith Self-esteem Inventory (Coopersmith, 1967) and the Rosenberg Self-esteem Scale (Rosenberg, 1965). This is consistent with the findings of several earlier studies, including Rosenberg and Pearlin (1978), Hare (1980), Bahr and Martin (1983) and Richman, Clark and Brown (1985). On the other hand, several other studies failed to find a relationship between social class and self-esteem, including Trowbridge (1970, 1972) and Maly (1992).

Hendry, Kloep and Olsson (1998) examined the relationship between social class and youth lifestyles in Sweden, Germany and Britain. Their data demonstrated that lifestyle socialisation in adolescence was still social-class based, although allowing for transitional variations within social-class boundaries. Despite opportunities for taste and choice to operate in contemporary western cultures, social class continues to differentiate among various lifestyles across the teenage years.

Two studies by Cooper, Smaje and Arber employed data from the British General Household Survey 1991–1994 to explore the relationship between social class and aspects of health among children and young people. In the first of these studies Cooper, Smaje and Arber (1998a) examined the use of health services by children and young people according to social class. They employed three outcome measures: consultations with a general practitioner within a two-week period, outpatient attendance within a three-month period, and inpatient stays within the past year. Social class emerged as a significant predictor of none of these outcome measures. In the second study Cooper, Smaje and Arber (1998b) investigated inequalities in children's reported morbidity by parental social class, compared with indicators of material disadvantage. The data demonstrated that the economic position of the family, and especially material deprivation, was more closely associated with children's health states than social class.

Cooper and Dunne (1998) examined social-class differences in children's responses to national curriculum mathematics testing. Data from the key stage two sample of 10–11 year olds showed a social-class effect in the response of children to questions which rooted the application of mathematics in 'realistic' settings. In this context some working-class children failed to demonstrate competencies which they possess.

Evaluation

The foregoing review has confirmed the importance of taking social class into account in mapping individual differences. The main issues still to be addressed concern the precise way in which social class should be operationalised in empirical research and the appropriateness of such operationalisation among 13–15 year olds.

In his review of the field Reid (1998, p. 10) argued for the following working definition:

> Social class is 'a grouping of people into categories on the basis of occupation'. This is not to suggest that social class is simply or only based on occupation, or for that matter any other single criterion such as income or education. It is to recognise that occupation has been seen and used as the best single indicator of a person's social standing and socio-economic circumstances.

Reid supported this argument with four further points. First, occupation has been consistently shown to be highly related to income, education and other factors associated with social class. Second, information on occupation is easy to collect and simple to treat. Third, occupation has been used extensively over a long time and as a consequence it enables comparisons to be made with studies over time. Fourth, it is 'official' in the sense that it is used by the Office for National Statistics in the census and related projects.

Occupational classification has been used since the 1911 census. The present categories derive from the 1921 census (Stevenson, 1928; Leete and Fox, 1977) and were reshaped by the 1971 census to form six distinct groups. Class one was defined as 'professional etc. occupations'; class two was defined as 'intermediate occupations'; class three was subdivided into 'skilled non-manual' and 'skilled manual' occupations; class four was defined as 'partly skilled occupations'; and class five was defined as 'unskilled occupations'. This classification system was further refined by the table of occupations prepared for the 1981 census (Office of Population Censuses and Surveys, 1980). According to this classification system occupations were graded 'according to the general standing within the community of the occupations concerned'. Class one included doctors, accountants and solicitors; class two, teachers, social workers and journalists; class three skilled non-manual, secretaries and clerks; class three skilled manual, lorry drivers and bus drivers; class four, partly skilled, postmen, machine operators and bricklayers; class five, unskilled, manual labourers, porters and messengers. Although this system was further modified for the 1991 census, there remains value in staying with the 1981 system in order to maintain comparability with earlier analyses.

Two major reservations against basing social class on occupational categories arise from the changing nature of work and employment in contemporary society and from the changing relationship between men and women within the household. A third reservation arises from the way in which this pragmatic operational definition maps onto the wider theoretical and conceptual issues relating to social-class (Crompton, 1993). Two further problems arise specifically in respect of occupational categories as the basis for attributing social-class classification to children. The first of these problems recognises that, traditionally, paternal occupation has been utilised to establish a child's social class. In spite of the contentious nature of this practice it is still generally considered to be a more accurate and stable indicator than maternal occupation on its own or attempts to combine maternal and paternal indicators. The second of these problems recognises that adolescent reporting of parental occupation may not be as accurate or as detailed as self-reports given by the parents themselves. In light of these reservations and problems it is important to be clear precisely what the analysis in the present chapter claims to be about and what it does not claim to be about. The empirical question is simply this: to establish the extent to which information provided by the pupils about paternal employment, categorised according to the classification proposed by the Office of Population Censuses and Surveys (1980), predicts individual differences in values among 13–15 year olds.

EXPLORING THE DATA

Aim

The aim of the present analysis is to divide the database into four distinct groups in order to compare young people whose fathers are engaged in employment classified as social class one or two, social class three non-manual, social class three manual, and social classes four and five. The practice of collapsing classes one and two and classes four and five is consistent with the policy adopted by the majority of the British Social Attitudes Survey cross-tabulations.

In view of the way in which, in this chapter, social class is calculated on the basis of paternal occupation, only those young people whose fathers were in employment and who provided sufficient detail regarding that employment are included in the analysis. This reduced the overall effective database to 27,717 cases, a loss of 18 per cent. Overall the data demonstrate that 53.1 per cent of the respondents come from non-manual backgrounds. This compared with 47 per cent of the male working population being classified as in non-manual occupations by the 1991 census (Reid, 1998).

The main body of the present analysis maps the relationship between paternal social class and the 15 areas explored by the survey, namely personal well-being, worries, counselling, school, work, religious beliefs, church and society, the supernatural, politics, social concerns, sexual morality, substance use, right and wrong, leisure and the local area. First, however, attention is given to the demographic characteristics between manual and non-manual employment categories.

Demographic characteristics

SEX

Similar proportions of males (53.3 per cent) and females (52.8 per cent) report that their fathers are engaged in non-manual occupations. This finding is consistent with the view that the sex of the child is irrelevant to the nature of paternal employment.

AGE

The older pupils in the sample are slightly more likely to locate their fathers within non-manual employment. Thus, 53.8 per cent of fathers of pupils in year ten are located in non-manual employment, compared with 52.5 per cent of fathers of pupils in year nine. This finding is consistent with the view that over the course of life men are more likely to move from manual to non-manual work than from non-manual to manual work.

RELIGION

Denominational membership remains a powerful predictor of differences in social class. Among the pupils who claimed no denominational allegiance, 48.5 per cent have fathers in non-manual employment. The proportion rises to 51.3 per cent among Roman Catholics, 58.9 per cent among Baptists, 59.5 per cent among Pentecostals, 61.8 per cent among Methodists, 66.1 per cent among Presbyterians and 70.1 per cent among Anglicans. The situation among members of other faith groups is as follows: Sikh 44.2 per cent, Muslim 50.4 per cent, Hindu 68.9 per cent and Jewish 82.6 per cent.

Personal well-being

Table 5.1 demonstrates that there is a significantly lower level of personal well-being among the young people from lower social-class backgrounds. This is perhaps seen most clearly in respect of the proportion of young people who have entertained suicidal ideation. Also, young people from lower social-class backgrounds are more likely to feel that they are not worth much as a person and are more likely to feel depressed. This is consistent with the second finding from this section that young people from higher social-class backgrounds are more likely to say that they feel their life has a sense of purpose and that they find life really worth living.

Table 5.1: Personal well-being: by social class

	1&2 (%)	3N (%)	3M (%)	4&5 (%)	χ^2	P<
I feel my life has a sense of purpose	61	58	55	54	83.4	.001
I find life really worth living	75	71	69	68	83.3	.001
I feel I am not worth much as a person	10	12	14	15	55.2	.001
I often feel depressed	49	50	53	52	31.0	.001
I have sometimes considered taking my own life	24	25	27	30	45.5	.001

Note: '1&2' = social class one and two
'3N' = social class three non-manual
'3M' = social class three manual
'4&5' = social class four and five

Worries

The relationship between social class and worries is less straightforward than the relationship between social class and personal well-being. Four features emerge from the data presented in Table 5.2. First, young people from non-manual backgrounds are more anxious than young people from manual backgrounds over relational issues: they are more inclined to worry about how they get on with other people and their attractiveness to the opposite sex. Second, anxiety about getting AIDS is higher among non-manual and manual social class three young people than among young people in either social classes one and two or social classes four and five. Third, it is young people from social classes four and five who are most likely to be worried about being attacked by pupils from other schools. Fourth, no significant pattern emerges between social class and worry about their sex life or worry about going out alone at night in their area.

Table 5.2: Worries: by social class

	1&2 (%)	3N (%)	3M (%)	4&5 (%)	χ^2	P<
I am worried about my sex life	17	19	17	16	9.0	NS
I am worried about my attractiveness to the opposite sex	38	38	33	33	86.3	.001
I am worried about getting AIDS	59	62	63	60	23.6	.001
I am worried about how I get on with other people	55	55	50	50	79.7	.001
I am worried about being attacked by pupils from other schools	18	19	19	22	12.9	.01
I am worried about going out alone at night in my area	32	33	31	32	9.2	NS

Counselling

Young people from the higher social-class backgrounds are more likely to express the view that they find it helpful to talk about their problems with others. This includes both close friends and parents. Already deriving help in this way from close friends and parents, young people from the higher social-class backgrounds are somewhat less likely to report that they often long for someone to turn to for advice. Table 5.3 also demonstrates that young people from lower social-class backgrounds are less reluctant to draw on the resources of professional people for advice: they are less reluctant to discuss their problems with a schoolteacher, youth leader, doctor, priest or social worker.

School

Table 5.4 shows a very clear relationship between social class and overall attitudes toward school. Young people from lower social-class backgrounds are much more likely to take the view that school is boring; they are less likely to be happy in their school; they are less likely to think that teachers do a good job. Consistent with this overall view, it is the young people from the higher social-class backgrounds who take their school work more seriously and display more anxiety over it; they are more likely to worry about their school work and about their exams at school. The data also demonstrate that young people from social-class one and two backgrounds are the most likely to feel that school is helping to prepare them for life and the least likely to be worried about being bullied at school. Finally, young people from all social-class backgrounds are equally likely to report that they like the people with whom they go to school.

Table 5.3: Counselling: by social class

	1&2 (%)	3N (%)	3M (%)	4&5 (%)	χ^2	P<
I often long for someone to turn to for advice	33	34	35	36	12.8	.01
I would be reluctant to discuss my problems with a schoolteacher	54	50	43	43	342.3	.001
I would be reluctant to discuss my problems with a youth club/group leader	56	52	44	43	271.6	.001
I would be reluctant to discuss my problems with a doctor	36	35	31	32	49.3	.001
I would be reluctant to discuss my problems with a Christian minister/vicar/priest	48	46	37	36	283.6	.001
I would be reluctant to discuss my problems with a social worker	46	41	37	36	155.2	.001
I find it helpful to talk about my problems with my mother	52	51	49	49	15.0	.01
I find it helpful to talk about my problems with my father	36	34	32	31	43.1	.001
I find it helpful to talk about my problems with close friends	66	65	63	62	18.4	.001

Table 5.4: School: by social class

	1&2 (%)	3N (%)	3M (%)	4&5 (%)	χ^2	P<
School is boring	28	34	39	41	244.2	.001
I am happy in my school	78	75	70	71	130.5	.001
I like the people I go to school with	89	90	90	91	6.3	NS
My school is helping to prepare me for life	73	70	67	70	70.5	.001
I often worry about my school work	65	66	63	62	13.3	.01
I am worried about my exams at school	79	73	73	72	30.6	.001
I am worried about being bullied at school	26	29	28	29	24.7	.001
Teachers do a good job	52	46	42	42	167.8	.001

Work

While there are some significant differences in work-related attitudes according to social class, the percentage figures reported in Table 5.5 make it clear that these differences are quite small. In fact exactly the same percentages of young people from social-class one and two backgrounds and from social-class four and five backgrounds agree that a job gives you a sense of purpose. Exactly the same percentages think that it is important to work hard when they get a job. Exactly the same percentages want to get to the top in their work when they get a job. More significant differences occur between the social classes, however, in respect of their attitudes toward unemployment. Young people from manual-class backgrounds are less likely than young people from non-manual-class backgrounds to say that they would not like to be unemployed. Young people from manual-class backgrounds are more likely than young people from non-manual-class backgrounds to take the view that most unemployed people could have a job if they really wanted to. Finally, there is no relationship between social class and young people preferring unemployment to a job which they do not like doing.

Table 5.5: Work: by social class

	1&2 (%)	3N (%)	3M (%)	4&5 (%)	χ^2	P<
A job gives you a sense of purpose	78	79	77	78	10.4	NS
I think it is important to work hard when I get a job	96	96	95	96	21.3	.001
I want to get to the top in my work when I get a job	88	89	86	88	34.9	.001
I would not like to be unemployed	90	89	85	84	152.5	.001
I would rather be unemployed on social security than get a job I don't like doing	16	17	18	18	8.9	NS
Most unemployed people could have a job if they really wanted to	50	50	54	55	41.5	.001

Religious beliefs

Table 5.6 confirms a clear link between social class and belief in God and Jesus. In particular young people from social-class one and two backgrounds are more likely to agree that they believe in God and that Jesus really rose from the dead. On the other hand, the percentages shown in Table 5.6 reveal only small social-class differences in the interpretation of Christian belief. Young people from manual-class backgrounds are slightly more likely than young people from non-manual backgrounds to subscribe to a theological view that God punishes people who do wrong. Young people from manual-class backgrounds are also slightly more likely to take the view that Christianity is the only true religion. Belief in life after death is highest among young people from non-manual-class-three backgrounds.

Table 5.6: Religious beliefs: by social class

	1&2 (%)	3N (%)	3M (%)	4&5 (%)	χ^2	P<
I believe in God	47	42	39	38	135.1	.001
I believe that Jesus really rose from the dead	35	30	29	28	100.9	.001
I believe in life after death	44	47	44	46	16.6	.001
I believe God punishes people who do wrong	19	19	20	22	15.0	.01
I think Christianity is the only true religion	16	15	16	17	23.3	.001
I believe that God made the world in six days and rested on the seventh	20	20	19	21	5.4	NS

Church and society

Table 5.7 confirms a clear link between social class and overall attitude toward the church. Young people from social-class one and two backgrounds are the least likely to dismiss the church as boring and the most likely to consider that the clergy do a good job; they are the most likely to consider that religious education should be taught in schools and that schools should hold a religious assembly every day; they are the most likely to want to get married in church and to want their own children to be baptised or christened in church. Young people from social-class one and two backgrounds are also the most likely to believe that they can be a Christian without going to church. On the other hand, young people from social-class one and two backgrounds are as likely as young people from manual backgrounds to dismiss the church and the Bible as irrelevant to life today.

Table 5.7: Church and society: by social class

	1&2 (%)	3N (%)	3M (%)	4&5 (%)	χ^2	P<
I believe that I can be a Christian without going to church	56	53	50	48	63.4	.001
The church seems irrelevant to life today	28	29	27	27	16.0	.01
The Bible seems irrelevant to life today	30	34	30	29	32.6	.001
I want my children to be baptised/ christened in church	59	54	55	55	34.2	.001
I want to get married in church	76	74	75	72	19.2	.001
Religious education should be taught in school	42	38	35	37	75.5	.001
Schools should hold a religious assembly every day	11	7	7	6	111.6	.001
Church is boring	47	52	53	55	67.6	.001
Christian ministers/vicars/priests do a good job	42	36	34	37	126.6	.001

The supernatural

Although young people from lower social-class backgrounds are less inclined to believe in God, Table 5.8 demonstrates that they are more inclined to believe in a range of supernatural phenomena. They are more inclined to believe in their horoscope, in ghosts, in black magic, to believe that fortune-tellers can tell the future, and to believe that it is possible to contact the spirits of the dead. At the same time, young people from lower social-class backgrounds are more likely to be apprehensive of the supernatural, in the sense that they would have more anxiety about going into a church alone. Belief in the Devil is highest among young people from non-manual-class-three backgrounds.

Politics

Table 5.9 confirms a clear link between social class and party-political preference: greatest support for the Conservative Party is found among pupils from social classes one and two while greatest support for the Labour Party is found among pupils from social classes four and five. Party political preference is also associated with traditional political ideologies. Greatest support for private schools is found among pupils from social classes one and two. Greatest antipathy for private medicine is found among pupils from social classes four and five. Levels of political apathy are also social-class related, with young people from the lower social classes being more inclined to maintain that it makes no difference which political party is in power. The relationship between social class and racist attitudes is somewhat more complex. Young people from working-class backgrounds are more likely than young people from non-manual backgrounds to agree that there are too many black people living in the country. On the other hand, it is young people from class one and two backgrounds who are most likely to think that immigration into Britain should be restricted.

Table 5.8: The supernatural: by social class

	1&2 (%)	3N (%)	3M (%)	4&5 (%)	χ^2	P<
I believe in my horoscope	27	34	38	38	213.9	.001
I believe in ghosts	34	40	42	44	117.5	.001
I believe in the Devil	21	23	21	21	11.4	.01
I believe in black magic	17	21	20	21	29.8	.001
I believe that fortune-tellers can tell the future	14	18	21	23	155.3	.001
I believe it is possible to contact the spirits of the dead	27	30	32	34	61.3	.001
I am frightened of going into a church alone	9	11	12	15	70.0	.001

Table 5.9: Politics: by social class

	1&2 (%)	3N (%)	3M (%)	4&5 (%)	χ^2	P<
It makes no difference which political party is in power	17	22	24	26	138.2	.001
I have confidence in the Conservative Party	22	17	12	11	326.5	.001
I have confidence in the Labour Party	13	16	22	25	264.0	.001
Private schools should be abolished	18	21	26	27	179.6	.001
Private medicine should be abolished	12	14	17	18	85.8	.001
There are too many black people living in this country	14	13	17	19	91.0	.001
I think that immigration into Britain should be restricted	34	31	31	31	14.9	.01

Social concerns

Just as young people from lower social-class backgrounds hold a more
cynical attitude toward politics, so they hold a more cynical attitude toward
the world's problems. According to Table 5.10 they are less inclined to feel
that they can do anything to help solve the world's problems. Second, Table
5.10 shows a clear correlation between social class and the level of concern
shown for a range of global issues; young people from higher social-class
backgrounds are more inclined to display concern about the risk of
pollution to the environment, about the poverty of the Third World and
about the risk of nuclear war. Third, Table 5.10 demonstrates that there is
no significant relationship between social class and attitudes toward
violence on television or toward the availability of pornography.

Table 5.10: Social concerns: by social class

	1&2 (%)	3N (%)	3M (%)	4&5 (%)	χ^2	P<
There is too much violence on television	19	19	19	21	6.1	NS
Pornography is too readily available	34	34	32	35	8.7	NS
I am concerned about the risk of pollution to the environment	73	70	63	62	235.6	.001
I am concerned about the poverty of the Third World	71	66	56	55	507.4	.001
I am concerned about the risk of nuclear war	61	56	54	53	90.6	.001
There is nothing I can do to help solve the world's problems	19	22	27	30	211.1	.001

Sexual morality

The data presented in Table 5.11 reveal four patterns in the relationship
between social class and sexual morality. First, it is young people from
social-class one and two backgrounds who are most likely to adopt a
conservative view on heterosexual ethics; they are more likely than young
people from other social-class backgrounds to agree that it is wrong to
have sexual intercourse outside marriage or that it is wrong to have sexual
intercourse under the legal age. Second, it is young people from manual-
class backgrounds who are most likely to adopt a conservative view on
homosexual ethics; they are more likely than young people from other
social-class backgrounds to agree that homosexuality is wrong. Third,
attitudes toward abortion are very strongly related to social class; young

people from social-class three non-manual backgrounds take a more conservative view on abortion than young people from social-class one and two backgrounds. Young people from social-class three manual backgrounds take a more conservative view on abortion than young people from social-class three non-manual backgrounds; young people from social-class four and five backgrounds take a more conservative view on abortion than young people from social-class three manual backgrounds. Fourth, young people from manual-class backgrounds take a slightly more conservative view on both contraception and divorce in comparison with young people from non-manual-class backgrounds.

Table 5.11: Sexual morality: by social class

	1&2 (%)	3N (%)	3M (%)	4&5 (%)	χ^2	P<
It is wrong to have sexual intercourse outside marriage	15	13	13	14	11.6	.01
It is wrong to have sexual intercourse under the legal age (16 years)	26	23	22	23	25.1	.001
Homosexuality is wrong	35	34	39	41	81.0	.001
Contraception is wrong	4	4	6	6	48.8	.001
Abortion is wrong	26	31	39	42	399.8	.001
Divorce is wrong	18	17	20	19	23.9	.001

Substance use

According to Table 5.12 young people from lower social-class backgrounds hold a more tolerant attitude toward the use of a range of substances; they are less likely to consider the use of tobacco, marijuana, heroin or glue to be wrong. On the other hand, attitudes toward sniffing butane gas and toward alcohol are not related to social-class background.

Table 5.12: Substance use: by social class

	1&2 (%)	3N (%)	3M (%)	4&5 (%)	χ^2	P<
It is wrong to smoke cigarettes	46	41	42	42	31.9	.001
It is wrong to become drunk	20	18	18	19	10.9	NS
It is wrong to use marijuana (hash or pot)	58	51	51	49	106.6	.001
It is wrong to use heroin	79	73	73	74	82.2	.001
It is wrong to sniff glue	81	78	78	77	29.3	.001
It is wrong to sniff butane gas	74	73	74	75	4.2	NS

Right and wrong

Two main conclusions emerge from Table 5.13 regarding the relationship between social class and law-abiding behaviours. First, in respect of several issues the real divide occurs between those from manual and those from non-manual backgrounds; young people from manual backgrounds tend to adopt a more liberal view than young people from non-manual backgrounds in respect of shoplifting, travelling without a ticket, cycling after dark without lights, playing truant from school and writing graffiti. Second, in respect of some other issues the real divide occurs between those from class-one and two backgrounds and the other social-class groups; young people from social-class one and two backgrounds are less likely than other young people to condone buying cigarettes under the legal age or buying alcoholic drinks under the legal age. Young people from social-class one and two backgrounds are also much more likely than other young people to consider that the police do a good job.

Table 5.13: Right and wrong: by social class

	1&2 (%)	3N (%)	3M (%)	4&5 (%)	χ^2	P<
There is nothing wrong in shoplifting	5	6	8	8	64.4	.001
There is nothing wrong in travelling without a ticket	17	19	21	21	44.4	.001
There is nothing wrong in cycling after dark without lights	12	15	18	19	132.7	.001
There is nothing wrong in playing truant (wagging) from school	13	14	18	18	117.0	.001
There is nothing wrong in buying cigarettes under the legal age (16 years)	25	29	30	29	62.2	.001
There is nothing wrong in buying alcoholic drinks under the legal age	39	42	43	42	25.4	.001
There is nothing wrong in writing graffiti (tagging) wherever you like	10	12	17	17	164.6	.001
The police do a good job	62	55	53	53	145.2	.001

Leisure

Table 5.14 demonstrates that there is a clear relationship between social class and attitudes toward leisure. Overall young people from social-class one and two backgrounds have a more positive experience of their leisure than young people from lower social-class backgrounds. Young people from social-class one and two backgrounds are the least likely to complain that they wish they had more things to do with their leisure time; they are the least likely to hang about with friends doing nothing in particular; they are the least likely to complain that their youth centre is boring. Young people from social-class one and two backgrounds are the least likely to feel that their parents prefer them to stay in as much as possible and they are also the least likely to feel that their parents do not agree with most of the things they do in their leisure time.

Table 5.14: Leisure: by social class

	1&2 (%)	3N (%)	3M (%)	4&5 (%)	χ^2	P<
I often hang about with my friends doing nothing in particular	62	69	70	72	166.7	.001
I wish I had more things to do with my leisure time	51	57	60	61	141.4	.001
My youth centre is boring	30	34	38	39	110.9	.001
My parents prefer me to stay in as much as possible	17	20	20	21	24.8	.001
My parents allow me to do what I like in my leisure time	49	47	49	50	8.3	NS
My parents do not agree with most of the things that I do in my leisure time	21	26	31	34	250.0	.001

My area

Table 5.15 demonstrates a clear and consistent gradient between social class and attitudes toward the local area. Young people from social-class one and two backgrounds have a more positive attitude toward the area in which they live than young people from social-class three non-manual backgrounds. Young people from social-class three non-manual backgrounds have a more positive attitude toward their area than young people from class-three manual backgrounds. Young people from class-three manual backgrounds have a more positive attitude toward their area than young people from class-four or five backgrounds. This is clearly reflected in their evaluation of crime, vandalism, violence, drunkenness and unemployment in their local area. The trend is also reflected, but less clearly so, in their evaluation of drug-taking in their local area. Looked at from another perspective, young people from higher social-class backgrounds are more likely to like living where they do. On the other hand, there is no relationship between social class and young people's likelihood to consider that their area cares about its young people.

Table 5.15: My area: by social class

	1&2 (%)	3N (%)	3M (%)	4&5 (%)	χ^2	P<
Crime is a growing problem in my area	37	41	43	47	99.5	.001
Vandalism is a growing problem in my area	38	44	47	51	149.1	.001
Drug-taking is a growing problem in my area	26	33	32	36	115.0	.001
Violence is a growing problem in my area	26	31	33	37	120.4	.001
Drunks are a growing problem in my area	18	23	27	29	188.7	.001
Unemployment is a growing problem in my area	29	34	36	39	128.6	.001
I like living in my area	79	75	74	73	58.7	.001
My area cares about its young people	20	21	22	21	8.4	NS

CONCLUSION

This chapter has profiled the relationship between social class and adolescent values over 15 specific areas. The data make it clear that there are significant differences over all 15 areas between young people who belong to different social-class backgrounds.

As a consequence of this analysis a clear profile can be drawn of the values associated with four distinct social-class groupings. For example, young people from social-class one and two backgrounds enjoy an overall higher level of psychological well-being; worry more about personal relationships; benefit from a closer relationship with parents and close friends; hold a more positive attitude toward school; show a greater abhorrence of unemployment; are more likely to believe in God but less likely to believe in their horoscopes; hold a more positive attitude toward the church; show more confidence in the Conservative Party and less confidence in the Labour Party; display more concern for the Third World, hold a more liberal attitude toward divorce, abortion and homosexuality; hold a more proscriptive attitude toward drug use; see the police in a more positive light, have a more positive view of their leisure time; and feel more positive about the area in which they live. These findings are consistent with the wider field of research which suggests that social class remains an important predictor of a range of individual differences.

Since the present data are based on a cross-sectional survey, the findings are, by definition, correlational rather than causational. Nonetheless, the causal inference can be advanced with some confidence on the grounds that few contaminating variables, not themselves intimately related to the construct of social class, are likely to be implicated in shaping the pattern of correlations reported. A clear weakness with the present analysis derives from the fact that social-class classification has been based on pupils' reporting the nature of their fathers' occupations rather than on objective data reported by the fathers themselves. However, the fact that so many strong and consistent relationships have been found in the data lends further confidence to the validity of the classifications of social class included in this study.

6

PARENTAL SEPARATION
OR DIVORCE

Data provided by the Office of Population Censuses and Surveys (1990, 1993) demonstrated the rising divorce rate in England and Wales since the mid-1960s. According to Haskey (1990) by the time they are 16 years old, one in four children were likely to have experienced parental divorce. In her review of lone parenthood and family disruption, Burghes (1994) argued that, as more and more children experience family change, research into the impact of family disruption on children will be increasingly important.

In order to chart a path through current research concerned with the potential impact of family disruption on the lives of those who experience such change during childhood, this chapter distinguishes between three main groups of studies: studies conducted among schoolchildren, studies conducted among students and studies conducted among adults.

Schoolchildren

One group of studies has looked at the relationship between parental divorce and differences in young people's behaviour, attitude or achievement during the school years. For example, Douglas (1970) studied bed-wetting among 15 year olds. He reported that adolescents whose parents had either separated or divorced during their first five years of life were twice as likely to be bed-wetting as those whose parents were together.

Ferri (1976) looked at school behaviour among 11 year olds. His analysis of the National Child Development Study data found that children whose parents had divorced had poorer behaviour at school and were considered less well-adjusted, although this relationship disappeared after controlling for other indices of deprivation.

Elliott and Richards (1991) explored disruptive behaviour and self-reported worry and unhappiness among 16 year olds in the National Child Development Study. Their data showed two findings. If parents divorced when children were between the ages of 7 and 16, the children had higher scores of unhappiness and worry and displayed more disruptive behaviour at the age of 16. They also scored higher on both indices at the age of 7, before their parents divorced. Elliott and Richards also looked at the relationship between marital disruption and educational achievement in maths and reading at the ages of 11 and 16 respectively. Again, significant differences among those whose parents had divorced and those continuing to live in intact families were reduced by controlling for other background variables.

Clark and Barber (1994) compared adolescent self-esteem in post-divorce, mother-headed families, and two-parent, always married families. No difference in self-esteem by family structure was found. On the other hand, the study by Martin-Lebrun et al. (1997) among first-year secondary pupils found that pupils from intact homes recorded higher self-esteem scores than pupils where parents had separated or divorced.

Suh, Schutz and Johanson (1996) examined the relationship between family structure and initiating non-medical drug use among adolescents. They found that 12–17-year-old adolescents from intact families were less likely to initiate non-medical drug use. Similarly, Jenkins and Zunguze (1998) examined the relationship of family structure to adolescent drug use and peer-related factors. They found that pupils from intact families reported less frequent drug use, fewer drug-using friends, and perceptions of more peer disapproval of drug use. Neher and Short (1998) also found that children of divorce reported significantly more substance-using friends and less use of coping and social skills than children from intact families.

Borkhuis and Patalano (1997) compared the personality profiles of 52 adolescents from divorced families and 55 adolescents from intact families. They found that the adolescents from divorced families demonstrated greater signs of overall emotional distress, depression, pessimism about the future, anxiety, somatic symptomatology, agitation, irritability, aggression and alienation. They also demonstrated lower levels of impulse control and lower self-esteem.

Max, Brokaw and McQueen (1997) investigated the relationship between adolescent religiosity and parental religiosity in intact families and in families disrupted by separation or divorce. They found that adolescents from disrupted families were less religious than adolescents from intact families. This finding is consistent with the results of an earlier study by Ambert and Saucier (1986) who found in a sample of 275 adolescents that those from separated or divorced families were less likely to attend church than those from intact families.

Giuliani, Iafrate and Rosnati (1998) examined the relationship between family structure and adolescents' friendships and romantic relationships. They found that compared with adolescents from intact homes, adolescents from homes which had experienced separation or divorce displayed a higher level of distrust of others, were less likely to see marriage as a certain step in their own lives and showed a higher degree of fear toward marriage.

Aseltine (1996) found a positive correlation between depression and parental separation and divorce. Rubenstein *et al.* (1998) reported a positive correlation between suicidal behaviour and parental separation and divorce among high school students.

Ely *et al.* (1999) re-analysed data from the three British birth cohorts of 1946, 1958 and 1970. They found lower educational attainment associated with parental divorce in all three cohorts.

Guijarro *et al.* (1999) found a significant relationship between adolescent pregnancy and parental separation in a study conducted among 135 females between the ages of 12 and 19 years.

Students

A second group of studies has looked at the relationship between parental divorce and differences in the behaviour, attitudes, personality or achievement of university and college students. For example, Crossman, Shea and Adams (1980) compared the level of ego development, locus of control, and identity achievement in 294 college students who came from intact, divorced, and divorced–remarriage family backgrounds. Divorce backgrounds were not predictive of lower scores on any of the three measures. Similarly, Parish (1981) examined the self-concept of 1,409 college students in the USA. He found no significant differences in self-concept between students from divorced families and students from intact families. Phillips and Asbury (1990) examined several indicators of self-concept and mental health among a sample of 900 black freshmen students, of whom 356 came from divorced or separated backgrounds. They found no significant differences on any of the measures. Garber (1991) also failed to find a relationship between parental divorce and self-concept in his sample of 324 undergraduates. Heyer and Nelson (1993) found no difference in autonomy scores in a sample of 388 college students between those whose parents were divorced and those from intact families, although those from divorced backgrounds recorded higher confidence and sexual identity scores.

Vess, Schwebel and Moreland (1983) compared the sex-role orientation and sex-role preference of two groups of college students; 84 students who had experienced parental divorce before the age of 10 and 135 students whose parents had never divorced or separated. No significant differences were found between the two groups.

Lopez, Campbell and Watkins (1988) examined aspects of adjustment to college among 255 students from intact homes and 112 students from non-intact homes in the USA. They found no significant differences between the two groups.

Gabardi and Rosén (1991) explored the relationship between several measures of adjustment and parental divorce among a sample of 500 college students in the USA. Multivariate analyses of variance indicated that students from divorced families had significantly more sexual partners and more negative attitudes toward marriage than students from intact families.

Jennings, Salts and Smith (1991) employed the Favourableness of Attitudes Towards Marriage Scale among 340 college freshmen, 67 of whom came from divorced families. They found a significantly less favourable attitude toward marriage among those whose parents had separated or divorced. Similarly, Greenberg and Nay (1982) studied attitudes toward divorce among college students. They found that those from broken homes were more favourable toward divorce than other young people. On the other hand, Livingston and Kordinak (1990) examined the relationship between parental divorce and marital role expectations among a sample of 80 college students. They found no simple relationship between these two variables.

Adults

A third group of studies has looked at the relationship between parental divorce and differences in the behaviour and attitudes of adult samples. For example, MacLean and Wadsworth (1988) examined educational qualifications, using the 1946 National Survey of Health and Development cohort. They concluded that those who experienced parental divorce during their school years were significantly more likely to have lower educational attainment, whatever the social class of their family origin. Similarly, Kuh and MacLean (1990) demonstrated that women whose parents had separated or divorced by the time they were 16 were significantly less likely to have any educational qualifications by the age of 26, compared with their contemporaries from intact families.

Kiernan (1992b) found significant differences in the ages when 'transitions' were made into young adulthood, comparing those who had experienced family disruption by the age of 16 with those who had not experienced such disruption. The transitions reviewed included leaving school, leaving home, forming partnerships and having children. For example, girls were shown to leave home earlier following parental divorce, than those living in intact families or those who had experienced the death of a parent. These data also demonstrated that women whose parents had divorced were more likely to have been teenage brides than their contemporaries from intact families. By the age of 36 they were also more likely to have been separated or divorced and twice as likely to have been married more than once. Similarly McLanahan and Bumpass (1988) found that women who spent part of their childhood in one-parent families were more likely to marry and bear children early, to give birth before marriage, and to have their own marriage break up.

Wadsworth's (1984) analysis of the National Survey of Health and Development data at the age of 26 concluded that those who had experienced family disruption were more likely to have had stomach, peptic or duodenal ulcers or a psychiatric disorder, although they were no more likely to have suffered from epilepsy, migraine, asthma or psoriasis.

Using two national surveys of the American adult population to test for the influence of parental divorce on adult adjustment, Kulka and Weingarten (1979) concluded that coming from a non-intact family had some negative significance for adult well-being. On the other hand, Amato (1988) found no relationship between parental divorce and current levels of self-esteem in a sample of 2,544 individuals between the ages of 18 and 34 years.

Estaugh and Power (1991) compared self-reported drinking at the age of 23, using the National Child Development Study, between young adults who had and who had not experienced family disruption during childhood. They found that individuals from disrupted families were not especially prone to heavy drinking.

A group of studies has looked at the relationship between parental divorce and their offspring's courtship patterns and marriage. Kulka and Weingarten (1979) found that individuals from disrupted homes were less likely to marry. Mueller and Pope (1977) found that women whose parents had divorced scored lower on predictors of marital stability. Booth, Brinkerhoff and White (1984) found that parental divorce increased courtship activity among offspring. Using a combined sample of US national data, for white respondents only, Keith and Finlay (1988) demonstrated that parental divorce was associated with lower educational attainment and earlier age at marriage for both sexes. Daughters of divorced parents had a higher probability of being divorced. For sons of divorced parents, the probability of ever marrying was lower and the probability of divorce was higher among those of lower social-class background. Kiernan and Cherlin (1999) drew on a longitudinal survey of a British cohort born in 1958. They found that by the age of 33 offspring of parents who divorced were more likely to have dissolved their first partnership.

In a meta-analysis of 37 studies dealing with aspects of the long-term consequences of parental divorce for adult well-being, Amato and Keith (1991) concluded that mean effect sizes were significant and negative for all outcomes, indicating that adults who had experienced parental divorce exhibited lower levels of well-being than did adults whose parents were continuously married. This general finding is further supported by Amato and Booth's (1991) analysis among 1,243 married respondents under the age of 55 years. On the other hand, the study by Gahler (1998) in Sweden failed to find a relationship between levels of well-being during adulthood and the experience of parental separation or divorce during childhood.

Palosaari, Aro and Laippala (1996) examined the relationship between parental divorce and depression among young people up to the age of 22 years. Depression was found to be more common among the offspring of divorced families. Using the 1958 National Child Development Study when the cohort had reached the age of 23, Chase-Lansdale, Cherlin and Kiernan (1995) found a significantly higher risk of serious emotional disorders among those whose parents had divorced.

Spruijt and deGoede (1997) examined the effects of family structure on physical health, thoughts of suicide, mental health, relational well-being and the employment situation of young people up to the age of 25 years. They found that young people from intact families were less likely to have relational problems and less likely to experience unemployment.

Tucker et al. (1997) examined the relationship between parental divorce and longevity. Both men and women from divorced families had higher risks of premature mortality. Men who had experienced parental divorce were more likely to have their own marriages end in divorce, obtained less education, and engaged in fewer service activities. Women who had experienced parental divorce smoked more and were themselves more likely to divorce.

Nurco et al. (1998) examined the relationship between narcotic addiction and early family circumstances among a sample of urban males.

They found that parental separation or divorce prior to the age of 11 was significantly associated with narcotic addiction.

Wolfinger (1998) examined the relationship between parental divorce and alcohol and tobacco consumption among adults. According to this study, parental divorce increased significantly the likelihood of being a smoker and, for men, a problem drinker.

O'Connor *et al.* (1999) examined the link between the experience of divorce in childhood and several indices of adjustment in adulthood in a large community sample of women. The findings confirmed the long-term correlation between parental divorce and depression and divorce in adulthood.

Evaluation

There are a number of problems associated with integrating and interpreting the wide range of research concerned with the relationship between parental separation or divorce and the developing lives of the schoolchildren, students and adults affected in this way (Kanoy and Cunningham, 1984; Demo and Acock, 1988; Demo, 1993). These problems include reservations about the representativeness of some of the samples studied, as well as the restrictions placed on both longitudinal and cross-sectional studies. There are significant difficulties in synthesising the findings of research generated in different cultures and at different points in history. What was shown to be the case in North America may not necessarily be the case in Britain. What was shown to be the case in Britain in the 1970s may not necessarily be the case in Britain in the twenty-first century. Recent research concerned with attitudes toward divorce and marital disruption clearly indicated both significant shifts over time and significant differences between countries and cultures (Harding, Phillips and Fogarty, 1986; Jowell, Brook and Dowds, 1993) or even within different parts of the UK (Jowell, Witherspoon and Brook, 1988). Moreover, while it is relatively straightforward to demonstrate a relationship between marital disruption and specific features of the young person's experience, it is much less easy to prove the *causal* nature of such relationships.

In spite of these significant difficulties and reservations, the overall impression generated by the research literature is that information about parental separation or divorce is by itself likely to be a significant predictor across a wide range of adolescent values and attitudes.

EXPLORING THE DATA

Aim

The aim of the present analysis is to divide the database into two discrete groups in order to compare the young people whose parents have experienced separation or divorce with the young people whose parents have not experienced separation or divorce. Overall the data demonstrate that more than one in five of the respondents (22.8 per cent) come from families whose parents have been separated or divorced.

The main body of the present analysis maps the relationship between parental separation or divorce and the 15 areas explored by the values survey, namely personal well-being, worries, counselling, school, work, religious beliefs, church and society, the supernatural, politics, social concerns, sexual morality, substance use, right and wrong, leisure and the local area. In the following tables the column headed 'intact' presents data for the young people whose parents have not experienced separation or divorce and the column headed 'broken' presents data for the young people whose parents have experienced separation or divorce. First, however, attention is given to the demographic characteristics of the two groups.

Demographic characteristics

SEX

Similar proportions of males and females report that they have experienced parental separation or divorce. This finding is consistent with the view that the sex of the child is irrelevant to the parental decision to separate or divorce.

AGE

The older pupils in the sample are slightly more likely to have experienced separation or divorce than the younger pupils. Thus, marital disruption has affected 22.5 per cent of the pupils in year nine and 23.3 per cent of the pupils in year ten. This finding is consistent with the view that the older children become the more likely they are to have experienced family disruptions.

SOCIAL CLASS

Social class is calculated on the classification system proposed by the Office of Population Censuses and Surveys (1980) applied to the pupils' reporting of paternal occupation. The data demonstrate that pupils whose fathers are employed in higher social-class occupations are less likely to report parental separation or divorce. Separation or divorce is reported by 12.5 per cent of pupils whose father is in class one or professional occupations, 15.3 per cent in class two or semi-professional occupations, 19.4 per cent in non-manual class-three occupations, 22.1 per cent in skilled manual class-three occupations, 22.5 per cent in semi-skilled manual class-four occupations and 30.3 per cent in unskilled manual class-five occupations.

RELIGION

Like social class, denominational membership is a powerful predictor of differences in parental divorce or separation. Among the pupils who claim no denominational allegiance, 26.4 per cent have parents who have experienced separation or divorce, compared with 25.6 per cent of Pentecostals, 21.9 per cent of Catholics, 19.7 per cent of Baptists, 19.6 per cent of Anglicans, 16.4 per cent of Methodists and 11.9 per cent of Presbyterians. The situation among members of other faith groups is as follows: Hindu 4.1 per cent, Moslem 6.9 per cent, Sikh 9.0 per cent and Jewish 19.2 per cent.

Personal well-being

Table 6.1 demonstrates that there is a significantly lower level of personal well-being among the young people whose parents have experienced separation or divorce. They are less likely to find life really worth living or to feel that their life has a sense of purpose. They are more likely to feel that they are not worth much as a person, to suffer from depression and to have considered taking their own life.

Table 6.1: Personal well-being: by parental separation or divorce

	intact (%)	broken (%)	χ^2	$P<$
I feel my life has a sense of purpose	57	52	64.6	.001
I find life really worth living	71	64	142.9	.001
I feel I am not worth much as a person	13	16	60.8	.001
I often feel depressed	51	58	124.8	.001
I have sometimes considered taking my own life	25	34	228.3	.001

Note: 'intact' refers to the young people whose parents have not experienced separation or divorce.
'broken' refers to the young people whose parents have experienced separation or divorce.

Worries

Young people whose parents have experienced separation or divorce are slightly more anxious about the sexual aspects of their own personal relationships. According to Table 6.2 they are a little more likely to worry about their sex life. They are more worried about getting AIDS. They are not, however, generally more anxious. They display no more worry than their contemporaries from intact families about their attractiveness to the opposite sex or about how they get on with other people. They are no more worried about being attacked by pupils from other schools. Indeed, they display a slightly higher level of autonomy in comparison with their contemporaries from intact families, in the sense that they are less worried about going out alone at night in their area.

Table 6.2: Worries: by parental separation or divorce

	intact (%)	broken (%)	χ^2	$P<$
I am worried about my sex life	17	19	11.0	.001
I am worried about my attractiveness to the opposite sex	35	35	0.8	NS
I am worried about getting AIDS	61	63	10.0	.01
I am worried about how I get on with other people	52	53	0.9	NS
I am worried about being attacked by pupils from other schools	19	19	0.9	NS
I am worried about going out alone at night in my area	32	30	12.2	.001

Counselling

Young people whose parents have experienced separation or divorce experience a greater need to turn to others for advice. According to Table 6.3 they derive less help than other young people from talking with their fathers or with their mothers, and, possibly as a consequence, are more likely to turn to close friends for help, advice and support. On the other hand, they are no more likely than young people from intact homes to want to turn to professional people for help, advice and support. There are no significant differences between the proportions of young people from intact homes and from homes affected by separation or divorce who show openness to discuss their problems with doctors, clergy, social workers, teachers or youth leaders.

Table 6.3: Counselling: by parental separation or divorce

	intact (%)	broken (%)	χ^2	P<
I often long for someone to turn to for advice	34	38	56.8	.001
I would be reluctant to discuss my problems with a schoolteacher	47	46	3.6	NS
I would be reluctant to discuss my problems with a youth club/group leader	48	47	3.7	NS
I would be reluctant to discuss my problems with a doctor	33	33	0.1	NS
I would be reluctant to discuss my problems with a Christian minister/vicar/priest	41	40	4.8	NS
I would be reluctant to discuss my problems with a social worker	40	39	4.1	NS
I find it helpful to talk about my problems with my mother	50	48	12.9	.001
I find it helpful to talk about my problems with my father	33	29	63.6	.001
I find it helpful to talk about my problems with close friends	63	66	18.2	.001

School

Table 6.4 demonstrates that young people whose parents have experienced separation or divorce hold a less positive attitude toward school: they are more inclined to regard school as boring and to feel that they are not happy in their school. They are less inclined to feel that teachers do a good job, or that their school is helping to prepare them for life. On the other hand, they are no less inclined than their contemporaries from intact families to like the people with whom they go to school. Moreover, young people from intact homes and from homes affected by separation or divorce display very similar levels of anxiety or worry about school: they are equally likely to worry about their school work, to worry about exams at school, and to worry about being bullied at school.

Work

Table 6.5 suggests that young people whose parents have experienced separation or divorce hold a slightly less positive attitude toward the world of work: they are slightly less inclined to think that it is important to work hard when they get a job. They hold a slightly more cavalier attitude toward the prospects of unemployment and they are slightly more inclined to think that they would rather be unemployed than get a job which they dislike. On the other hand, they are no less inclined to want to get to the top in their work than pupils from intact families. Young people from intact homes and from homes affected by separation or divorce hold very similar views on the importance of work for generating a sense of purpose in life.

Table 6.4: School: by parental separation or divorce

	intact (%)	broken (%)	χ^2	P<
School is boring	35	42	128.0	.001
I am happy in my school	73	65	186.8	.001
I like the people I go to school with	90	89	5.5	NS
My school is helping to prepare me for life	69	66	16.5	.001
I often worry about my school work	64	65	0.4	NS
I am worried about my exams at school	74	74	0.7	NS
I am worried about being bullied at school	28	28	0.2	NS
Teachers do a good job	46	41	45.5	.001

Table 6.5: Work: by parental separation or divorce

	intact (%)	broken (%)	χ^2	P<
A job gives you a sense of purpose	77	77	0.0	NS
I think it is important to work hard when I get a job	95	94	18.6	.001
I want to get to the top in my work when I get a job	87	86	5.6	NS
I would not like to be unemployed	86	84	23.7	.001
I would rather be unemployed on social security than get a job I don't like doing	18	20	26.0	.001
Most unemployed people could have a job if they really wanted to	51	52	2.5	NS

Religious beliefs

Young people whose parents have experienced separation or divorce are less inclined to subscribe to traditional Christian beliefs than young people from intact families. According to Table 6.6, they are less likely to believe in God; they are less likely to believe that Jesus Christ really rose from the dead; they are less likely to believe the Genesis account of creation. They are less likely to think that Christianity is the only true religion. On the other hand, they are slightly more inclined to believe in life after death. There are no significant differences in the proportions of young people from intact homes and from homes affected by separation or divorce who believe that God punishes people who do wrong.

Table 6.6: Religious beliefs: by parental separation or divorce

	intact (%)	broken (%)	χ^2	$P<$
I believe in God	43	36	115.4	.001
I believe that Jesus really rose from the dead	31	27	58.1	.001
I believe in life after death	45	47	10.3	.01
I believe God punishes people who do wrong	20	20	1.8	NS
I think Christianity is the only true religion	17	15	9.5	.01
I believe that God made the world in six days and rested on the seventh	21	17	48.8	.001

Church and society

Table 6.7 demonstrates that young people whose parents have experienced separation or divorce hold a less positive attitude toward the role of the church in contemporary society: they are more inclined to think that the church and the Bible are irrelevant for life today. They are more inclined to dismiss the church as boring. They are less inclined to consider that the clergy do a good job. They are less inclined to want to get married in church or to have their children baptised or christened in church than pupils from intact families. They are less inclined to support the view that schools should hold a religious assembly every day.

The supernatural

Although young people whose parents have experienced separation or divorce are less inclined to believe in God, Table 6.8 demonstrates that they are more inclined to believe in a range of supernatural phenomena. Thus, they are more likely to believe in their horoscope, or to believe that fortune-tellers can tell the future. They are more likely to believe in ghosts and that it is possible to contact the spirits of the dead. They are more likely to believe in black magic and the Devil. At the same time, they are slightly more likely to be apprehensive of the supernatural, in the sense that they would show more anxiety about going into a church alone.

Table 6.7: Church and society: by parental separation or divorce

	intact (%)	broken (%)	χ^2	P<
I believe that I can be a Christian without going to church	51	50	2.6	NS
The church seems irrelevant to life today	27	29	13.6	.001
The Bible seems irrelevant to life today	30	32	10.2	.01
I want my children to be baptised/christened in church	56	51	50.4	.001
I want to get married in church	74	71	35.0	.001
Religious education should be taught in school	38	36	6.5	NS
Schools should hold a religious assembly every day	8	7	24.8	.001
Church is boring	50	56	87.1	.001
Christian ministers/vicars/priests do a good job	37	32	52.8	.001

Table 6.8: The supernatural: by parental separation or divorce

	intact (%)	broken (%)	χ^2	P<
I believe in my horoscope	33	41	168.3	.001
I believe in ghosts	39	47	172.8	.001
I believe in the Devil	21	23	12.1	.001
I believe in black magic	19	24	91.2	.001
I believe that fortune-tellers can tell the future	18	25	189.9	.001
I believe it is possible to contact the spirits of the dead	29	38	202.2	.001
I am frightened of going into a church alone	11	13	28.8	.001

Politics

Two main conclusions emerge from Table 6.9 regarding the relationship between separation or divorce and adolescents' attitudes toward politics. First, young people whose parents have experienced separation or divorce hold a more cynical attitude toward politics: they are more inclined to feel that it makes no difference which political party is in power. Second, young people whose parents have experienced separation or divorce adopt a more left-wing political stance: they are likely to have more confidence in the Labour Party and less confidence in the Conservative Party; they are more inclined to argue against private schools and against private medical practice. On the other hand, young people from intact homes and from homes affected by separation or divorce hold very similar views on issues concerned with racial integration.

Table 6.9: Politics: by parental separation or divorce

	intact (%)	broken (%)	χ^2	P<
It makes no difference which political party is in power	22	25	46.8	.001
I have confidence in the Conservative Party	16	13	30.3	.001
I have confidence in the Labour Party	19	21	9.9	.01
Private schools should be abolished	23	26	43.7	.001
Private medicine should be abolished	15	18	34.7	.001
There are too many black people living in this country	16	16	2.8	NS
I think that immigration into Britain should be restricted	31	30	6.3	NS

Social concerns

Just as young people whose parents have experienced separation or divorce hold a more cynical attitude toward politics, so they also hold a more cynical attitude toward the world's problems. According to Table 6.10 they are less inclined to feel that they can do anything to help solve the world's problems. Table 6.10 also demonstrates that they are less inclined to be concerned about global issues, like the risk of pollution to the environment, the risk of nuclear war, and the poverty of the Third World. On the other hand, young people from disrupted families are neither more conservative nor more liberal than young people from intact families in their attitudes toward violence on television or pornography.

Sexual morality

Table 6.11 demonstrates that there is a significantly more permissive attitude toward sexual morality among the young people whose parents have experienced separation or divorce. They are less likely to think that it is wrong to have sexual intercourse under the legal age or outside marriage; they are less likely to think that divorce is wrong; they are less likely to think that homosexuality is wrong. On the other hand, they are more likely than young people from intact families to think that abortion is wrong. Young people from intact homes and from homes affected by separation or divorce hold very similar views on the acceptability of contraception.

Table 6.10: Social concerns: by parental separation or divorce

	intact (%)	broken (%)	x^2	P<
There is too much violence on television	20	19	3.2	NS
Pornography is too readily available	33	34	0.3	NS
I am concerned about the risk of pollution to the environment	67	63	51.9	.001
I am concerned about the poverty of the Third World	62	56	73.0	.001
I am concerned about the risk of nuclear war	56	54	10.2	.01
There is nothing I can do to help solve the world's problems	24	28	42.3	.001

Table 6.11: Sexual morality: by parental separation or divorce

	intact (%)	broken (%)	χ^2	P<
It is wrong to have sexual intercourse outside marriage	15	11	58.4	.001
It is wrong to have sexual intercourse under the legal age (16 years)	25	20	68.0	.001
Homosexuality is wrong	38	36	8.1	.01
Contraception is wrong	5	6	1.4	NS
Abortion is wrong	35	39	40.2	.001
Divorce is wrong	20	17	34.8	.001

Substance use

Just as young people whose parents have experienced separation or divorce hold a more liberal attitude toward sexual morality, so they also hold a more liberal attitude toward substance use. According to Table 6.12 they are more likely to condone smoking cigarettes and becoming drunk;

they are more likely to condone the use of marijuana and heroin; they are more likely to condone glue-sniffing and the sniffing of butane gas.

Table 6.12: Substance use: by parental separation or divorce

	intact (%)	broken (%)	χ^2	P<
It is wrong to smoke cigarettes	44	37	104.0	.001
It is wrong to become drunk	20	16	66.0	.001
It is wrong to use marijuana (hash or pot)	52	45	130.6	.001
It is wrong to use heroin	74	71	40.0	.001
It is wrong to sniff glue	78	76	13.4	.001
It is wrong to sniff butane gas	73	72	7.6	.01

Right and wrong

According to Table 6.13 young people whose parents have experienced separation or divorce are less likely to think that there is anything wrong in a variety of antisocial or criminal activities. They are less likely to think that there is anything wrong in writing graffiti, playing truant or cycling after dark without lights. They are more likely to condone travelling without a ticket, shoplifting or buying alcoholic drinks or cigarettes under the legal age. They hold a much less positive attitude toward the police.

Table 6.13: Right and wrong: by parental separation or divorce

	intact (%)	broken (%)	χ^2	P<
There is nothing wrong in shoplifting	7	9	68.8	.001
There is nothing wrong in travelling without a ticket	19	23	66.2	.001
There is nothing wrong in cycling after dark without lights	16	20	74.2	.001
There is nothing wrong in playing truant (wagging) from school	15	21	151.3	.001
There is nothing wrong in buying cigarettes under the legal age (16 years)	27	37	289.7	.001
There is nothing wrong in buying alcoholic drinks under the legal age (18 years)	40	47	108.0	.001
There is nothing wrong in writing graffiti (tagging) wherever you like	14	17	37.1	.001
The police do a good job	56	50	77.3	.001

Leisure

Two main conclusions emerge from Table 6.14 regarding the relationship between separation or divorce and adolescents' attitudes toward their leisure. First, young people whose parents have experienced separation or divorce hold a less positive attitude toward their leisure; they are more likely to long for more things to do with their leisure time; they are more likely to hang about with their friends doing nothing in particular; they are more likely to be critical of their local youth centre. Second, young people whose parents have experienced separation or divorce tend to feel that their parents are more critical of the ways in which they spend their leisure time. On the other hand, they are neither more nor less aware of parental restrictions being placed on their leisure time than young people from intact families.

Table 6.14: Leisure: by parental separation or divorce

	intact (%)	broken (%)	χ^2	P<
I often hang about with my friends doing nothing in particular	67	72	69.7	.001
I wish I had more things to do with my leisure time	57	61	32.3	.001
My youth centre is boring	35	38	26.8	.001
My parents prefer me to stay in as much as possible	20	21	0.1	NS
My parents allow me to do what I like in my leisure time	48	49	2.5	NS
My parents do not agree with most of the things that I do in my leisure time	27	35	188.6	.001

My area

Table 6.15 demonstrates that young people whose parents have experienced separation or divorce hold a less positive attitude toward the area in which they live. They are significantly less likely than young people from intact homes to agree that they like living in their area. They are significantly more likely than young people from intact homes to share the perception of their area as being one in which problems are growing; they are more inclined to feel that crime, vandalism, drug-taking, violence, drink-related problems and unemployment are all on the increase in their local area. On the other hand, young people from intact homes and from

homes affected by separation or divorce hold similar views on the extent
to which their local area cares for its young people.

Table 6.15: My area: by parental separation or divorce

	intact (%)	broken (%)	χ^2	P<
Crime is a growing problem in my area	41	45	30.1	.001
Vandalism is a growing problem in my area	44	47	26.7	.001
Drug taking is a growing problem in my area	30	36	79.5	.001
Violence is a growing problem in my area	31	35	35.2	.001
Drunks are a growing problem in my area	24	28	63.1	.001
Unemployment is a growing problem in my area	35	38	25.7	.001
I like living in my area	76	68	190.5	.001
My area cares about its young people	21	20	6.3	NS

CONCLUSION

This chapter has profiled the relationship between parental separation or
divorce and adolescent values over 15 specific areas. The data make it
clear that there are significant differences over all 15 areas between those
young people whose parents have experienced separation or divorce and
those whose parents have not. It is important to be clear just what kind of
conclusions can be drawn from these findings and what kind of
conclusions cannot be drawn from these findings. Two main observations
need to be made.

First, it is possible on the basis of these data to conclude that, as a group,
young people whose parents have experienced separation or divorce differ
in significant ways from young people whose parents have not. As a group
they experience lower personal well-being; worry more about sex; long
more to be able to turn to others for advice; hold less positive attitudes
toward school and work; are less likely to believe in conventional religion
but more likely to believe in superstitions; are more cynical about politics
and issues of global concern; tend to prefer left-wing political views; are
more liberal in their attitudes toward sexual morality and substance use;
are more inclined to condone antisocial behaviour; are less satisfied with
their leisure time; and hold a less positive view of the area in which they
live. These findings are consistent with the wider field of research which

suggests that parental separation and divorce function as a significant predictor of values and behaviour not only during the years of schooling but also during university and college life and during adulthood.

Second, however, it is not possible on the basis of the present analysis to conclude that these very real differences are necessarily or wholly a consequence of parental separation or divorce. In a cross-sectional study of this nature there are a number of correlates, like social class and religious background, which need to be taken into consideration in exploring the adequacy of a causal account. These findings, at least, confirm the value of undertaking such further analyses. The present findings also clearly demonstrate that it would be a fundamental error not to take parental separation and divorce into account in understanding, interpreting and predicting individual differences in the values debate among adolescents.

7

CHURCH ATTENDANCE

SETTING THE SCENE

Questions regarding the social significance of religion within England and Wales have been handled in several different ways by recent commentators. In an often-cited study, Davie (1994) distinguished between the key dimensions of religion which she characterised as 'believing' and as 'belonging'. For Davie believing was associated with notions like belief in God, and belonging was associated with practices like church attendance. According to these definitions Davie was able to describe the current religious ethos of England and Wales as one of 'believing without belonging'. Using language in a somewhat different way, Francis (1994a) distinguished between three key dimensions of religion which he characterised as 'belonging', 'believing' and 'practising'. For Francis belonging was associated with self-identified religious affiliation, believing was associated with belief in God, and practising was associated with church attendance. According to these definitions Francis would describe the current religious ethos of England and Wales as 'belonging without practising'. Each of the three dimensions of religion have been subjected to closer scrutiny by different studies including Fane (1999) on belonging, Kay (1997) and Gill, Hadaway and Marler (1998) on believing and Brierley (1991a, 1991b) and Francis and Lankshear (1991) on practising.

Given the complexity of the debate regarding the significance of these three distinct markers of religiosity, the present chapter proposes to concentrate on just one of them, namely church attendance. The relationship between church attendance and the wider issues of values is charted by giving attention to two bodies of literature, namely what is known from the British Social Attitudes Survey, and what is known from other studies conducted among children and adolescents. Because the review is concentrating specifically and exclusively on identifying the power of church attendance to predict individual differences, attention is not being given to related issues like denominational identity or belief in God. Moreover, the review is focused specifically on the Christian tradition. Related areas of research have dealt with other faith traditions and varying levels of practice within these traditions.

British Social Attitudes Survey

From its inception the British Social Attitudes Survey included a question on frequency of church attendance. Little use, however, has been made of this variable in the annual reports based on the survey. For example, no reference to analyses by church attendance appeared in the indices for 1984, 1985, 1986, 1987, 1988, 1991, 1994, 1995, 1996, 1997 and 1999, although on closer inspection several of these volumes actually included analyses by church attendance.

In the 1985 report an examination of moral attitudes concerning right and wrong in public life by Johnson and Wood (1985) included a cross-tabulation by frequency of church attendance of the following scenario. A man offers refuse collectors £5 to take away rubbish they are not supposed to pick up. According to the data 44 per cent of weekly churchgoers judged this to be wrong, compared with 33 per cent of those who attended church once a year or less.

In the 1988 report Johnson (1988) examined the relationship between church attendance and personal standards of honesty. He found that 12 per cent of weekly churchgoers would over claim on insurance by £100, compared with 30 per cent of non-churchgoers. Similarly 6 per cent of weekly churchgoers would keep £5 extra change given by mistake in a large store, compared with 29 per cent of non-churchgoers. In the 1989 report Davis and Jowell (1989) compared the level of church attendance in Britain with that in other countries, but they did not explore the correlates of church attendance.

In the 1990 report Curtice and Gallagher (1990) compared the relationship between church attendance and certain moral issues in Northern Ireland and Great Britain. For example, in Great Britain they found that 30 per cent of those who attended religious services weekly considered premarital sex always wrong, compared with 9 per cent of those who attended church less than twice a year. Homosexual relationships were judged always wrong by 70 per cent of weekly attenders and 54 per cent of those who attended less than twice a year. Two-thirds (65 per cent) of weekly attenders said that pornography should be banned altogether, compared with one-third (34 per cent) of those who attended less than twice a year. Abortion should not be allowed in cases where there is a strong chance of defect in the baby according to 25 per cent of weekly attenders and 6 per cent of those who attended less than twice a year.

In the 1992 report Greeley (1992) traced the relationship between church attendance and religious affiliation. He found that 30 per cent of Roman Catholics attended services two or three times a month, compared with 31 per cent of Free Church members, 25 per cent of Presbyterians and 14 per cent of Anglicans. Overall 19 per cent of women attended two or three times a month, compared with 12 per cent of men. In the 1993 report Heath, Taylor and Toka (1993) compared the importance of church attendance and denominational affiliation (Catholic and Pentecostal) for predicting family values. They concluded that practice was a more important factor than affiliation.

In the 1996 report, Donnison and Bryson (1996) constructed a scale to measure pro-euthanasia attitudes. They found significantly less acceptance of euthanasia among weekly churchgoers. In the 1997 report Barnett and Thomson (1997) constructed indices of tolerance of screen and television violence and portrayal of sex. They found that church attendance was associated with a more restrictive view. In the 1998 report Bryson and Curtice (1998) found that church attendance was associated with lower scores on their scale of post-materialism, lower scores on their scale of sexual liberalism, and higher scores on their scale of national pride. In the 1999 report Stratford, Marteau and Bobrow (1999) found that church attendance was correlated with a less positive attitude toward prenatal genetic testing.

Given the paucity of use made of church attendance in the annual reports of the British Social Attitudes Survey, much remained to be extracted by secondary analyses. In his book *Churchgoing and Christian Ethics* Gill (1999) turned attention to this possibility. In particular Gill concentrated on the relationship between church attendance and the three themes of faith, moral order and love. Each of these three themes will be reviewed in order.

First, drawing on the 1991 database in respect of faith, Gill found that 21 per cent of non-churchgoers believed that there is a God who concerns himself personally with every human being, compared with 84 per cent of weekly churchgoers. A quarter (27 per cent) of non-churchgoers believed that right and wrong should be based on God's laws, compared with 77 per cent of weekly churchgoers. One in eight (12 per cent) of non-churchgoers believed that the course of our life is decided by God, compared with 53 per cent of weekly churchgoers.

Regarding traditional tenets of Christian belief, 89 per cent of weekly churchgoers believed in heaven and so did 45 per cent of non-churchgoers. By way of comparison, 62 per cent of weekly churchgoers believed in hell and so did 19 per cent of non-churchgoers. Belief in life after death was held by 83 per cent of weekly churchgoers and 39 per cent of non-churchgoers. Belief in religious miracles was held by 81 per cent of weekly churchgoers and 28 per cent of non-churchgoers.

Regarding wider issues of belief in the supernatural, non-churchgoers were more likely to be believers than churchgoers. For example, 28 per cent of non-churchgoers believed that a person's star sign at birth, or horoscope, can affect the course of that person's future, compared with 19 per cent of weekly churchgoers. Two-fifths (41 per cent) of non-churchgoers believed that some fortune-tellers can really foresee the future, compared with 33 per cent of weekly churchgoers. A quarter (25 per cent) of non-churchgoers believed that good-luck charms sometimes do bring good luck, compared with 14 per cent of weekly churchgoers. Finally, 66 per cent of weekly churchgoers believed that there should be daily prayers in all state schools, compared with 28 per cent of non-churchgoers.

Second, in respect of moral order, Gill combined data from the 1983 and 1984 surveys to examine how churchgoers and non-churchgoers would respond to the following question: 'In general would you say that people should obey the law without exception, or are there exceptional occasions on which people should follow their own conscience even if it means breaking the law?' He found that 57 per cent of weekly churchgoers agreed that people should obey the law without exception, compared with 44 per cent of non-churchgoers. Asking the same question of the 1994 database, Gill found that the gap had widened (51 per cent and 31 per cent).

Taking a different perspective on the 1994 database, Gill examined the relationship between church attendance and political activity. He found that 68 per cent of weekly churchgoers said that they would contact their MP if they thought a law being considered by Parliament was really unjust and harmful, compared with 54 per cent of non-churchgoers. Gill also found that in 1989 and 1991 twice as many weekly churchgoers (32 per cent) as non-churchgoers (15 per cent) said that they had actually taken that kind of action.

On the question of people who avoid paying income tax in full, according to the 1983 database, 86 per cent of weekly churchgoers agreed that they should not be allowed to get away with it, compared with 64 per cent of non-churchgoers. According to the 1991 database, 56 per cent of weekly churchgoers argued that it was wrong to pay a plumber cash to avoid VAT, compared with 38 per cent of non-churchgoers.

Regarding the issue of divorce, in the combined 1983 and 1984 surveys, Gill found that 54 per cent of weekly churchgoers considered that divorce in Britain should be more difficult, compared with 28 per cent of non-churchgoers. In the 1994 database the contrast had widened to 61 per cent and 27 per cent.

According to the combined 1983 and 1984 surveys, 64 per cent of weekly churchgoers believed that it is always or mostly wrong if a man and a women have sexual relations before marriage, compared with 26 per cent of non-churchgoers. In the 1994 database the contrast remained, although both groups had become somewhat more liberal. The figures stood at 53 per cent and 13 per cent. Also according to the 1994 database, 87 per cent of weekly churchgoers agreed that people who want children ought to get married, compared with 74 per cent of non-churchgoers.

On the question of homosexuality, the combined 1983 and 1984 surveys showed that 79 per cent of weekly churchgoers judged homosexuality to be always or mostly wrong, compared with 66 per cent of non-churchgoers. In the 1993 database the figures stood at 80 per cent and 69 per cent. According to the combined 1983 and 1984 survey, 61 per cent of weekly churchgoers and 60 per cent of non-churchgoers considered that homosexuals should not be allowed to teach in schools. In the 1993 database the figures stood at 42 per cent and 44 per cent.

Gill cites several indicators concerned with the relationship between smoking and church attendance. For example, 15 per cent of weekly churchgoers reported that they smoked cigarettes, compared with 37 per cent of non-churchgoers. At the same time, 80 per cent of weekly churchgoers agreed that all cigarette advertising should be banned, compared with 57 per cent of non-churchgoers.

Third, in respect of love, Gill derived three distinct tests of altruism from the British Social Attitudes database. The first test of altruism examined whether churchgoers were more involved in voluntary service to the community. Using the 1994 database, Gill found that 15 per cent of weekly churchgoers were members of a community or voluntary group, compared with 3 per cent of non-churchgoers.

The second test of altruism examined whether churchgoers were particularly concerned about the vulnerable and needy. Using the 1989 database, Gill found that 28 per cent of weekly churchgoers cited 'to help others' as the most important factor in choosing a new job, compared with 6 per cent of non-churchgoers. In the 1983 database, 55 per cent of weekly churchgoers agreed that children should look after aged parents, compared with 39 per cent of non-churchgoers. In the combined 1983, 1984 and 1985 databases, churchgoers showed themselves to be less in favour of capital punishment than non-churchgoers. For example, 58 per cent of weekly churchgoers favoured capital punishment for police murder, compared with 76 per cent of non-churchgoers. In the 1993 and 1994 database, the comparable figures stood at 63 per cent and 74 per cent. Finally, in the combined 1983–87 surveys churchgoers showed themselves to be less prejudiced than non-churchgoers. For example, 76 per cent of weekly churchgoers described themselves as not prejudiced at all against people of other races, compared with 58 per cent of non-churchgoers.

The third test of altruism contained a mixture of attitudes and behaviours. According to the 1993 database, weekly churchgoers took the needs of the poor overseas more seriously than did other people. Thus, 67 per cent of weekly churchgoers gave a high priority to such charitable causes, compared with 32 per cent of non-churchgoers. According to the 1994 survey, churchgoers showed greater support for national lottery money helping overseas causes and less support for animal causes at home. Thus, 22 per cent of weekly churchgoers considered that it was not good to spend lottery money on the starving overseas, compared with 54 per cent of non-churchgoers. At the same time, 35 per cent of weekly churchgoers considered that it was not good to spend lottery money on preventing cruelty to animals in Britain, compared with 14 per cent of non-churchgoers. According to the combined 1991 and 1993 database, 60 per cent of weekly churchgoers agreed that they cannot refuse when someone comes to the door with a collecting tin, compared with 51 per cent of non-churchgoers.

Children and adolescents

Five main strands of research regarding the role of religion within childhood and adolescence have flourished in Britain during the past two decades. One strand, based on ethnographic methods, has profiled the identity of young people growing up within a range of faith traditions. Jackson (1997) has provided an overview of this work. A second strand, concentrating on mapping children's spirituality, has been documented by Hay and Nye (1998). A third strand, developed by the Children and Worldviews Project, has been documented by Erricker *et al.* (1997). A fourth strand has concentrated on mapping the correlates of a positive attitude toward Christianity. Kay and Francis (1996) have provided an overview of this work. The fifth strand, largely developed by Francis and his colleagues, has developed a series of independent studies which have included church attendance as a predictor of individual differences among children and adolescents. It is with this fifth strand that the present chapter is concerned. Many of the issues covered by this chapter have been previewed by Francis and Kay (1995).

Within this tradition several studies have explored the relationship between church attendance and attitude toward Christianity. Drawing on a database of 2,000 pupils between the ages of 11 and 16 years, Francis (1989) compared the views of those who attended church weekly with the rest of the sample. This study involved references to five areas: God, Jesus, prayer, the Bible and the church. The data demonstrated that 13 per cent of the weekly churchgoers found it hard to believe in God, compared with 46 per cent of the rest of the sample. Two-thirds (64 per cent) of the weekly churchgoers felt that Jesus helped them, compared with 25 per cent of the rest of the sample. Over half (53 per cent) of the weekly churchgoers reported that saying prayers helped them a lot, compared with 23 per cent of the rest of the sample. The Bible was dismissed as out of date by 9 per cent of weekly churchgoers and 28 per cent of the rest of the sample. Church services were described as boring by 17 per cent of weekly churchgoers and 54 per cent of the rest of the sample.

The responses to the same set of items by 673 self-identified Roman Catholic pupils between the ages of 12 and 16 were analysed against church attendance by Burton and Francis (1996). This analysis demonstrated, for example, that 18 per cent of weekly churchgoers found it hard to believe in God, compared with 43 per cent of non-churchgoers; 66 per cent of weekly churchgoers believed that Jesus helped them, compared with 19 per cent of non-churchgoers; 58 per cent of weekly churchgoers found praying helps them a lot, compared with 18 per cent of non-churchgoers; 42 per cent of weekly churchgoers found church services boring, compared with 67 per cent of non-churchgoers.

Francis, Gibson and Fulljames (1990) extended the same set of items to include attitudes toward creationism and scientism in a study among 6,095 11–15-year-old pupils in Scotland. This study found a positive correlation between church attendance and creationism and a negative correlation between church attendance and scientism. For example, while 16 per cent of weekly churchgoers agreed that nothing should be believed unless it can be proved scientifically, the proportion rose to 31 per cent among the rest of the sample.

A further extension of this same set of items is reported by Francis (1992a) in a study among 3,863 pupils between the ages of 12 and 16. The questions were extended to include perceptions about Christians and the role of the church in society. The data indicated that 91 per cent of monthly churchgoers considered that they wanted to get married in church, and so did 74 per cent of non-churchgoers. While 84 per cent of monthly churchgoers wanted their children to be baptised in church, so did 49 per cent of non-churchgoers.

Drawing on a sample of 3,762 11-year-old pupils, Francis (1992b) examined the relationship between church attendance and attitude toward school. This study employed seven semantic differential scales of attitude toward school, English lessons, maths lessons, music lessons, games lessons, religious education lessons and school assemblies. The data demonstrated that church attendance was a significant predictor of positive attitudes toward school, English, music, maths, religious education and assemblies, but not games lessons.

The relationship between church attendance and television-viewing time and programme preferences was studied by Francis and Gibson (1993) on data provided by a sample of 5,432 pupils between the ages of 11 and 15 years. This study distinguished between four types of programmes described as soap, sport, light entertainment and current awareness. The data demonstrated that weekly churchgoers watched less television overall. Regarding viewing preferences, weekly churchgoers gave more priority to current awareness programmes and less priority to sport programmes. On the other hand, church attendance was not correlated with preferences for soaps or for light entertainment programmes.

A study by Francis and Evans (1996) mapped the relationship between church attendance and purpose in life in a sample of 4,014 12–15 year olds. The data demonstrated that 69 per cent of the weekly churchgoers reported a sense of purpose in life, compared with 43 per cent of the non-churchgoers. This finding confirmed the results of an earlier study conducted among Catholic adolescents by Francis and Burton (1994).

Francis (1997a) explored the relationship between church attendance and the 'closed mind', as assessed by Rokeach's (1960) dogmatism scale, among a sample of 711 16 year olds. The data failed to find either a positive or negative correlation between dogmatism and church attendance. This finding is consistent with the findings of earlier studies among high-school pupils reported by Wilson (1985), among students reported by Primavera, Tantillo and DeLisio (1980) and among adult church members reported by Schlangen and Davidson (1985). Other earlier studies, however, have reported a positive correlation between dogmatism and church attendance (Kilpatrick, Sutker and Sutker, 1970; MacDonald, 1970; Steininger, Durso and Pasquariello, 1972).

Francis (1997b) drew on a database of 20,968 pupils between the ages of 13 and 15 to examine the relationship between church attendance and concern about environmental pollution. The data demonstrated that, after taking into account sex, age and personality, greater frequency of church attendance was associated with a higher level of environmental concern. Taken alongside the findings of two other studies conducted in the USA by Woodrum and Hoban (1994) and Kanagy and Nelsen (1995) these findings challenge Lynn White's (1967) classic criticism of the Christian traditions as promoting the exploitation of nature and hastening the ecological crisis. On the other hand, another recent study in the USA by Boyd (1999) failed to find any relationship between church attendance and environmental concern.

Francis (1997c) explored the relationship between church attendance and attitude toward substance use among 11,173 pupils between the ages of 13 and 15 years. The scale of attitude toward substance use included references to alcohol, tobacco, glue, marijuana, butane gas and heroin. The data demonstrated a significant positive correlation between frequency of church attendance and a negative attitude toward substance use. This finding is consistent with a series of studies which have reported a negative association between church attendance and drinking patterns among students (Amoateng and Bahr, 1986; Faulkner, Alcorn and Garvin, 1989; Long and Boik, 1993) and among adults (Lubben, Chi and Kitano, 1988; Clarke, Beeghley and Cochran, 1990; Cochran, Beeghley and Bock, 1992). On the other hand Francis (1994b) found no significant relationship between frequency of church attendance and reported drinking behaviour among his adult sample in England. More generally, an inverse relationship between church attendance and several types of drug use among young people has been reported over a number of years (Burkett and White, 1974; Linden and Currie, 1977; Higgins and Albrecht, 1977; McIntosh et al., 1981; Nelsen and Rooney, 1982; Hadaway, Elifson and Petersen, 1984; Adlaf and Smart, 1985; Sloane and Potvin, 1986; Francis and Mullen, 1993; Mullen and Francis, 1995).

In an innovative study in the USA, Wallace and Forman (1998) examined the relationship between church attendance and health-promoting behaviours among a sample of nearly 5,000 high-school seniors. They found that church attendance was negatively correlated with a range of risky behaviours, including interpersonal violence, driving while drinking, smoking, binge-drinking and marijuana use. At the same time they found that church attendance was positively correlated with a range of health-promoting behaviours, including seatbelt use, diet, exercise and sleep.

Francis and Greer (1999b) explored the relationship between church attendance and attitude toward science among a sample of 1,549 pupils in Northern Ireland between the ages of 13 and 16 years. They employed an instrument developed by Menis (1989) designed to distinguish three components of attitude toward science: the importance of science, science as a career, and science in the school curriculum. The data demonstrated that pupils who never attended church held a significantly more positive attitude than churchgoing pupils toward science in the school curriculum and toward the importance of science. Churchgoers and non-churchgoers, however, did not differ in their attitude toward science as a career. The negative correlation between church attendance and science-related attitudes is consistent with the findings of an earlier study in Scotland reported by Fulljames, Gibson and Francis (1991).

Evaluation

The present review has concentrated on studies which have provided information about the predictive power of church attendance in isolation from other information about religiosity. Many of these studies have gone on to demonstrate the additional information which can be conveyed through multivariate models which introduce alongside church attendance such factors as age, sex, patterns of belief, denominational affiliation, religious orientation, personal prayer and personality. Such refinements do not detract, however, from the directness and simplicity of taking levels of church attendance seriously in their own right. The overall impression generated by the research literature is that information about church attendance is by itself likely to be a significant predictor across a whole range of adolescent values and attitudes.

EXPLORING THE DATA

Aim

The aim of the present study is to isolate one clear aspect of religiosity, namely church attendance. The questionnaire invited the young people to categorise their level of church attendance on a five-point scale, anchored by 'nearly every week', 'at least once a month', 'sometimes', 'once or twice a year' and 'never'. For the purposes of clarity in the analysis these five categories will be collapsed into three, distinguishing between those who attend church weekly, those who attend church less frequently than weekly and those who never attend church.

In the British Social Attitudes Survey the question about attendance was only asked of those who identified with a specific religious group. The problem with that approach is that it excludes the category of those individuals who attend but who do not affiliate. In the present study of teenagers the question about attendance was asked of the whole sample. The problem with this approach is that attenders include those who attend not only Christian churches but also other places of worship. For this reason the following analyses have excluded all respondents who identified with a non-Christian faith group. This reduced the overall effective database to 32,743 cases, a loss of 3.7 per cent. Overall, the data demonstrate that 14.3 per cent of the respondents attended church weekly, 36.5 per cent attended less frequently than weekly, and 49.1 per cent never attended church.

The main body of the present analysis maps the relationship between church attendance and the 15 areas explored by the survey, namely personal well-being, worries, counselling, school, work, religious beliefs, church and society, the supernatural, politics, social concerns, sexual morality, substance use, right and wrong, leisure and the local area. First, however, attention is given to the demographic characteristics associated with frequency of church attendance.

Demographic characteristics

SEX

A higher proportion of females (15.5 per cent) than males (13.2 per cent) report weekly church attendance. At the same time, a higher proportion of males (53.4 per cent) than females (44.7 per cent) report never attending church. This sex difference is consistent with a large number of findings identifying higher levels of religiosity among females during childhood, adolescence and adulthood (Francis, 1997d).

AGE

The older pupils in the sample are slightly less likely to report weekly church attendance. Thus, 13.7 per cent of the pupils in year ten classify themselves as weekly churchgoers, compared with 14.9 per cent of the pupils in year nine. This finding is consistent with the evidence provided from other studies regarding the persistent and consistent drift from the churches during the teenage years (Francis, 1989).

SOCIAL CLASS

Social class is calculated on the classification system proposed by the Office of Population Censuses and Surveys (1980) applied to the pupils' reporting of paternal occupation. The data demonstrate that pupils whose fathers are employed in higher social-class occupations are more likely to attend church. Weekly church attendance is reported by 28.4 per cent of pupils whose father is in class one or professional occupations, 20.1 per cent in class two or semi-professional occupations, 15.8 per cent in non-manual class-three occupations, 10.8 per cent in skilled manual occupations, 10.1 per cent in semi-skilled manual class-four occupations, and 11.9 per cent in unskilled manual class-five occupations. The proportions of pupils who never attend church are as follows: 30.5 per cent in class one, 37.0 per cent in class two, 44.5 per cent in class three non-manual, 55 per cent in class three manual, 57.9 per cent in class four and 54.4 per cent in class five. This social-class difference is consistent with a large number of findings associating higher levels of church attendance with the higher social classes (Beit-Hallahmi and Argyle, 1997).

RELIGION

Like social class, denominational affiliation is a significant predictor of levels of church attendance. According to the data, weekly church attendance is practised by 65.8 per cent of Pentecostals, 48.3 per cent of Presbyterians, 42.9 per cent of Roman Catholics, 42 per cent of Baptists, 36.7 per cent of Methodists and 16.6 per cent of Anglicans. Looked at from the opposite perspective, the following proportions of different denominational groups never attend church: 31.1 per cent of Anglicans, 16.8 per cent of Methodists, 16.7 per cent of Baptists, 11.6 per cent of Roman Catholics, 7.9 per cent of Presbyterians and 4.3 per cent of Pentecostals. Three-quarters (73.5 per cent) of the young people who claim no religious affiliation also report never attending church. These differences in the level of church attendance practised by those who affiliate with different denominations are consistent with the findings from a number of studies concerned with the issue of religious nominalism (Fane, 1999). In particular the Anglican church in England and Wales has a large number of affiliates who rarely or never practise (Greeley, 1992).

Personal well-being

According to Table 7.1 there is a clear and consistent relationship between frequency of church attendance and personal well-being. The most striking comparison occurs in respect of purpose in life. Weekly churchgoers are much more likely to feel that their lives have a sense of purpose; they are also somewhat more likely to say that they find life really worth living. Although there is comparatively little variation in the perceptions of weekly churchgoers and non-churchgoers who often feel depressed, such feelings of depression are less likely to translate into suicidal ideation among weekly churchgoers.

Table 7.1: Personal well-being: by church attendance

	never (%)	sometimes (%)	weekly (%)	χ^2	P<
I feel my life has a sense of purpose	49	59	70	732.5	.001
I find life really worth living	68	70	73	53.6	.001
I feel I am not worth much as a person	14	13	12	5.2	NS
I often feel depressed	52	54	50	17.8	.001
I have sometimes considered taking my own life	28	26	23	55.2	.001

Note: This analysis has excluded all respondents who identified with a non-Christian faith.

Worries

Table 7.2 demonstrates that young churchgoers emerge as displaying a higher level of worry and anxiety over a range of issues in comparison with young people who never attend church. In particular churchgoers are more likely to worry about personal relationships, including how they get on with other people, their attractiveness to the opposite sex and their sex life. Young churchgoers are also more likely to worry about going out alone at night in their area or about being attacked by pupils from other schools. Only in respect of getting AIDS do young churchgoers display a lower level of worry than young people who never attend church.

Table 7.2: Worries: by church attendance

	never (%)	sometimes (%)	weekly (%)	χ^2	P<
I am worried about my sex life	16	19	19	61.7	.001
I am worried about my attractiveness to the opposite sex	31	38	41	235.6	.001
I am worried about getting AIDS	62	64	57	60.1	.001
I am worried about how I get on with other people	47	57	59	362.6	.001
I am worried about being attacked by pupils from other schools	17	20	24	141.4	.001
I am worried about going out alone at night in my area	27	34	40	327.4	.001

Counselling

It is clear from Table 7.3 that young churchgoers benefit from a high level of personal support both from their parents and from their close friends: weekly churchgoers are more likely to say that they find it helpful to talk about their problems with their mother, with their father and with close friends. In spite of indicating that they are more likely to talk with others about their problems, young churchgoers are also more likely to report that they often long for someone to turn to for advice. Young churchgoers also differ significantly from non-churchgoers regarding the categories of people to whom they are willing to turn for advice. Young churchgoers are more willing to turn to the clergy for advice, but less willing to turn to schoolteachers, youth leaders, doctors and social workers.

Table 7.3: Counselling: by church attendance

	never (%)	*sometimes* (%)	*weekly* (%)	χ^2	*P<*
I often long for someone to turn to for advice	32	37	38	108.4	.001
I would be reluctant to discuss my problems with a schoolteacher	45	49	48	44.1	.001
I would be reluctant to discuss my problems with a youth club/group leader	45	51	50	79.6	.001
I would be reluctant to discuss my problems with a doctor	32	34	35	21.7	.001
I would be reluctant to discuss my problems with a Christian minister/vicar/priest	42	43	37	41.0	.001
I would be reluctant to discuss my problems with a social worker	39	40	43	23.3	.001
I find it helpful to talk about my problems with my mother	46	53	55	173.7	.001
I find it helpful to talk about my problems with my father	30	33	38	93.7	.001
I find it helpful to talk about my problems with close friends	60	66	68	185.2	.001

School

Table 7.4 demonstrates that young churchgoers hold a significantly more positive attitude toward school than young people who never attend church.

Young churchgoers are much less likely to dismiss school as boring; they are much more likely to be happy in their school and they are more likely to feel that school is helping to prepare them for life; and they feel much more positive about their teachers than young people who never attend church. At the same time, young churchgoers experience a higher level of anxiety and stress concerning their school life. They are more likely than non-churchgoers to worry about their school work and to worry about their exams at school. They are more worried about being bullied at school. They are slightly less likely to like the people with whom they go to school

Table 7.4: School: by church attendance

	never (%)	sometimes (%)	weekly (%)	χ^2	P<
School is boring	43	32	27	569.6	.001
I am happy in my school	68	75	77	246.6	.001
I like the people I go to school with	90	90	88	16.6	.001
My school is helping to prepare me for life	63	72	74	322.4	.001
I often worry about my school work	59	68	69	355.5	.001
I am worried about my exams at school	70	77	79	279.9	.001
I am worried about being bullied at school	25	30	33	158.3	.001
Teachers do a good job	37	49	57	719.0	.001

Work

Table 7.5 demonstrates a positive relationship between church attendance and work-related attitudes. Young churchgoers are significantly more likely to think that it is important to work hard when they get a job and to want to get to the top in their work. They are more likely to feel that a job gives people a sense of purpose. It is consistent with this view that young churchgoers record a higher level of distaste for being unemployed. Finally, young churchgoers have a slight but significantly greater tendency to reject the view that most unemployed people could have a job if they really wanted.

Religious beliefs

The relationship between religious beliefs and frequency of church attendance is very strong. The data in Table 7.6 also show that a considerable proportion of weekly churchgoers do not fully share the conventional beliefs promoted by the churches. One in five churchgoers do not believe in God; two in five churchgoers do not believe in life after death. At the same time, there is quite a high level of religious belief among people who never attend church. One in five non-churchgoers believe in God; two in five non-churchgoers believe in life after death. Quite a high proportion of weekly churchgoers hold conservative Christian beliefs. Half of them believe that God made the world in six days and rested on the seventh. More than a third of them think that Christianity is the only true religion. Nearly a third of them believe that God punishes people who do wrong.

Table 7.5: Work: by church attendance

	never (%)	*sometimes* (%)	*weekly* (%)	χ^2	*P<*
A job gives you a sense of purpose	74	80	79	123.0	.001
I think it is important to work hard when I get a job	93	96	97	188.0	.001
I want to get to the top in my work when I get a job	85	89	87	92.4	.001
I would not like to be unemployed	83	88	89	218.0	.001
I would rather be unemployed on social security than get a job I don't like doing	19	17	18	27.7	.001
Most unemployed people could have a job if they really wanted to	52	51	49	15.8	.001

Table 7.6: Religious beliefs: by church attendance

	never (%)	*sometimes* (%)	*weekly* (%)	χ^2	*P<*
I believe in God	21	49	82	6028.6	.001
I believe that Jesus really rose from the dead	15	35	72	5725.4	.001
I believe in life after death	38	47	60	754.2	.001
I believe God punishes people who do wrong	13	21	32	820.7	.001
I think Christianity is the only true religion	11	17	37	1742.0	.001
I believe that God made the world in six days and rested on the seventh	10	20	48	3444.2	.001

Church and society

Table 7.7 makes it clear that there is quite a lot of support for the social role of the church among young people who never attend church services. Two out of every three young people who never attend church nonetheless consider that they want to get married in church. Two out of every five young people who never attend church consider that they want their children to be baptised or christened in church. Table 7.7 also makes it clear that a number of young people who attend church weekly nonetheless feel quite negative about the church. One in four weekly churchgoers feel that the church is boring; one in five feel that the church or the Bible is irrelevant for life today; one in three are not convinced that the clergy do a good job. Although they are themselves in regular contact with the church, half of the weekly churchgoers believe that they can be a Christian without going to church. Finally, attitudes toward religious education in schools are closely related to personal church attendance. Nonetheless, one in four of the young people who never attend church still support the place of religious education in school, while one in three of the young people who attend church weekly remain unconvinced about teaching religious education in school. Even among weekly churchgoers support for daily religious assemblies in school runs very low.

Table 7.7: Church and society: by church attendance

	never (%)	sometimes (%)	weekly (%)	χ^2	P<
I believe that I can be a Christian without going to church	43	65	47	1194.2	.001
The church seems irrelevant to life today	34	23	17	745.5	.001
The Bible seems irrelevant to life today	38	26	18	898.7	.001
I want my children to be baptised/ christened in church	41	66	79	2896.5	.001
I want to get married in church	67	82	88	1240.8	.001
Religious education should be taught in school	25	44	63	2631.1	.001
Schools should hold a religious assembly every day	3	9	19	1347.9	.001
Church is boring	67	44	24	3096.8	.001
Christian ministers/vicars/priests do a good job	23	43	66	3309.1	.001

The supernatural

Table 7.8 makes it clear that weekly churchgoers are much less likely than young people who never attend church to entertain belief in their horoscope, in ghosts, in black magic, in fortune-tellers and in the possibility of contacting the spirits of the dead. The young people who do not attend church and who are more likely to reject Christian belief nonetheless are more likely than young churchgoers to inhabit a world which has room for many expressions of the supernatural. Young people who do not attend church also show a greater apprehension of the supernatural in the sense that a higher proportion of them claim to be frightened of going into a church alone.

Table 7.8: The supernatural: by church attendance

	never (%)	sometimes (%)	weekly (%)	χ^2	P<
I believe in my horoscope	36	37	24	302.3	.001
I believe in ghosts	41	43	34	94.3	.001
I believe in the Devil	19	20	36	621.4	.001
I believe in black magic	22	19	14	126.4	.001
I believe that fortune-tellers can tell the future	21	20	14	109.0	.001
I believe it is possible to contact the spirits of the dead	33	32	24	123.2	.001
I am frightened of going into a church alone	12	12	7	98.0	.001

Politics

The data presented in Table 7.9 draw attention to four main correlations between church attendance and political views. First, young churchgoers are less apathetic about politics than young people who never attend church; a somewhat smaller proportion of young churchgoers claim that it makes no difference which political party is in power. Second, young churchgoers show more confidence in the Conservative Party, while young people who never attend church show more confidence in the Labour Party. Third, young people who never attend church reveal a greater tendency to wish to abolish private schools and private medicine. Fourth, young churchgoers are less likely than young people who never attend church to voice racist views; they are much less likely to feel that there are too many black people living in this country and they are a little less likely to think that immigration into Britain should be restricted.

Table 7.9: Politics: by church attendance

	never (%)	sometimes (%)	weekly (%)	χ^2	$P<$
It makes no difference which political party is in power	25	21	20	71.7	.001
I have confidence in the Conservative Party	14	16	18	63.7	.001
I have confidence in the Labour Party	20	19	17	12.1	.01
Private schools should be abolished	27	21	18	248.9	.001
Private medicine should be abolished	17	15	13	52.0	.001
There are too many black people living in this country	19	13	11	263.8	.001
I think that immigration into Britain should be restricted	32	31	29	14.1	.001

Social concerns

Young churchgoers display a considerably higher level of concern over social issues than young people who never attend church. Table 7.10 demonstrates that a much higher proportion of churchgoers are concerned about the poverty of the Third World and about the risk of pollution to the environment. Young churchgoers are also more concerned about the level of violence shown on the television and about the general availability of pornography. Young churchgoers are more concerned about the risk of nuclear war. However, not only are young churchgoers more concerned about social issues, they also feel more empowered to do something about them: they are less inclined than young people who never attend church to feel that there is nothing they can do to help solve the world's problems.

Sexual morality

Young churchgoers tend to hold more conservative views on issues of heterosexual morality in comparison with those young people who never attend church: according to Table 7.11 churchgoers are more likely to consider that it is wrong to have sexual intercourse outside marriage and that it is wrong to have sexual intercourse under the legal age. At the same time, young churchgoers are also more likely to speak out against abortion and against divorce. Views on homosexuality follow a somewhat different pattern. It is the occasional churchgoers who hold the more liberal attitude toward homosexuality in contrast with both those young people who never attend church and those young people who attend church every week.

Table 7.10: Social concerns: by church attendance

	never (%)	sometimes (%)	weekly (%)	χ^2	P<
There is too much violence on television	16	21	28	366.0	.001
Pornography is too readily available	29	35	43	305.0	.001
I am concerned about the risk of pollution to the environment	59	72	75	662.4	.001
I am concerned about the poverty of the Third World	50	68	78	1595.2	.001
I am concerned about the risk of nuclear war	50	61	60	358.1	.001
There is nothing I can do to help solve the world's problems	30	21	17	502.6	.001

Table 7.11: Sexual morality: by church attendance

	never (%)	sometimes (%)	weekly (%)	χ^2	P<
It is wrong to have sexual intercourse outside marriage	10	12	28	1034.0	.001
It is wrong to have sexual intercourse under the legal age (16 years)	18	23	39	836.5	.001
Homosexuality is wrong	40	32	41	198.4	.001
Contraception is wrong	9	4	6	40.8	.001
Abortion is wrong	34	33	47	325.6	.001
Divorce is wrong	17	17	29	393.4	.001

Substance use

Table 7.12 demonstrates that there is a very clear relationship between church attendance and attitude toward substance use. Young people who never attend church adopt a more liberal attitude across a wide range of substances. Young churchgoers are more likely to consider that it is wrong to become drunk and that it is wrong to smoke cigarettes. Young churchgoers are also more likely to reject the use of heroin and marijuana and are more likely to consider it wrong to sniff glue or gas.

Table 7.12: Substance use: by church attendance

	never (%)	sometimes (%)	weekly (%)	χ^2	P<
It is wrong to smoke cigarettes	39	43	49	151.0	.001
It is wrong to become drunk	16	18	28	367.5	.001
It is wrong to use marijuana (hash or pot)	47	54	60	298.4	.001
It is wrong to use heroin	70	76	81	272.8	.001
It is wrong to sniff glue	75	80	82	127.0	.001
It is wrong to sniff butane gas	71	75	77	72.9	.001

Right and wrong

Religion seems to remain a formative influence in shaping young people's ideas of right and wrong across a wide range of issues. Table 7.13 makes it clear that young people who never attend church are significantly less likely to think that there is anything wrong in buying cigarettes or alcoholic drinks under the legal age; they are significantly less likely to think that there is anything wrong in travelling without a ticket, in cycling after dark without lights, in playing truant from school or in writing graffiti; they are significantly less likely to think that there is anything wrong in shoplifting. Consistent with the more permissive attitude of the young people who never attend church is the difference between churchgoers and non-churchgoers in the way in which they see the police. Young churchgoers display a significantly more positive attitude toward the police in comparison with young people who never attend church

Leisure

According to Table 7.14 two main differences emerge in respect of leisure-related attitudes between the young people who attend church and those who do not. First, in general, the young churchgoers hold a more positive view of their leisure time; they are less likely to report that they often hang about with their friends doing nothing in particular and are less likely to complain that their youth centre is boring. They are slightly less likely to say that they wish they had more things to do with their leisure time. Second, the young churchgoers feel that their parents somehow keep greater control over their leisure time than is the case among young people who never attend church. For example, young churchgoers are significantly less likely to feel that their parents allow them to do what they like in their leisure time. They are slightly more likely to feel that their parents prefer them to stay in as much as possible. Perhaps as a consequence of these differences, young churchgoers are more likely to feel that their parents agree with things they do in their leisure time.

Table 7.13: Right and wrong: by church attendance

	never (%)	sometimes (%)	weekly (%)	χ^2	P<
There is nothing wrong in shoplifting	10	5	4	270.3	.001
There is nothing wrong in travelling without a ticket	25	17	13	457.3	.001
There is nothing wrong in cycling after dark without lights	21	13	10	489.8	.001
There is nothing wrong in playing truant (wagging) from school	21	13	10	500.8	.001
There is nothing wrong in buying cigarettes under the legal age (16 years)	35	27	20	432.8	.001
There is nothing wrong in buying alcoholic drinks under the legal age (18 years)	47	40	31	464.8	.001
There is nothing wrong in writing graffiti (tagging) wherever you like	18	12	10	308.3	.001
The police do a good job	50	58	63	360.1	.001

Table 7.14: Leisure: by church attendance

	never (%)	sometimes (%)	weekly (%)	χ^2	P<
I often hang about with my friends doing nothing in particular	71	68	62	141.1	.001
I wish I had more things to do with my leisure time	58	58	55	12.7	.01
My youth centre is boring	39	35	26	234.5	.001
My parents prefer me to stay in as much as possible	19	19	23	39.4	.001
My parents allow me to do what I like in my leisure time	52	47	41	193.7	.001
My parents do not agree with most of the things that I do in my leisure time	32	26	23	229.7	.001

My area

To a large extent church attendance does not colour the way in which young people perceive the problems facing the environment in which they live. Church attenders and non-attenders look out on the same local world. For example, there is no significant difference in the perceptions of weekly churchgoers and non-churchgoers who have come to the view that crime, vandalism, drug-taking, drunks or unemployment constitute a growing problem in their area. Weekly churchgoers are only marginally more likely than non-churchgoers to have come to the view that violence constitutes a growing problem in their area. Although church attendance does not colour the way in which young people perceive the problems facing the environment in which they live, church attendance does seem to impact a little on their overall evaluation of that environment. The data presented in Table 7.15 demonstrate that young churchgoers are slightly more likely to report that they like living in their area. They are also a little more likely to feel that their area cares about its young people.

Table 7.15: My area: by church attendance

	never (%)	sometimes (%)	weekly (%)	χ^2	P<
Crime is a growing problem in my area	42	42	43	1.8	NS
Vandalism is a growing problem in my area	45	44	45	4.0	NS
Drug-taking is a growing problem in my area	32	32	30	6.2	NS
Violence is a growing problem in my area	32	31	34	11.4	.01
Drunks are a growing problem in my area	25	23	25	13.2	.01
Unemployment is a growing problem in my area	36	35	37	2.9	NS
I like living in my area	73	76	76	38.4	.001
My area cares about its young people	19	22	23	38.8	.001

CONCLUSION

This chapter has profiled the relationship between church attendance and adolescent values over 15 specific areas. The data make it clear that there are significant differences over all 15 areas between young people who attend church and those who do not.

As a consequence of this analysis, a clear profile can be drawn, for example, of the young churchgoer in comparison with the young person who never attends church. Young churchgoers enjoy a higher level of personal well-being and a greater sense of purpose in life. They are, however, more anxious about their personal relationships and more fearful about how other young people treat them. Young churchgoers benefit from greater support from parents and close friends, yet are more likely to long for others to turn to for advice. Young churchgoers hold a much more positive attitude toward their school, yet are more likely to worry about their school work. They also hold a more positive attitude regarding their future working lives. Not only do young churchgoers hold more conventional religious beliefs, they are also more likely to reject beliefs in horoscopes, ghosts and fortune-tellers. Young churchgoers hold a more positive view of the role of the church in society, although there is far from unanimous and unambiguous enthusiasm for the church among the practising group. Young churchgoers are less apathetic about political issues and are less racist in their attitudes. Overall young churchgoers show more support for the Conservative Party and less support for the Labour Party. Young churchgoers are more confident about their ability to do something positive about the world's problems and show a much higher level of concern over world issues, including environmental matters and world development matters. Young churchgoers hold more conservative attitudes on issues of heterosexual morality. They are less inclined to support the use of substances. They hold generally more law-abiding attitudes. Young churchgoers hold a more positive attitude toward their leisure time, although they are more likely to feel that their parents exercise greater control over how that time is used. Young churchgoers hold a slightly more positive attitude toward the area in which they live.

Since the present data are based on a cross-sectional survey, the findings are, by definition, correlational rather than causational. Nevertheless, the consistency of these findings across all 15 areas and the consistency of these findings with overall impressions generated from the earlier research reviewed in the first part of this chapter lend weight to the view that church attendance by itself needs to be taken seriously as a predictor of understanding and interpreting individual differences in the attitudes held by young people. There are, however, two weaknesses with the present analysis. First, the relationship between church attendance and attitude formation may vary from one denomination to another according to the distinctive social and ethical perspectives adopted by that denomination.

Further research needs to cross-tabulate church attendance with denominational groupings. Second, the apparent relationship between church attendance and attitudes may be contaminated by other external factors, such as social class for example, which may influence both church attendance and certain attitudinal areas. Further research needs to build the appropriate multivariate models in order to control for the possible contaminating influence of such factors. Nonetheless, what remains very clear is that future research which fails to take church attendance into account in profiling individual differences among teenage attitudes and values must also fail to provide an adequate account of the young person's world-view. In spite of widespread rumours about the pervasiveness of secularisation, religious practice seems to persist as a formative influence in shaping young lives.

8

TELEVISION

A number of studies of young people in the United Kingdom draw attention to the central role of television in their lives. Murdock and Phelps (1973) identified watching television as the most common leisure activity at evenings and weekends. Fogelman's (1976) study of 16 year olds found that 'watching television was the leading recreation'. More recently Furnham and Gunter (1983) confirmed that television was the most popular home-based leisure activity among young people. This finding has been viewed both positively and negatively by different commentators. The contrast is aptly illustrated by the titles of two reviews published around the same time. Gunter and McAleer (1990) decided to subtitle their study, *The One Eyed Monster?* Davies (1989) chose for her study the direct title, *Television is Good for Your Kids*.

In order to chart a path through current research concerned with the potential impact of television on the lives of young people, this chapter distinguishes between five groups of studies concerned with violence and antisocial behaviour, food and body image, physical and mental health, school-related attitudes and performance, and world-views and social attitudes.

Violence and antisocial behaviour

There has been a long history of research concerned with the potential link between television and violence or other forms of antisocial behaviour. For example, in a study among 80 boys between the ages of 5 and 12

Cline, Croft and Courrier (1973) found a correlation between high television exposure and desensitisation to violence. In a three-year longitudinal study of pupils in grades one through five, Eron *et al.* (1983) found positive correlations among boys and girls between television-violence viewing and peer-nominated aggression.

In a three-year longitudinal study among two cohorts of children starting in grade two and grade four Wiegman, Kuttschreuter and Baarda (1992) found a correlation between aggression and television-violence viewing. This relationship disappeared almost completely, however, when controlling for the starting level of aggression and intelligence. More recently, in a study among 470 teenagers, Aluja-Fabregat and Torrubia-Beltri (1998) found a positive relationship between viewing mass media violence and the display of aggressive behaviour patterns.

Singer *et al.* (1999) found a positive relationship between self-reported violent behaviours in a sample of 2,245 pupils between the ages of 7 and 15 years and the number of hours they spent watching television and their preference for watching violent television programmes. They also found a negative relationship between self-reported violent behaviours and parental monitoring of their children's viewing habits.

Krcmar and Valkenburg (1999), in a study among 158 children, found that watching television violence influenced the way in which violence was perceived. Moreover, those who watched more violence used less advanced moral reasoning strategies to justify their moral judgements about violence.

Food and body image

A second strand of research has given considerable attention to the interrelationship between television viewing, eating habits and body image. For example, Robinson and Killen (1995) in a sample of 1,912 pupils in grade 9 found a significant correlation between total weekly hours of television viewing and dietary fat intake. Similarly, in a study among 427 fourth- and fifth-grade students Signorielli and Staples (1997) found a significant correlation between television viewing and having unhealthy perceptions of nutrition. In a study of pupils between the ages of 12 and 15 years Woodward *et al.* (1997) found a significant relationship between television watching and food choices. Students who watched television more extensively tended to eat healthy foods less often and unhealthy foods more often.

Other studies have been concerned to relate diet to the influence of advertising. Within this tradition, in a study conducted among 44 children between the ages of 9 and 11 years, Hitchings and Moynihan (1998) found a positive relationship between television food advertisements and actual food consumed.

Tiggemann and Pickering (1996) conducted a study among 94 adolescent women. They found that the amount of time spent watching soaps, movies and (negatively) sport predicted body dissatisfaction, and the watching of music videos predicted drive for thinness. Botta (1999) examined the relationship between television images and body-image disturbance among a sample of 214 adolescent girls. Media variables emerged as significant predictors of the drive for thinness, body dissatisfaction and bulimic behaviour.

Gortmaker et al. (1996), in a study of 746 young people between the ages of 10 and 15, found that the odds of being overweight were 4.6 times greater for those watching more than five hours of television per day compared with those watching less than three hours. In a study among 4,063 children aged 8 through 16 years Anderson et al. (1998) found that boys and girls who watched four or more hours of television each day had greater body fat and a greater body mass index than those who watched less than two hours per day.

Robinson (1999) conducted a randomised school-based trial among 192 third- and fourth-grade pupils to assess the effects of reducing television, videotape and video game use on obesity. He found a statistically significant relative decrease in body mass index among the experimental group which had reduced television use, but not among the control group.

Hernandez et al. (1999) found a positive association between television viewing and obesity in a study among 461 young people between the ages of 9 and 16 years. In a study among 176 men and 705 women between the ages of 25 and 40, Crawford, Jeffery and French (1999) found a positive relationship between television viewing and obesity among women, but not among men.

Physical and mental health

A third strand of research has concentrated on the relationship between television and aspects of physical and mental health. For example, Attina, Catalano and Surace (1997), in a study among 1,368 children, found a clear inverse relationship between television watching and physical activity. Similarly, Armstrong et al. (1998) found an inverse relationship between television viewing and physical activity in a sample of 588 children. On the other hand, Tucker and Hager (1996) found no relationship between time spent watching television and muscular fitness in a study among 262 children between the ages of 9 and 10.

In a study conducted among 495 children from kindergarten through fourth grade, Owens *et al.* (1999) found a relationship between television-viewing practices and sleep disturbance. Higher levels of television viewing, especially at bedtime, were associated with bedtime resistance, sleep onset delay, anxiety around sleep and shorter sleep duration.

Page *et al.* (1996), in a study of 1,915 adolescents, found that females who were heavy viewers used significantly more drugs and smokeless tobacco than light and moderate viewers. Among males heavy viewers got drunk significantly more often than light or moderate viewers. In addition heavy viewers used illicit drugs and cigarettes more frequently than moderate viewers. Similarly, in a study among 1,533 14 year olds, Robinson, Chen and Killen (1998) found a positive correlation between hours of television viewing and the onset of alcohol use.

The relationship between television and suicide has been the subject of a number of studies. For example, Gould and Shaffer (1986) found a relationship between suicide in television movies and levels of attempted suicide. Philips and Carstensen (1986) found clustering of teenage suicides after television news stories about suicides. Taking a somewhat different focus, Martin (1996) found higher depression scores and a greater incidence of suicide attempts among 14 year olds who claimed more than two exposures to television suicide.

Dittmar (1994) found a positive correlation between hours of television watching and clinical depression scores on the MMPI among college students. In a comparison between 22 upper elementary school pupils who seldom watched television and 24 pupils who frequently watched television, Hopf and Weiss (1996) found higher scores on death anxiety and on guilt anxiety among the frequent viewers. In a study conducted among 2,245 pupils in grades three through eight, Singer *et al.* (1998) found a relationship between heavy television viewing and higher levels of trauma, depression and anxiety. In a study among undergraduates Johnston and Davey (1997) demonstrated that negatively toned television news programmes can exacerbate a range of personal concerns that are not specifically relevant to the content of the programme.

School-related attitudes and performance

A fourth strand of research has focused on the relationship between television and school-related attitudes and performance. For example, using a database of 20,308 high school students, Gaddy (1986) found significant negative correlations between television viewing and achievement across a range of measures. In a study of 183 grade nine and ten pupils, Hagborg (1995) found a negative correlation between television viewing and attitude toward school. In a three-year longitudinal study among elementary school children, Koolstra and van der Voort (1996) found a negative relationship between television viewing and book reading, deterioration of attitude to book reading, and deterioration of ability to concentrate on reading. As part of the same study, Koolstra, van der Voort and van der Kamp (1997) found a negative relationship between television viewing and reading comprehension, after controlling for IQ and socioeconomic status.

In a study among 50 11-year-old boys, Myrtek *et al.* (1996) found that high television consumption was associated with diminished activities outside the home and a tendency for reduced school-related homework. In a study among 30 pre-schoolers Clarke and Kurtz-Costes (1997) concluded that television-viewing time was negatively related to school-readiness skills.

A more positive view of the role of television is presented by a series of studies concerned specifically with the influence of television news broadcasts and information-based programmes. For example, Conway, Stevens and Smith (1975) studied the impact of television news on civic awareness among 284 pupils in grades four, five and six. They found a positive correlation between the two variables. More recently Cairns (1990) studied the impact of television news exposure on 570 children's perceptions of violence in Northern Ireland. He found that accurate estimates of actual violence levels were associated with more frequent news exposure. Brothers, Fortner and Mayer (1991) studied the impact of television news on public environmental knowledge. They found that news programmes increased knowledge levels significantly. Mangleburg and Bristol (1998) found a relationship between the extent of television viewing and adolescents' scepticism toward advertising.

World-view and social attitudes

A fifth strand of research has been concerned with the relationship between television and world-view or social attitudes. Within this tradition a number of early studies focused on perceptions of violence and danger. For example, Gerbner and Gross (1976) demonstrated the relationship between television viewing and fear of victimisation and violence. Doob and MacDonald (1979) also found a correlation between media usage and estimated likelihood of being a victim of crime. This correlation was reduced, however, when controlling for the actual level of crime in the local area. Similarly, Wober and Gunter (1982) found that the correlation reduced when the influence of locus of control was partialled out.

In a study conducted among 619 pupils in grades six through twelve, Carlson (1983) found that heavy viewers of crime programmes were likely to show less support for civil liberties and to be harsher toward criminals. In a more recent study Davis and Mares (1998) investigated the effects of talk-show viewing on social-reality beliefs among 282 high school students. They found that viewers were more likely to overestimate the frequency of deviant behaviours in society.

Cheung and Chan (1996) found high levels of television viewing associated with higher scores of mean world values, in terms of materialism and trivialisation of moral values, in a study among 402 high school students. Shanahan (1995) found a relationship between socio-political authoritarianism and television viewing in a study conducted among 1,190 high school students. This finding was replicated in a subsequent study by Shanahan (1998). Signorielli and Lears (1992) found a positive relationship between television viewing and sex-stereotyped attitudes among fourth- and fifth-grade pupils.

A more positive view of the influence of television on social attitudes is provided in two studies. Gunter and Wober (1983), in a study among 488 adults, found a positive relationship between just world beliefs and television viewing. In a study of 308 adolescents, Potter (1990) found that those who watched a high level of television were more inclined to believe that hard work yields rewards and that good wins over evil.

Ward and Rivadeneyra (1999) examined the relationship between television and sexual attitudes and awareness among a sample of 314 students between 18 and 20 years of age. They found that higher levels of viewing and greater involvement with television sexual content were associated with stronger endorsement of recreational attitudes toward sex, higher expectations of the sexual activity of peers and more extensive sexual experience.

Two analyses concerned with the relationship between television and religious attitudes are reported by Francis and Gibson (1992, 1993a). Both studies, conducted among over 5,000 pupils between the ages of 11 and 15 years, demonstrated a significant negative correlation between the total time spent watching television and attitudes toward Christianity. In addition, one of these studies pointed to the positive correlation between attitudes toward Christianity and watching popular religious television. The other study found no relationship between attitudes toward Christianity and preference for watching programmes concerned with teenage pop culture.

Wider context

In addition to the foregoing five major themes, other studies have explored the relationship between television and aggressive behaviour (Huesmann and Eron, 1986), beliefs about the police (Gunter, McAleer and Clifford,

1991), leisure activities (Selnow and Reynolds, 1984), lifestyle preferences (Hendry and Thornton, 1976), listening to music (Telfer and Kann, 1984), moral judgement (Tidhar and Peri, 1990), occupational knowledge (de Fleur and de Fleur, 1967), pro-social behaviour (Gunter, 1984), racial attitudes (Zuckerman, Singer and Singer, 1980), recognition of sexual reference (Silverman-Watkins and Sprafkin, 1983), response to advertising (Collins, 1990b), sex-appeal awareness (Tan, 1979), sexual knowledge (Kelley, Buckingham and Davies), social interaction (Johnson-Smaragdi, 1983) and toy preferences (Cobb, Stevens-Long and Goldstein, 1982).

Other studies have explored young people's motivations in watching television (Boeckmann and Hipfl, 1987), their programme preferences (Collins, 1990a), their identification with television characters (Sheehan, 1983), their perception of how much influence television has on them (Krendl, Lasky and Dawson, 1989) the nature of parental influence on and interaction with sons' and daughters' viewing habits (Lawrence and Wozniak, 1989), and the influence of such factors as age, sex, social class and religion on television-viewing time and programme preferences (Francis and Gibson, 1993b).

Evaluation

Integration of the findings from this wide range of research concerned with the relationship between television viewing and young lives encounters a range of problems. There are significant difficulties in synthesising the findings of research generated in different cultures and at different points in history. In spite of such difficulties and reservations, the overall impression generated by the research literature is that information about television-viewing habits is by itself likely to be a significant predictor across a wide range of adolescent values and attitudes.

EXPLORING THE DATA

Aim

One of the major difficulties encountered by attempts to integrate the existing pool of empirical studies concerns the variety of definitions of television viewing employed. The aim of this chapter, therefore, is to isolate one clear issue and attempt to define and profile the teenage television addict. Previous research suggests that many teenagers go home from school and watch television in a fairly indiscriminate way. The contention of the present chapter is that young people who watch more than four hours of television after school on a normal day may be described as comparatively undiscriminating addicts. If this is so, it is likely that the world-view of this subset of young people is distinguished in a variety of ways from the world-view of other young people. Overall the data demonstrate that almost one in four of the respondents (24.5 per cent) watched more than four hours of television on the previous day.

The main body of the present analysis maps the relationship between watching more than four hours of television on the previous day and the 15 areas explored by the values survey, namely personal well-being, worries, counselling, school, work, religious beliefs, church and society, the supernatural, politics, social concerns, sexual morality, substance use, right and wrong, leisure and the local area. In the following tables the column headed 'tv addict' presents data for those who watched more than four hours of television and the column headed 'control group' presents data for those who watched less than that amount of television. First, however, attention is given to the demographic characteristics of the two groups.

Demographic characteristics

SEX

A higher proportion of boys (27.5 per cent) watch more than four hours of television than is the case among girls (21.4 per cent). This finding is consistent with other general surveys of adolescent leisure activities.

AGE

The older pupils in the sample are less likely than the younger pupils to come within the category of television addicts. Thus, 22.7 per cent of the year-ten pupils watch more than four hours of television compared with 26.2 per cent of year-nine pupils.

SOCIAL CLASS

Social class is calculated on the classification system proposed by the Office of Population Censuses and Surveys (1980) applied to the pupils' reporting of paternal occupation. The data demonstrate that pupils whose fathers are employed in higher social-class occupations are less likely to report having watched more than four hours of television on the previous day. Watching more than four hours of television was reported by 12.7 per cent of pupils whose fathers are in class one or professional occupations, 15.8 per cent in class two or semi-professional occupations, 22.7 per cent in non-manual class-three occupations, 28.2 per cent in skilled manual class-three occupations, 29.4 per cent in semi-skilled manual class-four occupations and 35.5 per cent in unskilled manual class-five occupations.

RELIGION

Like social class religious background is a significant predictor of differences in level of television watching. Generally adolescents who report membership of one of the Christian denominations tend to watch less television. While 26.8 per cent of the adolescents who report no religious affiliation watched more than four hours of television on the previous day, the proportions fell to 17.3 per cent among Presbyterians, 17.3 per cent among Pentecostals, 19.7 per cent among Methodists, 19.8 per cent among Baptists, and 20.5 per cent among Anglicans. On the other hand, 27.8 per cent of Roman Catholics reported watching more than four hours of television on the previous day. The situation among members of other faith groups is as follows: 18.2 per cent among Hindus, 16.2 per cent among Jews, 27.3 per cent among Sikhs and 32.3 per cent among Moslems.

Personal well-being

Table 8.1 demonstrates that there is a significantly lower level of personal well-being among the young television addicts. They are less likely to find life really worth living or to feel that their life has a sense of purpose; they are more likely to feel that they are not worth much as a person and to suffer from depression; they are more likely to have considered taking their own life.

Table 8.1: Personal well-being: by television viewing

	control group (%)	tv addict (%)	χ^2	P<
I feel my life has a sense of purpose	58	53	57.8	.001
I find life really worth living	70	64	70.2	.001
I feel I am not worth much as a person	12	16	77.1	.001
I often feel depressed	51	55	38.1	.001
I have sometimes considered taking my own life	25	32	105.8	.001

Note: 'tv addict' refers to those who watched more than four hours of television on the day before the survey; 'control group' refers to those who watched less than four hours.

Worries

Table 8.2 demonstrates that young television addicts are slightly less concerned than other young people about aspects of human relationships: they are slightly less worried about their attractiveness to the opposite sex and about how they get on with other people. On the other hand, young television addicts are neither more nor less worried than other young people about their sex life or about the risks of getting AIDS. Generally young television addicts are neither more nor less worried than other young people about going out alone at night on their own. However, young television addicts are slightly more worried than other young people about being attacked by pupils from other schools.

Table 8.2: Worries: by television viewing

	control group (%)	tv addict (%)	χ^2	$P<$
I am worried about my sex life	18	18	0.0	NS
I am worried about my attractiveness to the opposite sex	37	33	30.5	.001
I am worried about getting AIDS	62	63	1.5	NS
I am worried about how I get on with other people	55	52	10.4	.01
I am worried about being attacked by pupils from other schools	18	21	20.0	.001
I am worried about going out alone at night in my area	31	31	0.3	NS

Counselling

Table 8.3 demonstrates that young television addicts experience the same level of need to turn to someone for advice as other young people. On the other hand, they are considerably less likely to derive benefit from talking with either parents or close friends. Significantly fewer of the young television addicts report that they find it helpful to talk about their problems with their mother, their father or with close friends: in this sense young television addicts emerge as more isolated than their contemporaries. While young television addicts are less likely to draw on the resources of parents and friends, they are more open than other young people to the possibilities of discussing their problems with a range of professional people, including teachers, youth club leaders, social workers and clergy. All young people are more open to discussing their problems with a doctor than with members of other caring professions. Young television addicts are neither more nor less open to talking with doctors than other young people.

Table 8.3: Counselling: by television viewing

	control group (%)	tv addict (%)	χ^2	P<
I often long for someone to turn to for advice	35	35	0.0	NS
I would be reluctant to discuss my problems with a schoolteacher	48	43	51.6	.001
I would be reluctant to discuss my problems with a youth club/group leader	49	43	69.4	.001
I would be reluctant to discuss my problems with a doctor	33	33	0.4	NS
I would be reluctant to discuss my problems with a Christian minister/vicar/priest	43	38	42.1	.001
I would be reluctant to discuss my problems with a social worker	40	37	8.9	.01
I find it helpful to talk about my problems with my mother	51	46	62.9	.001
I find it helpful to talk about my problems with my father	33	30	17.0	.001
I find it helpful to talk about my problems with close friends	66	56	175.4	.001

School

Table 8.4 demonstrates that young television addicts hold a considerably less positive attitude toward school than other young people. They are much more likely to dismiss school as boring. They are much less likely to report that they are happy in their school or to feel that school is helping to prepare them for life; they are much less likely to feel that teachers do a good job. They are even slightly less likely to report that they like the people they go to school with. As well as being less happy at school, young television addicts are less likely to take their school work seriously: they are less likely to worry about their work or exams at school.

Work

Table 8.5 suggests that young television addicts hold a slightly less positive attitude toward the world of work. They are slightly less inclined to think that it is important to work hard when they get a job; they are slightly less inclined to think that a job generates a sense of purpose; they hold a slightly more cavalier attitude toward the prospects of unemployment; they are slightly more inclined to think that they would rather be unemployed than get a job which they dislike. They are also less inclined to want to get to the top in their work than other young people. Young television addicts are more inclined than other young people to think that most unemployed people could have a job if they really wanted to.

Table 8.4: School: by television viewing

	control group (%)	tv addict (%)	χ^2	P<
School is boring	33	47	392.1	.001
I am happy in my school	74	64	208.0	.001
I like the people I go to school with	90	88	21.0	.001
My school is helping to prepare me for life	71	63	142.0	.001
I often worry about my school work	65	61	32.5	.001
I am worried about my exams at school	76	72	40.0	.001
I am worried about being bullied at school	29	30	2.5	NS
Teachers do a good job	47	37	179.0	.001

Table 8.5: Work: by television viewing

	control group (%)	tv addict (%)	χ^2	P<
A job gives you a sense of purpose	79	77	16.2	.001
I think it is important to work hard when I get a job	97	94	92.1	.001
I want to get to the top in my work when I get a job	88	86	11.0	.001
I would not like to be unemployed	87	81	125.2	.001
I would rather be unemployed on social security than get a job I don't like doing	17	22	78.7	.001
Most unemployed people could have a job if they really wanted to	50	54	31.1	.001

Religious beliefs

Table 8.6 demonstrates that young television addicts are less inclined to believe in God than other young people. They are also less inclined to subscribe to the central tenet of the Christian faith that Jesus really rose from the dead. On the other hand, young television addicts hold the same level of belief as other young people in life after death and in the creationist view that God made the world in six days and rested on the seventh. Young television addicts are just as likely as other young people to believe that God punishes people who do wrong or to regard Christianity as the only true religion.

Table 8.6: Religious beliefs: by television viewing

	control group (%)	tv addict (%)	χ^2	P<
I believe in God	42	38	33.9	.001
I believe that Jesus really rose from the dead	31	28	19.4	.001
I believe in life after death	46	45	1.9	NS
I believe God punishes people who do wrong	19	20	1.9	NS
I think Christianity is the only true religion	16	16	1.4	NS
I believe that God made the world in six days and rested on the seventh	19	18	0.7	NS

Church and society

Table 8.7 demonstrates that young television addicts hold a less positive attitude toward the role of the church in contemporary society: they are more inclined to think that the church and the Bible are irrelevant for life today and they are more inclined to dismiss the church as boring. They are less inclined to value the contribution made by clergy. They are less inclined to want to be associated with the church for major rites of passage like wanting to get married in church or wanting to have their children christened in church. At the same time, young television addicts hold a more negative attitude toward the place of religious education and the place of a religious assembly in school.

Table 8.7: Church and society: by television viewing

	control group (%)	tv addict (%)	χ^2	P<
I believe that I can be a Christian without going to church	52	48	39.2	.001
The church seems irrelevant to life today	27	30	23.9	.001
The Bible seems irrelevant to life today	30	33	23.5	.001
I want my children to be baptised/ christened in church	55	53	7.4	.01
I want to get married in church	75	73	6.7	.01
Religious education should be taught in school	38	33	42.0	.001
Schools should hold a religious assembly every day	8	7	12.7	.001
Church is boring	51	58	105.1	.001
Christian ministers/vicars/priests do a good job	37	33	38.3	.001

The supernatural

Although young television addicts are less inclined to believe in God, Table 8.8 demonstrates that they are more inclined to believe in a range of supernatural phenomena. Thus, they are more likely to believe in their horoscope, or to believe that fortune-tellers can tell the future; they are more likely to believe in ghosts and that it is possible to contact the spirits of the dead; they are more likely to believe in black magic and the Devil. At the same time, compared with other young people, young television addicts are more inclined to be apprehensive about going into a church alone.

Politics

Two main conclusions emerge from Table 8.9 regarding the relationship between watching more than four hours of television and adolescents' attitudes toward politics. First, young television addicts hold a more cynical attitude toward politics; they are more inclined to feel that it makes no difference which political party is in power. Second, young television addicts adopt a more left-wing political stance: they are likely to have more confidence in the Labour Party. Young television addicts also show less sympathy for institutions like private schools and private health care.

Table 8.9 also indicates that young television addicts are more likely than other young people to hold racist views and to maintain that there are too many black people living in this country. On the other hand, young television addicts are no more likely than other young people to take the view that immigration into Britain should be restricted.

Table 8.8: The supernatural: by television viewing

	control group (%)	tv addict (%)	χ^2	P<
I believe in my horoscope	34	39	70.2	.001
I believe in ghosts	39	44	46.8	.001
I believe in the Devil	21	25	60.7	.001
I believe in black magic	19	25	121.4	.001
I believe that fortune-tellers can tell the future	19	24	71.5	.001
I believe it is possible to contact the spirits of the dead	30	35	61.2	.001
I am frightened of going into a church alone	11	14	32.6	.001

Table 8.9: Politics: by television viewing

	control group (%)	tv addict (%)	χ^2	P<
It makes no difference which political party is in power	21	27	92.3	.001
I have confidence in the Conservative Party	15	14	4.7	NS
I have confidence in the Labour Party	19	25	97.9	.001
Private schools should be abolished	22	30	191.0	.001
Private medicine should be abolished	15	19	44.2	.001
There are too many black people living in this country	13	18	112.4	.001
I think that immigration into Britain should be restricted	29	29	0.0	NS

Social concerns

Just as young television addicts hold a more cynical attitude toward politics, so they also hold a more cynical attitude toward the world's problems. According to Table 8.10 they are much less inclined to feel that they can do anything to help solve the world's problems. Table 8.10 also demonstrates that young television addicts are much less inclined to be concerned about global issues, such as the risk of pollution to the environment, the poverty of the Third World or the risk of nuclear war. According to Table 8.10 young television addicts are less concerned than other young people about the availability of pornography or the level of violence screened on television.

Table 8.10: Social concerns: by television viewing

	control group (%)	tv addict (%)	χ^2	P<
There is too much violence on television	20	17	32.1	.001
Pornography is too readily available	34	29	57.9	.001
I am concerned about the risk of pollution to the environment	72	61	304.6	.001
I am concerned about the poverty of the Third World	65	51	390.9	.001
I am concerned about the risk of nuclear war	57	52	63.2	.001
There is nothing I can do to help solve the world's problems	21	31	295.5	.001

Sexual morality

Table 8.11 demonstrates that young television addicts tend to hold a more conservative, not a more liberal, attitude toward a range of issues concerned with sexual morality. They are more likely to think that homosexuality, abortion, contraception and divorce are wrong. On the other hand, young television addicts adopt a more liberal attitude than other young people concerning sexual intercourse under the legal age.

Substance use

In contrast with their attitudes toward sexual morality, Table 8.12 demonstrates that young television addicts hold a more liberal, not a more conservative, attitude toward a range of issues concerned with the use of substances. They are more likely to condone glue-sniffing and sniffing butane gas; they are more likely to condone the use of marijuana and heroin; they are more likely to support smoking tobacco. Only on the issue of alcohol are young television addicts indistinguishable from other young people, but young people in general hold a much more permissive attitude toward alcohol than toward other substances.

Table 8.11: Sexual morality: by television viewing

	control group (%)	tv addict (%)	χ^2	P<
It is wrong to have sexual intercourse outside marriage	14	13	1.6	NS
It is wrong to have sexual intercourse under the legal age (16 years)	24	20	42.3	.001
Homosexuality is wrong	35	41	83.8	.001
Contraception is wrong	4	9	155.3	.001
Abortion is wrong	34	42	109.9	.001
Divorce is wrong	18	21	34.2	.001

Table 8.12: Substance use: by television viewing

	control group (%)	tv addict (%)	χ^2	P<
It is wrong to smoke cigarettes	43	39	42.1	.001
It is wrong to become drunk	18	18	1.2	NS
It is wrong to use marijuana (hash or pot)	51	47	44.2	.001
It is wrong to use heroin	75	69	107.5	.001
It is wrong to sniff glue	79	73	109.1	.001
It is wrong to sniff butane gas	74	70	47.4	.001

Right and wrong

According to Table 8.13 young television addicts are less likely to think that there is anything wrong in a variety of antisocial or criminal activities. They are less likely to think that there is anything wrong in writing graffiti, playing truant or cycling after dark without lights. They are more likely to condone travelling without a ticket or shoplifting. They are more likely to condone buying cigarettes and alcohol under the legal age. Young television addicts are less likely than other young people to feel that the police do a good job.

Table 8.13: Right and wrong: by television viewing

	control group (%)	tv addict (%)	χ^2	P<
There is nothing wrong in shoplifting	7	11	225.1	.001
There is nothing wrong in travelling without a ticket	19	26	156.3	.001
There is nothing wrong in cycling after dark without lights	14	22	204.9	.001
There is nothing wrong in playing truant (wagging) from school	14	22	224.4	.001
There is nothing wrong in buying cigarettes under the legal age (16 years)	29	35	82.9	.001
There is nothing wrong in buying alcoholic drinks under the legal age (18 years)	40	48	115.3	.001
There is nothing wrong in writing graffiti (tagging) wherever you like	13	21	267.0	.001
The police do a good job	55	50	41.5	.001

Leisure

Two main conclusions emerge from Table 8.14 regarding the relationship between watching more than four hours of television and adolescents' attitudes toward their leisure. First, young television addicts hold a less positive attitude toward their leisure. They are more likely to long for more things to do with their leisure time. They are more likely to hang about with their friends doing nothing in particular; they are more likely to be critical of their local youth centre. Second, young television addicts are more likely to feel that their parents allow them to do what they like in their leisure time. However, they also feel that their parents are more critical of the ways in which they spend their leisure time. At the same time young television addicts are more inclined than other young people to feel that their parents prefer them to stay in as much as possible.

My area

Table 8.15 demonstrates that young television addicts tend to feel a little less positive toward their area than other young people: they are less likely to say that they like living in their area. They are more inclined to consider that drunks, vandalism and violence are growing problems in their area. On the other hand, young television addicts and other young people share similar perceptions regarding the levels of crime, drug-taking and unemployment in their area. Young television addicts and other young people share similar perceptions regarding the extent to which their area cares about its young people.

Table 8.14: Leisure: by television viewing

	control group (%)	tv addict (%)	χ^2	P<
I often hang about with my friends doing nothing in particular	65	69	55.5	.001
I wish I had more things to do with my leisure time	56	61	51.0	.001
My youth centre is boring	33	39	64.1	.001
My parents prefer me to stay in as much as possible	19	22	20.0	.001
My parents allow me to do what I like in my leisure time	48	52	43.2	.001
My parents do not agree with most of the things that I do in my leisure time	27	34	119.5	.001

Table 8.15: My area: by television viewing

	control group (%)	tv addict (%)	χ^2	P<
Crime is a growing problem in my area	41	42	2.8	NS
Vandalism is a growing problem in my area	43	46	13.8	.001
Drug-taking is a growing problem in my area	33	33	0.4	NS
Violence is a growing problem in my area	31	33	16.5	.001
Drunks are a growing problem in my area	24	29	73.9	.001
Unemployment is a growing problem in my area	36	38	3.3	NS
I like living in my area	76	73	25.3	.001
My area cares about its young people	22	23	0.4	NS

CONCLUSION

This analysis has profiled the relationship between watching more than four hours of television on a normal school day and adolescent values over 15 specific areas. The data make it clear that there are significant differences over all 15 areas between young television addicts and those young people who watch less television. It is important to be clear just what kind of conclusions can be drawn from these findings and what kind of conclusions cannot be drawn from these findings. Two main observations need to be made.

First, it is possible on the basis of these data to conclude that, as a group, young television addicts differ in significant ways from other young people. As a group they enjoy lower personal well-being; worry less about relationships; receive much less personal support from parents and close friends; are more willing to confide in teachers and other caring professionals; hold less positive attitudes toward school and work; are less likely to believe in conventional religion but more likely to believe in superstitions; are more cynical about politics and issues of global concern; tend to prefer left-wing political views; hold more conservative attitudes toward sexual morality; are more permissive toward pornography and violence on television; are more inclined to hold racist views; are more liberal in their attitudes toward substance use; are more inclined to condone antisocial behaviour; and are less satisfied with their leisure time.

Second, however, it is not possible on the basis of the present analysis to conclude that these very real differences are necessarily or wholly a consequence of addiction to television. In a cross-sectional study of this nature there are a number of correlates, such as social class and religious background, which need to be taken into consideration in exploring the adequacy of a causal account. The present findings, at least, confirm the value of undertaking such further analyses, since there is no doubt that teenage television addicts project a highly distinctive sociopsychological profile.

CONCLUSION

This study set out to profile the world-view of year-nine and year-ten pupils, between the ages of 13 and 15 years. The new and unique database provided by nearly 34,000 pupils throughout England and Wales enables two main types of conclusion to be drawn. The first conclusion provides a values profile of young people in general. The second conclusion draws attention to the significance of six key predictors of individual differences in the values held by young people. These two conclusions will be summarised in turn, drawing together the major summaries from the previous chapters. Here is the voice of the pupils making their distinctive contribution to the values debate in education.

VALUES PROFILE

The values survey was designed to provide information about 15 key areas defined as personal well-being, worries, counselling, school, work, religious belief, church and society, the supernatural, politics, social concerns, sexual morality, substance use, right and wrong, leisure and the local area. The following findings emerged.

Personal well-being

The data provide a profile of a generation of young people, the majority of whom find life worth living but who at the same time experience mood swings and feelings of depression. A significant minority, however, lack a sense of purpose in life, have a low self-esteem and entertain suicidal thoughts. The job of values education is to take this significant minority seriously and address the issues of self-worth, purpose in life and enhanced self-concept.

Worries

The data provide a profile of a generation of young people who are accepting their developing sexual identity but who are anxious about growing up in a world in which AIDS is so well established. A large number of these young people, however, feel insecure in their personal relationships and a significant minority doubt their own attractiveness to the opposite sex. A significant minority are anxious about their personal safety. The job of values education is to address enhanced confidence and skills in interpersonal relationships and to enable young people to confront anxieties over personal safety.

Counselling

The data provide a profile of a generation of young people who draw particularly heavily on their peer group for support and who are reluctant to seek advice and help from professionals. The job of values education is to equip young people with the skills required to listen effectively to their friends and to offer good counsel and support. It is also necessary to help young people appreciate the resources available to them through the caring professions and perhaps in particular to build up greater trust and confidence in doctors.

School

The data provide a profile of a generation of young people who remain basically well disposed toward their schooling. Many of them, however, are under considerable pressure to perform well. An unacceptably high number of them live under the fear of being bullied. Respect for the teaching profession is not high. The job of values education is to take seriously the significant minority who are not convinced about the value of education and who are not convinced about the job done by teachers. Considerable attention needs to be given to the culture and climate of schools which can breed such fear of bullying.

Work

The data provide a profile of a generation of young people who remain committed to a world of work, whose future identity hinges on appropriate employment and who may hold an unrealistic view regarding the availability of job opportunities. A significant minority, however, have set their sights on a jobless future and on being supported by the state. The job of values education is to take seriously the shifting world of employment and prepare young people for a future which will not only require dedication to the employment market but also the ability to build self-identity independently of the work environment.

Religious belief

The data provide a profile of a generation of young people who are divided between theists, agnostics and atheists. Large numbers have no real opinion to declare on issues like the resurrection of Jesus, life after death and the exclusivist claims of Christianity. The danger may be that young people who are not forming views on religious matters may become vulnerable to the persuasion of cults and quasi-religious systems. The job of values education is to equip young people to think rationally and intelligently about contrasting and conflicting religious claims within a rapidly changing pluralist society.

Church and society

The data provide a profile of a generation of young people who have separated their Christian heritage from the institution and practice of the church. Many want to retain the notion of being Christian, to have the church involved in their weddings and to bring their children for christening. Many feel neutral about the contribution made to life by the Bible, the church and the clergy. When it comes to school worship, however, their stance of neutrality passes over into active hostility. The job of values education is to help young people think through the religious heritage of their culture, to appreciate more fully the positive role of religion within the lives of practising adherents, and to explore more positively the personal, social, cultural and spiritual dimensions of the school assembly.

The supernatural

The data provide a profile of a generation of young people who have not rejected the world of the supernatural to inhabit a materialistic and mechanistic universe. Two out of every three leave the door open for horoscopes, ghosts and communication with the spirits of the dead. One out of every two leave the door open for fortune-telling and black magic. The job of values education is to leave space for a spirituality which embraces the transcendent and enables young people to make rational and informed choices regarding the ways in which they conceptualise the horizons of their universe.

Politics

The data provide a profile of a generation of young people who are cynical about political institutions, who have comparatively little confidence in the long-established political parties and whose political views are often unformed. They are not, however, generally racist in their attitudes. The job of values education is to help equip young people for a more active and better informed part in the democratic process which is the responsibility of all citizens.

Social concerns

The data provide a profile of a generation of young people who are quite concerned about world issues such as pollution and poverty, but who are much less concerned about domestic issues such as pornography and violence on television. On balance they remain hopeful that it is within their power to improve the world in which they live. The job of values education is to build on the commitment of these young people toward responsible global citizenship and to address seriously the significant minority who are still making up their minds where they stand on such issues.

Sexual morality

The data provide a profile of a generation of young people who have adopted a liberal stance on sex outside marriage and divorce. They remain more conservative in their attitude toward homosexuality. Nearly a third have not made up their minds about abortion. The job of values education is to steer a careful path between discussing traditional family values and respecting the range of alternative lifestyles represented within the pupils' own immediate and wider home environment.

Substance use

The data provide a profile of a generation of young people who are very tolerant about alcohol and quite tolerant about tobacco. They are less tolerant about marijuana and generally quite intolerant about heroin and solvents. The job of values education is to help young people make mature decisions about the use of alcohol and tobacco and about the attendant risks of these substances. Moreover, it is clear from the data that drugs-related education needs to remain vigilant in respect of hard drugs and solvents.

Right and wrong

The data provide a profile of a generation of young people who are largely law-abiding in respect of issues which they feel really matter. When, however, the law restricts their freedom to express the maturity they feel they have properly attained, then they are more inclined to flout such laws. Overall their attitude toward the police is not entirely positive. The job of values education is to develop proper respect for the law as befits good citizenship and to work on the basic goodwill for the law which many young people display.

Leisure

The data provide a profile of a generation of young people who spend a great deal of time hanging about with friends doing nothing in particular. The majority of them are content with how they spend their leisure time; and the majority of them do not experience conflict with their parents over how they choose to spend their leisure time. The job of values education is to help young people assess creatively their use of leisure and to develop their sense of using leisure time for the benefit of themselves and for the benefit of others as growing and responsible citizens.

My area

The data provide a profile of a generation of young people who hold a basically positive attitude toward their local area, although they feel that their area does not really care about its young people. At the same time, a number of them perceive the social conditions of their local area to be worsening. The job of values education is to help young people integrate more positively and successfully within their local community and make an active contribution to community life. In this way young citizens may make a more effective contribution to their local area and also derive a more affirming sense that they matter to that community.

INDIVIDUAL DIFFERENCES

The values survey has been employed to examine the significance of six key factors to understand and interpret individual differences in the values held by young people. The six key factors are defined as age, sex, social class, parental separation or divorce, church attendance and excessive exposure to television. The following findings emerged.

Age

The chapter concerned with age difference compares the values of pupils in year nine with the values of pupils in year ten. The data make it clear that there are some significant detectable differences in values across even this very narrow age range.

In comparison with pupils in year nine, year-ten pupils have grown in self-confidence; derive more support from close friends and less support from parents; have become more reluctant to discuss their problems with many professionals; hold a less positive attitude toward school but worry more about their school work; show a greater abhorrence of unemployment; are less likely to believe in God; feel less positive about the role of the church in society; display more racist attitudes; feel more positive about their effect on the world's future; hold more permissive attitudes toward sex outside marriage, abortion and divorce; hold more liberal attitudes toward substance use across a range of substances; see the police in a less positive light; experience more conflict with their parents over their use of leisure time; and feel less positive about the area in which they live. These findings are consistent with the wider field of research which demonstrates that age is a significant predictor of individual differences in values held by young people.

Sex

The chapter concerned with sex differences makes it clear that there are significant differences between young women and young men across all 15 areas. Young women and young men not only inhabit different bodies, they also inhabit and shape quite different world-views. Sex is an important predictor of individual differences in values among young people.

As a group young women experience a lower level of personal well-being, are more inclined to worry about personal safety and relationships; are more likely to long for someone to turn to for advice and derive a lot of support from talking problems through with close friends; derive more support from mother and less support from father; project a more positive attitude toward school but experience higher levels of school-related anxiety; show a slightly lower sense of purpose and ambition in work but a greater dislike for unemployment; are more likely to believe in God; hold a more positive attitude toward the role of the church in society; are more likely to believe in the potentially positive aspects of the supernatural although less likely to believe in the potentially negative aspects; show a lower level of interest in party politics; are less racist in their attitudes; are more concerned about world issues; are more accepting of homosexuality and divorce but less accepting of under-age sex and abortion; are less permissive about most substances but more accepting of tobacco; generally hold more law-abiding attitudes; generally experience less satisfaction with their leisure time but more parental control over what they do; and are generally less content with the area where they live.

This profile of young women can be inverted in order to generate a profile of young men in terms of the characteristics which distinguish them from young women of comparable age. As a group young men enjoy a higher level of personal well-being; are less inclined to worry about personal safety and relationships; are less likely to long for someone to turn to for advice and derive less support from close friends; derive more support from father and less support from mother; experience lower levels of school-related anxiety but project an overall less positive attitude toward school; show a slightly higher sense of purpose and ambition in work but a greater acceptance of unemployment; are less likely to believe in God; hold a less positive attitude toward the role of the church in society; are more likely to believe in the potentially negative aspects of the supernatural although less likely to believe in the potentially positive aspects; show a higher level of interest in party politics; are more racist in their attitudes; are less concerned about world issues, are more accepting of under-age sex and abortion but less accepting of divorce and homosexuality; are less accepting of tobacco but more permissive about many other substances; generally hold less law-abiding attitudes; generally experience more satisfaction with their leisure time and less parental control over what they do; and are generally more content with the area where they live.

Social class

The chapter concerned with social-class differences makes it clear that there are significant differences over all 15 areas between young people who belong to different social-class backgrounds.

As a consequence of this analysis a clear profile can be drawn of the values associated with four distinct social-class groupings. For example, young people from social-class one and two backgrounds enjoy an overall higher level of psychological well-being; worry more about personal relationships; benefit from a closer relationship with parents and close friends; hold a more positive attitude toward school, show a greater abhorrence of unemployment; are more likely to believe in God but less likely to believe in their horoscopes; hold a more positive attitude toward the church; show more confidence in the Conservative Party and less confidence in the Labour Party; display more concern for the Third World; hold a more liberal attitude toward divorce, abortion and homosexuality; hold a more proscriptive attitude toward drug use; see the police in a more positive light; have a more positive view of their leisure time; and feel more positive about the area in which they live. These findings are consistent with the wider field of research which suggests that social class remains an important predictor of a range of individual differences.

Parental separation or divorce

The chapter concerned with parental separation or divorce makes it clear that there are significant differences over all 15 areas between those young people whose parents have experienced separation or divorce and those whose parents have not experienced such separation or divorce.

It is possible on the basis of these data to conclude that, as a group, young people whose parents have experienced separation or divorce differ in significant ways from young people whose parents have not. As a group they experience lower personal well-being; worry more about sex; long more to be able to turn to others for advice; hold less positive attitudes toward school and work; are less likely to believe in conventional religion but more likely to believe in superstitions; are more cynical about politics and issues of global concern; tend to prefer left-wing political views; are more liberal in their attitudes toward sexual morality and substance use; are more inclined to condone antisocial behaviour; are less satisfied with their leisure time; and hold a less positive view of the area in which they live. These findings are consistent with the wider field of research which suggests that parental separation and divorce function as a significant predictor of values and behaviour not only during the years of schooling, but also during university and college life and during adulthood.

Church attendance

The chapter concerned with church attendance makes it clear that there are significant differences over all 15 areas between young people who attend church and those who do not.

As a consequence of this analysis, a clear profile can be drawn, for example, of the young churchgoer in comparison with the young person who never attends church. Young churchgoers enjoy a higher level of personal well-being and a greater sense of purpose in life. They are, however, more anxious about their personal relationships and more fearful about how other young people treat them. Young churchgoers benefit from greater support from parents and close friends, yet are more likely to long for others to turn to for advice. Young churchgoers hold a much more positive attitude toward their school, yet are more likely to worry about their school work. They also hold a more positive attitude regarding their future working lives. Not only do young churchgoers hold more conventional religious beliefs, they are also more likely to reject beliefs in horoscopes, ghosts and fortune-tellers. Young churchgoers hold a more positive view of the role of the church in society, although there is far from unanimous and unambiguous enthusiasm for the church among the practising group. Young churchgoers are less apathetic about political issues and are less racist in their attitudes. Overall young churchgoers show more support for the Conservative Party and less support for the Labour Party. Young churchgoers are more confident about their ability to do something positive about the world's problems and show a much higher level of concern over world issues, including environmental matters and world development matters. Young churchgoers hold more conservative attitudes on issues of heterosexual morality. They are less inclined to support the use of substances. They hold generally more law-abiding attitudes. Young churchgoers hold a more positive attitude toward their leisure time, although they are more likely to feel that their parents exercise greater control over how that time is used. Young churchgoers hold a slightly more positive attitude toward the area in which they live.

Television

The chapter concerned with television profiles the relationship between watching more than four hours of television on a normal school day and adolescent values over the 15 specific areas. The data make it clear that there are significant differences over all 15 areas between young television addicts and those young people who watch less television.

It is possible on the basis of these data to conclude that, as a group, young television addicts differ in significant ways from other young people. As a group they enjoy lower personal well-being; worry less about relationships; receive much less personal support from parents and close friends; are more willing to confide in teachers and other caring professionals; hold less positive attitudes toward school and toward work; are less likely to believe in conventional religion; but more likely to believe in superstitions; are more cynical about politics and issues of global concern; tend to prefer left-wing political views; hold more conservative attitudes toward sexual morality; are more permissive toward pornography and violence on television; are more inclined to hold racist views; are more liberal in their attitudes toward substance use; are more inclined to condone antisocial behaviour, and are less satisfied with their leisure time.

POSTSCRIPT

The young people profiled in this book have grown up and formed their values in a Britain shaped by Margaret Thatcher and sustained by John Major. In a real sense they are Thatcher's children, not 'generation X' of the USA but 'generation T' of the UK. Margaret Thatcher would have much to be proud of in generation T. Here is a generation of young people who are firmly committed to the work-based culture of self-sufficiency, who encourage private enterprise and often rate individual self-expression above social collectivity. Here, too, is a generation of young people who live in constant anxiety about the pressure of performing well at school and meeting the criteria of external assessment. Here is a generation of people who accept as normal a high level of suicidal ideation among their peers. It remains to be seen if Tony Blair is successful in shaping a different face for tomorrow's generation.

REFERENCES

Adelson, J. and O'Neil, R. (1966), 'Growth of political ideas in adolescence: the sense of community', *Journal of Personality and Social Psychology*, 4, pp. 295–306.

Adlaf, E.M. and Smart, R.G. (1985), 'Drug use and religious affiliation, feelings and behaviour', *British Journal of Addiction*, 80, pp. 163-71.

Advisory Group on Citizenship (1998), *Education for Citizenship and Teaching of Democracy in Schools*, London, Qualifications and Curriculum Authority.

Airey, C. (1984), 'Social and moral values', in R. Jowell and C. Airey (eds), *British Social Attitudes: The 1984 Report*, pp. 121–56, Aldershot, Gower.

Airey, C. and Brook, L. (1986), 'Interim report: social and moral issues', in R. Jowell, S. Witherspoon and L. Brook (eds), *British Social Attitudes: The 1986 Report*, pp. 149–72, Aldershot, Gower.

Aluja-Fabregat, A. and Torrubia-Beltri, R. (1998), 'Viewing of mass media violence, perceptions of violence, personality and academic achievement', *Personality and Individual Differences*, 25, pp. 973–89.

Amato, P.R. (1988), 'Long-term implications of parental divorce for adult self-concept', *Journal of Family Issues*, 9, pp. 201–13.

Amato, P.R. and Booth, A. (1991), 'Consequences of parental divorce and marital unhappiness for adult well-being', *Social Forces*, 69, pp. 895–914.

Amato, P.R. and Keith, B. (1991), 'Parental divorce and adult well-being: a meta-analysis', *Journal of Marriage and the Family*, 53, pp. 43–58.

Ambert, A.M. and Saucier, J.F. (1986), 'Adolescents' overt religiosity and parents' marital status', *International Journal of Comparative Sociology*, 27, pp. 87–95.

Amoateng, A.Y. and Bahr, S.J. (1986), 'Religion, family and adolescent drug use', *Sociological Perspectives*, 29, pp. 53–76.

Anderson, R.E., Crespo, C.J., Bartlett, S.J., Cheskin, L.J. and Pratt, M. (1998), 'Relationship of physical activity and television watching with body weight and level of fatness among children: results from the third national health and nutrition examination survey', *Journal of the American Medical Association*, 279, pp. 938–42.

Argyle, M. (1994), *The Psychology of Social Class*, London, Routledge.

Argyle, M. and Beit-Hallahmi, B. (1975), *The Social Psychology of Religion*, London, Routledge & Kegan Paul.

Armstrong, C.A., Sallis, J.F., Alcaraz, J.E., Kolody, B., McKenzie, T.L. and Hovell, M.F. (1998), 'Children's television viewing, body fat and physical fitness', *American Journal of Health Promotion*, 12, pp. 363–8.

Aseltine, R.H. (1996), 'Pathways linking parental divorce with adolescent depression', *Journal of Health and Social Behaviour*, 37, pp. 133–48.

Ashford, S. (1987), 'Family matters', in R. Jowell, S. Witherspoon and L. Brook (eds), *British Social Attitudes: The 1987 Report*, pp. 121–52, Aldershot, Gower.

Attina, D.A., Catalano, G. and Surace, C. (1997), 'Physical exercise, sport and television: cross-sectional analyses among 1368 children attending compulsory school', *Medicina Dello Sport*, 50, pp. 9–14.

Austin, A. (1977), *Four Critical Years*, San Francisco, CA, Jossey-Bass.

Bagley, C. and Verma, G. (eds) (1975), *Race and Education across Cultures*, London, Heinemann.

Bahr, H.M. and Martin, T.K. (1983), '"And thy neighbour as thy self": self-esteem and faith in people as correlates of religiosity and family solidarity among Middletown high school students', *Journal for the Scientific Study of Religion*, 22, pp. 132–44.

Bailey, E.I. (1986), 'The religion of the people', in T. Moss (ed.), *In Search of Christianity*, pp. 178–88, London, Firethorn Press.

Bailey, E.I. (1997), *Implicit Religion in Contemporary Society*, Kampen, Netherlands, Kok Pharos.

Balding, J. (1993), *Young People in 1992*, Exeter, Schools Health Education Unit, University of Exeter.

Balding, J. (1997), *Young People in 1996*, Exeter, Schools Health Education Unit, University of Exeter.

Balding, J. (1998), *Young People in 1997*, Exeter, Schools Health Education Unit, University of Exeter.

Balding, J. (1999), *Young People in 1998*, Exeter, Schools Health Education Unit, University of Exeter.

Barker-Lunn, J.C. (1972), 'The influence of sex, achievement level and social class on junior school children's attitudes', *British Journal of Educational Psychology*, 42, pp. 70–4.

Barling, N. and Moore, S. (1990), 'Adolescents' attitudes towards AIDS precautions and intention to use condoms', *Psychological Reports*, 67, pp. 883–90.

Barnett, S. and Saxon-Harrold, S. (1992), 'Interim report: charitable giving', in R. Jowell, L. Brook, G. Prior and B. Taylor (eds), *British Social Attitudes: The Ninth Report*, pp. 195–208, Aldershot, Dartmouth.

Barnett, S. and Thomson, K. (1997), 'How we view violence', in R. Jowell, J. Curtice, A. Park, L. Brook, K. Thomson and C. Bryson (eds), *British Social Attitudes: The Fourteenth Report*, pp. 169–96, Aldershot, Ashgate.

Beck, T., Ward, C.H., Mendelson, M., Hock, J. and Erbaugh, J. (1961), 'An inventory for measuring depression', *Archives of General Psychiatry*, 7, pp. 158–216.

Beit-Hallahmi, B. and Argyle, M. (1997), *The Psychology of Religious Belief and Experience*, London, Routledge.

Bem, S.L. (1981), *Bem Sex Role Inventory: Professional Manual*, Palo Alto, CA, Consulting Psychologists Press.

Ben-Shlomo, Y., Sheiham, A. and Marmot, M. (1991), 'Smoking and health', in R. Jowell, L. Brook and B. Taylor (eds), *British Social Attitudes: The Eighth Report*, pp. 155–74, Aldershot, Dartmouth.

Boeckmann, K. and Hipfl, B. (1987), 'How can we learn about children and television?', *Journal of Educational Television*, 13, pp. 217–29.

Booth, A., Brinkerhoff, D.B. and White, L.K. (1984), 'The impact of parental divorce on courtship', *Journal of Marriage and the Family*, 46, pp. 85–94.

Borkhuis, G.W. and Patalano, F. (1997), 'MMPI personality differences between adolescents from divorced and non-divorced families', *Psychology*, 34, pp. 37–41.

Bosanquet, N. (1984), 'Social policy and the welfare state', in R. Jowell and C. Airey (eds), *British Social Attitudes: The 1984 Report*, pp. 75–104, Aldershot, Gower.

Bosanquet, N. (1986), 'Interim report: public spending and the welfare state', in R. Jowell, S. Witherspoon and L. Brook (eds), *British Social Attitudes: The 1986 Report*, pp. 127–39, Aldershot, Gower.

Bosanquet, N. (1988), 'An ailing state of National Health', in R. Jowell, S. Witherspoon and L. Brook (eds), *British Social Attitudes: The Fifth Report*, pp. 93–108, Aldershot, Gower.

Bosanquet, N. (1994), 'Improving health', in R. Jowell, J. Curtice, L. Brook and D. Ahrendt (eds), *British Social Attitudes: The Eleventh*

Report, pp. 51–60, London, Dartmouth.

Botta, R.A. (1999), 'Television images and adolescent girls' body image disturbance', *Journal of Communication*, 49 (2), pp. 22–41.

Boyd, A. (1996), *Dangerous Obsessions: Teenagers and the Occult*, London, Marshal Pickering.

Boyd, H.H. (1999), 'Christianity and the environment in the American public', *Journal for the Scientific Study of Religion*, 38, pp. 36–44.

Bradburn, N.M. (1969), *The Structure of Psychological Well-being*, Chicago, IL, Aldine.

Brierley, P. (1991a), *'Christian' England: What the English Church Census Reveals*, London, MARC Europe.

Brierley, P. (ed.) (1991b), *Prospects for the Nineties: All England*, London, MARC Europe.

Brook, L. (1988), 'The public's response to AIDS', in R. Jowell, S. Witherspoon and L. Brook (eds), *British Social Attitudes: The Fifth Report*, pp. 71–91, Aldershot, Gower.

Brothers, C.C., Fortner, R.W. and Mayer, V.J. (1991), 'The impact of television news on public environmental knowledge', *Journal of Environmental Education*, 22 (4), pp. 22–9.

Bryson, C. and Curtice, J. (1998), 'The end of materialism?', in R. Jowell, J. Curtice, A. Park, L. Brook, K. Thomson and C. Bryson (eds), *British Social Attitudes: The Fifteenth Report*, pp. 125–48, Aldershot, Ashgate.

Budgell, P. (1983), 'Working with pupils who refuse to attend school', in G. Lindsay (ed.), *Problems of Adolescence in the Secondary School*, pp. 182–208, London, Croom Helm.

Burghes, L. (1994), *Lone Parenthood and Family Disruption: The Outcomes for Children*, London, Family Policy Studies Centre.

Burkett, S. and White, M. (1974), 'Hellfire and delinquency: another look', *Journal for the Scientific Study of Religion*, 13, pp. 455–62.

Burton, L. and Francis, L.J. (1996), 'Growing up Catholic today: the teenage experience', in L.J. Francis, W.K. Kay and W.S. Campbell (eds), *Research in Religious Education*, pp. 359–81, Leominster, Gracewing.

Cairns, E. (1990), 'Impact of television news exposure on children's perceptions of violence in Northern Ireland', *Journal of Social Psychology*, 130, pp. 447–52.

Carlson, J.M. (1983), 'Crime show viewing by preadults: the impact on attitudes toward civil liberties', *Communication Research*, 10, pp. 529–52.

Chase-Lansdale, P.L., Cherlin, A.J. and Kiernan, K.E. (1995), 'The long-term effects of parental divorce on the mental health of young adults: a developmental perspective', *Child Development*, 66, pp. 1614–34.

Cheung, C.K. and Chan, C.F. (1996), 'Television viewing and mean world value in Hong Kong's adolescents', *Social Behaviour and Personality*, 24, pp. 351–64.

Child, D. (1969), 'A comparative study of personality, intelligence and social class in a technological university', *British Journal of Educational Psychology*, 39, pp. 40–6.

Christie, D., Maitles, H. and Halliday, J. (eds) (1998), *Values Education for Democracy and Citizenship*, Glasgow, University of Strathclyde Faculty of Education.

Clark, J. and Barber, B.L. (1994), 'Adolescents in post-divorce and always-married families: self-esteem and perceptions of fathers' interest', *Journal of Marriage and the Family*, 56, pp. 608–14.

Clarke, A.T. and Kurtz-Costes, B. (1997), 'Television viewing, educational quality of the home environment and school readiness', *Journal of Educational Research*, 90, pp. 279–85.

Clarke, L., Beeghley, L. and Cochran, J.K. (1990), 'Religiosity, social class, and alcohol use: an application of reference group theory', *Sociological Perspectives*, 33, pp. 201–18.

Cline, V.B., Croft, R.G. and Courrier, S. (1973), 'Desensitisation of children to television violence', *Journal of Personality and Social Psychology*, 27, pp. 360–5.

Cobb, N.J., Stevens-Long, J. and Goldstein, S. (1982), 'The influence of televised models on toy preference in children', *Sex Roles*, 8, pp. 1075–80.

Cochran, J.K., Beeghley, L. and Bock, E.W. (1992), 'The influence of religious stability and homogamy on the relationship between religiosity and alcohol use among Protestants', *Journal for the Scientific Study of Religion*, 31, pp. 441–56.

Collins, J. (1990a), 'Television and secondary school children', *Educational Media International*, 27, pp. 128–34.

Collins, J. (1990b), 'Television and primary school children in Northern Ireland: the impact of advertising', *Journal of Educational Television*, 16, pp. 31–9.

Conway, M.M., Stevens, A.J. and Smith, R.G. (1975), 'The relation between media use and children's civic awareness', *Journalism Quarterly*, 52, pp. 531–8.

Cooper, B. and Dunne, M. (1998), 'Anyone for tennis? Social class differences in children's responses to national curriculum mathematics testing', *Sociological Review*, 46, pp. 115–48.

Cooper, H., Smaje, C. and Arber, S. (1998a), 'Use of health services by children and young people according to ethnicity and social class:

secondary analysis of a national survey', *British Medical Journal*, 317, pp. 1047–51.

Cooper, H., Smaje, C. and Arber, S. (1998b), 'Social class or deprivation? Structural factors and children's limiting longstanding illness in the 1990s', *Sociology of Health and Illness*, 20, pp. 289–311.

Coopersmith, S. (1967), *The Antecedents of Self-esteem*, San Francisco, CA, Freeman.

Cox, E. and Cairns, J.M. (1989), *Reforming Religious Education: The Religious Clauses of the 1988 Education Reform Act*, London, Kogan Page.

Crawford, D.A., Jeffery, R.W. and French, S.A. (1999), 'Television viewing, physical inactivity and obesity', *International Journal of Obesity*, 23, pp. 437–40.

Crompton, R. (1993), *Class and Stratification: An Introduction to Current Debates*, Cambridge, Polity.

Crossman, S.M., Shea, J.A. and Adams, G.R. (1980), 'Effects of parental divorce during early childhood on ego development and identity formation of college students', *Journal of Divorce*, 3, pp. 263–72.

Crumbaugh, J.C. (1968), 'Cross-validation of Purpose in Life Test based on Frankl's concepts', *Journal of Individual Psychology*, 24, pp. 74–81.

Crumbaugh, J.C. and Maholick, L.T. (1969), *Manual of Instruction for the Purpose in Life Test*, Munster, IN, Psychometric Affiliates.

Cumberbatch, G., Lee, M., Hardy, G. and Jones, I. (1987), *The Portrayal of Violence on British Television*, London, British Broadcasting Corporation.

Curtice, J. (1986), 'Political partnership', in R. Jowell, S. Witherspoon and L. Brook (eds), *British Social Attitudes: The 1986 Report*, pp. 39–58, Aldershot, Gower.

Curtice, J. and Gallagher, T. (1990), 'The Northern Irish dimension', in R. Jowell, S. Witherspoon and L. Brook (eds), *British Social Attitudes: The Seventh Report*, pp. 183–216, Aldershot, Gower.

Davie, G. (1994), *Religion in Britain since 1945: Believing without Belonging*, Oxford, Blackwell.

Davies, M.M. (1989), *Television is Good for your Kids*, London, Hilary Shipman.

Davis, J.A. and Jowell, R. (1989), 'Measuring national differences', in R. Jowell, S. Witherspoon and L. Brook (eds), *British Social Attitudes: The Sixth Report*, pp. 1–13, Aldershot, Gower.

Davis, S. and Mares, M.L. (1998), 'Effects of talk show viewing on adolescents', *Journal of Communication*, 48 (3), pp. 69–86.

de Fleur, M. and de Fleur, L. (1967), 'The relative contribution of television as a learning source for children's occupational knowledge', *American Sociological Review*, 32, pp. 777–89.

Demo, D.H. (1993), 'The relentless search for effects of divorce: forging new traits or tumbling down the beaten path?', *Journal of Marriage and the Family*, 55, pp. 42–5.

Demo, D.H. and Acock, A.C. (1988), 'The impact of divorce on children', *Journal of Marriage and the Family*, 50, pp. 619–48.

Department of Education and Science (1983), *Young People in the '80s: A Survey*, London, HMSO.

Department of Education and Science (1989), *The Education Reform Act 1988: Religious Education and Collective Worship*, London, DES, circular 3/89.

Desforges, M. (1983), 'Drugs, adolescents and adults', in G. Lindsay (ed.), *Problems of Adolescence in the Secondary School*, pp. 161–81, London, Croom Helm.

Diekstra, R.F., Kienhorst, C.W.M. and de Wilde, E.J. (1995), 'Suicide and suicidal behaviour among adolescents', in M. Rutter and D.J. Smith (eds), *Psychosocial Disorders in Young People: Time Trends and their Causes*, pp. 686–761, Chichester, John Wiley & Sons.

Diener, E., Emmons, R.A., Larsen, R.J. and Griffen, S. (1985), 'The satisfaction with life scale', *Journal of Personality Assessment*, 49, pp. 71–5.

Dittmar, M.L., (1994), 'Relations among depression, gender and television viewing of college students', *Journal of Social Behaviour and Personality*, 9, pp. 317–28.

Donnison, D. and Bryson, C. (1996), 'Matters of life and death: attitudes to euthanasia', in R. Jowell, A. Park, L. Brook and K. Thomson (eds), *British Social Attitudes: The Thirteenth Report*, pp. 161–83, Aldershot, Dartmouth.

Doob, A.N. and MacDonald, G.E. (1979), 'Television viewing and fear of victimisation: is the relationship causal?' *Journal of Personality and Social Psychology*, 37, pp. 170–9.

Douglas, J.W.B. (1970), 'Broken families and child behaviour', *Journal of the Royal College of Physicians*, 4, pp. 203–10.

Dowds, L. and Ahrendt, D. (1995), 'Fear of crime', in R. Jowell, J. Curtice, A. Park, L. Brook and D. Ahrendt (eds), *British Social Attitudes: The Twelfth Report*, pp. 19–41, Aldershot, Dartmouth.

Elliott, B.J. and Richards, M.P.M. (1991), 'Children and divorce: educational performance and behaviour before and after parental separation', *International Journal of Law and the Family*, 5, pp. 258–76.

Ely, M., Richards, M.P.M., Wadsworth, M.E.J. and Elliott, B.J. (1999), 'Secular changes in the association of parental divorce and children's educational attainment: evidence from three British birth cohorts', *Journal of Social Policy*, 28, pp. 437–55.

Eron, L.D., Huesmann, L.R., Brice, P., Fischer, P. and Mermelstein, R. (1983), 'Age trends in the development of aggression, sex typing and related television habits', *Developmental Psychology*, 19, pp. 71–7.

Erricker, C., Erricker, J., Sullivan D., Ota, C. and Fletcher, M. (1997), *The Education of the Whole Child*, London, Cassell.

Estaugh, V. and Power, C. (1991), 'Family disruption in early life and drinking in young adulthood', *Alcohol and Alcoholism*, 26, pp. 639–44.

Eysenck, H.J. (1951), 'Primary social attitudes as related to social class and political party', *British Journal of Sociology*, 2, pp. 198–209.

Eysenck, H.J. (1954), *The Psychology of Politics*, London, Routledge & Kegan Paul.

Eysenck, H.J. (1958), 'A short questionnaire for the measurement of two dimensions of personality', *Journal of Applied Psychology*, 42, pp. 14–17.

Eysenck, H.J. (1959), *Manual for the Maudsley Personality Inventory*, London, University of London Press.

Eysenck, H.J. (1971), 'Social attitudes and social class', *British Journal of Social and Clinical Psychology*, 10, pp. 201–12.

Eysenck, H.J. and Eysenck, S.B.G. (1964), *Manual of the Eysenck Personality Inventory*, London, University of London Press.

Eysenck, H.J. and Eysenck, S.B.G. (1969), *Personality Structure and Measurement*, London, Routledge & Kegan Paul.

Eysenck, H.J. and Eysenck, S.B.G. (1975), *Manual of the Eysenck Personality Questionnaire (Adult and Junior)*, London, Hodder & Stoughton.

Eysenck, S.B.G. (1960), 'Social class, sex, and response to a five-part personality inventory', *Educational and Psychological Measurement*, 20, pp. 47–54.

Fane, R.S. (1999), 'Is self-assigned religious affiliation socially significant?', in L.J. Francis (ed.), *Sociology, Theology and the Curriculum*, pp. 113–24, London, Cassell.

Farrington, D.P. (1990), 'Age, period, cohort and offending', in D.M. Goltfredson and R.V. Clarke (eds), *Policy and Theory in Criminal Justice: Contributions in Honour of Leslie T. Wilkins*, pp. 51–75, Aldershot, Avebury.

Faulkner, K.K., Alcorn, J.D. and Garvin, R.B. (1989), 'Prediction of alcohol consumption among fraternity pledges', *Journal of Alcohol and Drug Education*, 34 (2), pp. 12–20.

Ferri, E. (1976), *Growing Up in a One-parent Family*, Slough, National Foundation for Educational Research.

Fisher, S. and Holder, S. (1981), *Too Much Too Young?*, London, Pan.

Fitt, A.B. (1956), 'An experimental study of children's attitudes to school in Auckland, New Zealand', *British Journal of Educational Psychology*, 26, pp. 25–30.

Fogelman, K. (ed.) (1976), *Britain's Sixteen Year Olds*, London, National Child Bureau.

Ford, J. and Burrows, R. (1999), 'To buy or not to buy? A home of one's own', in R. Jowell, J. Curtice, A. Park and K. Thomson (eds), *British Social Attitudes: The Sixteenth Report*, pp. 97–112, Aldershot, Ashgate.

Francis, L.J. (1979), 'School influence and pupil attitude towards religion', *British Journal of Educational Psychology*, 49, pp. 107–23.

Francis, L.J. (1982a), *Youth in Transit: A Profile of 16–25 year olds*, Aldershot, Gower.

Francis, L.J. (1982b), *Experience of Adulthood: A Profile of 26–39 year olds*, Aldershot, Gower.

Francis, L.J. (1984a), *Young and Unemployed*, Tunbridge Wells, Costello.

Francis, L.J. (1984b), *Teenagers and the Church: A Profile of Church-going Youth in the 1980s*, London, Collins Liturgical Publications.

Francis, L.J. (1986), 'Denominational schools and pupil attitude towards Christianity', *British Educational Research Journal*, 12, pp. 145–52.

Francis, L.J. (1987), *Religion in the Primary School: Partnership between Church and State?*, London, Collins Liturgical Publications.

Francis, L.J. (1989), 'Drift from the churches: secondary school pupils' attitudes toward Christianity', *British Journal of Religious Education*, 11, pp. 76–86.

Francis, L.J. (1992a), 'Christianity today: the teenage experience', in J. Astley and D.V. Day (eds), *The Contours of Christian Education*, pp. 340–68, Great Wakering, McCrimmons.

Francis, L.J. (1992b), 'The influence of religion, gender and social class on attitudes toward school among eleven year olds in England', *Journal of Experimental Education*, 60, pp. 339–48.

Francis, L.J. (1994a), *Believing without Belonging: The Teenage Experience*, London, Unitarian and Free Christian Churches.

Francis, L.J. (1994b), 'Denominational identity, church attendance and drinking behaviour among adults in England', *Journal of Alcohol and Drug Education*, 39(3), pp. 27–33.

Francis, L.J. (1997a), 'Personal and social correlates of the "closed mind" among sixteen year old adolescents in England', *Educational Studies*, 23, pp. 429–37.

Francis, L.J. (1997b), 'Christianity, personality and concern about environmental pollution among 13 to 15 year olds', *Journal of Beliefs and Values*, 18, pp. 7–16.

Francis, L.J. (1997c), 'The impact of personality and religion on attitude towards substance use among 13–15 year olds', *Drug and Alcohol Dependence*, 44, pp. 95–103.

Francis, L.J. (1997d), 'The psychology of gender differences in religion: a review of empirical research', *Religion*, 27, pp. 81–96.

Francis, L.J. (1999), 'The benefits of growing up in rural England: a study among 13–15 year old females', *Educational Studies*, 25, pp. 335–41.

Francis, L.J. and Burton, L. (1994), 'The influence of personal prayer on purpose in life among Catholic adolescents', *Journal of Beliefs and Values*, 15(2), pp. 6–9.

Francis, L.J. and Evans, T.E. (1996), 'The relationship between personal prayer and purpose in life among churchgoing and non-churchgoing 12–15 year olds in the UK', *Religious Education*, 91, pp. 9–21.

Francis, L.J., Fulljames, P. and Gibson, H.M. (1992), 'Does creationism commend the gospel? A developmental study among 11–17 year olds', *Religious Education*, 87, pp. 19–27.

Francis, L.J. and Gibson, H.M. (1992), 'Popular religious television and adolescent attitudes towards Christianity', in J. Astley and D.V. Day (eds), *The Contours of Christian Education*, pp. 369–81, Great Wakering, McCrimmons.

Francis, L.J. and Gibson, H.M. (1993a), 'Television, pop culture and the drift from Christianity during adolescence', *British Journal of Religious Education*, 15, pp. 31–7.

Francis, L.J. and Gibson, H.M. (1993b), 'The influence of age, sex, social class and religion on television viewing time and programme preferences among 11–15 year olds', *Journal of Educational Television*, 19, pp. 25–35.

Francis, L.J., Gibson, H.M. and Fulljames, P. (1990), 'Attitude towards Christianity, creationism, scientism and interest in science among 11–15 year olds', *British Journal of Religious Education*, 13, pp. 4–17.

Francis, L.J. and Greer, J.E. (1999a), 'Attitudes towards creationism and evolutionary theory: the debate among secondary pupils attending Catholic and Protestant schools in Northern Ireland', *Public Understanding of Science*, 8, pp. 93–103.

Francis, L.J. and Greer, J.E. (1999b), 'Attitude toward science among secondary school pupils in Northern Ireland: relationship with sex, age and religion', *Research in Science and Technological Education*, 17, pp. 67–74.

Francis, L.J. and Jones, S.H. (1994), 'The relationship between Eysenck's personality factors and fear of bullying among 13–15 year olds in England and Wales', *Evaluation and Research in Education*, 8, pp. 111–18.

Francis, L.J. and Jones, S.H. (1996), 'Social class and self-esteem', *Journal of Social Psychology*, 136, pp. 405–6.

Francis, L.J. and Kay, W.K. (1995), *Teenage Religion and Values*, Leominster, Gracewing.

Francis, L.J. and Lankshear, D.W. (1991), *Continuing in the Way: Children, Young People and the Church*, London, National Society.

Francis, L.J. and Lewis, J.M. (1996), 'Who wants RE? A socio-psychological profile of adolescent support for religious education', in J. Astley and L.J. Francis (eds), *Christian Theology and Religious Education: Connections and Contradictions*, pp. 223–46, London, SPCK.

Francis, L.J., Littler, K.T. and Thomas, T.H. (2000), 'Fenced fonts or open doors? An empirical survey of baptismal policy among clergy in the Church in Wales', *Implicit Religion*, 3, pp. 73–86.

Francis, L.J. and Mullen, K. (1993), 'Religiosity and attitudes towards drug use among 13–15 year olds in England', *Addiction*, 88, pp. 665–72.

Francis, L.J. and Pearson, P.R. (1989), 'The relationship between social class and neuroticism among English 16 year olds', *Journal of Social Psychology*, 129, pp. 695–7.

Francis, L.J., Pearson, P.R. and Lankshear, D.W. (1990), 'The relationship between social class and attitude towards Christianity among ten and eleven year old children', *Personality and Individual Differences*, 11, pp. 1019–27.

Francis, L.J. and Wilcox, C. (1996), 'Religion and gender orientation', *Personality and Individual Differences*, 20, pp. 119–21.

Francis, L.J. and Wilcox, C. (1998), 'Religiosity and femininity: do women really hold a more positive attitude toward Christianity?', *Journal for the Scientific Study of Religion*, 37, pp. 462–9.

Fulljames, P., Gibson, H.M. and Francis, L.J. (1991), 'Creationism, scientism, Christianity and science: a study in adolescent attitudes', *British Educational Research Journal*, 17, pp. 171–90.

Furnham, A. and Gunter, B. (1983), 'Political knowledge and awareness in adolescents', *Journal of Adolescence*, 6, pp. 373–85.

Furnham, A. and Gunter, B. (1987), 'Young people's political knowledge', *Educational Studies*, 13, pp. 91–104.

Furnham, A. and Gunter, B. (1989), *The Anatomy of Adolescence: Young*

People's Social Attitudes in Britain, London, Routledge.

Gabardi, L. and Rosén, L.A. (1991), 'Differences between college students from divorced and intact families', *Journal of Divorce and Remarriage*, 15, pp. 175–91.

Gaddy, G.D. (1986), 'Television's impact on high school achievement', *Public Opinion Quarterly*, 50, pp. 340–59.

Gahler, M. (1998), 'Self-report psychological well-being among adult children of divorce in Sweden', *Acta Sociologica*, 41, pp. 209–25.

Garber, R.J. (1991), 'Long-term effects of divorce on the self-esteem of young adults', *Journal of Divorce and Remarriage*, 17(1), pp. 131–7.

Gerbner, G. and Gross, L. (1976), 'Living with television: the violence profile', *Journal of Communication*, 26, pp. 173–99.

Gibson, H.M. (1989), 'Attitudes to religion and science among school children aged 11 to 16 years in a Scottish city', *Journal of Empirical Theology*, 2, pp. 5–26.

Gibson, H.M., Francis, L.J. and Pearson, P.R. (1990), 'The relationship between social class and attitude towards Christianity among fourteen- and fifteen-year-old adolescents', *Personality and Individual Differences*, 11, pp. 631–5.

Gill, R. (1999), *Churchgoing and Christian Ethics*, Cambridge, Cambridge University Press.

Gill, R., Hadaway, C.K. and Marler, P.L. (1998), 'Is religious belief declining in Britain?', *Journal for the Scientific Study of Religion*, 37, pp. 507–16.

Giuliani, C., Iafrate, R. and Rosnati, R. (1998), 'Peer-group and romantic relationships in adolescents from intact and separated families', *Contemporary Family Therapy*, 20, pp. 95–105.

Glendinning, A., Shucksmith, J. and Hendry, L. (1994), 'Social class and adolescent smoking behaviour', *Social Science and Medicine*, 38, pp. 1449–60.

Glock, C.Y., Wuthnow, R., Piliavin, J.A. and Spencer, M. (1975), *Adolescent Prejudice*, New York, Harper & Row.

Goddard, E. (1991), *Drinking in England and Wales in the late 1980s*, London, HMSO.

Goggin, M. (1993), 'Gay and lesbian adolescence', in S. Moore and D. Rosenthal (eds), *Sexuality in Adolescence*, pp. 102–23, London, Routledge.

Goldman, R.J. and Goldman J. (1982), *Children's Sexual Thinking*, London, Routledge.

Goldman, R.J. and Goldman J. (1988), *Show Me Yours*, Harmondsworth, Penguin.

Goldney, R.D., Winefield, A.H., Tiggeman, M., Winefield, H.R. and Smith, S. (1989), 'Suicidal ideation in a young adult population', *Acta Psychiatrica Scandanavica*, 79, pp. 481–9.

Goldstein, H. (1984), 'Educational issues and priorities', in R. Jowell and C. Airey (eds), *British Social Attitudes: The 1984 Report*, pp. 105–19, Aldershot, Gower.

Goldstein, H. (1986), 'Interim report on education', in R. Jowell, S. Witherspoon and L. Brook (eds), *British Social Attitudes: The 1986 Report*, pp. 115–26, Aldershot, Gower.

Goldthorpe, J. and Heath, A. (1992), *Revised Class Schema 1992*, London, JUSST.

Goodhardt, G. (1985), 'Prices, incomes and consumer issues', in R. Jowell and S. Witherspoon (eds), *British Social Attitudes: The 1985 Report*, pp. 33–54, Aldershot, Gower.

Gortmaker, S.L., Must, A., Sobol, A.M., Peterson, K., Colditz, G.A. and Dietz, W.H. (1996), 'Television viewing as a cause of increasing obesity among children in the United States: 1986-1990', *Archives of Pediatrics and Adolescent Medicine*, 150, pp. 356–62.

Gould, M.S. and Shaffer, D. (1986), 'The impact of suicide in television movies', *New England Journal of Medicine*, 315, pp. 690–4.

Greeley, A. (1992), 'Religion in Britain, Ireland and the USA', in R. Jowell, L. Brook, G. Prior and B. Taylor (eds), *British Social Attitudes: The Ninth Report*, pp. 51–70, Aldershot, Dartmouth.

Green, G., MacIntyre, S., West, P. and Ecob, R. (1991), 'Like parent like child: associations between drinking and smoking-behaviour of parents and their children', *British Journal of Addiction*, 86, pp. 745–58.

Greenberg, E. and Nay, W. (1982), 'The intergenerational transmission of marital instability reconsidered', *Journal of Marriage and the Family*, 44, pp. 335–47.

Guijarro, S., Naranjo, J., Padilla, M., Gutierez, R., Lammers, C. and Blum, R.W. (1999), 'Family risk factors associated with adolescent pregnancy: study of a group of adolescent girls and their families in Ecuador', *Journal of Adolescent Health*, 25, pp. 166–72.

Gunter, B. (1984), 'Television as a facilitator of good behaviour among children', *Journal of Moral Education*, 13, pp. 152–9.

Gunter, B. and McAleer, J.L. (1990), *Children and Television: The One Eyed Monster?*, London, Routledge.

Gunter, B., McAleer, J.L. and Clifford, B.R. (1991), 'Television police dramas and children's beliefs about the police', *Journal of Educational Television*, 17, pp. 81–100.

Gunter, B. and Wober, M. (1983), 'Television viewing and public trust',

British Journal of Social Psychology, 22, pp. 174–6.

Hadaway, C.K., Elifson, K.W. and Petersen, D.M. (1984), 'Religious involvement and drug use among urban adolescents', *Journal for the Scientific Study of Religion*, 23, pp. 109–28.

Hagborg, W.J. (1995), 'High school student television viewing time: a study of school performance and adjustment', *Child Study Journal*, 25, pp. 155–67.

Hall, G.S. (1904), *Adolescence: Its Psychology, and its Relations to Physiology, Anthropology, Sociology, Sex, Crime, Religion and Education*, New York, D. Appleton.

Halsey, A.H. (1991), 'Failing education?', in R. Jowell, L. Brook and B. Taylor (eds), *British Social Attitudes: The Eighth Report*, pp. 43–58, Aldershot, Dartmouth.

Halstead, J.M. and Taylor, M.J. (eds) (1996), *Values in Education and Education in Values*, Lewes, Falmer Press.

Halstead, J.M. and Taylor, M.J. (2000), *The Development of Values, Attitudes and Personal Qualities: A Review of Recent Research*, Slough, NFER.

Hammer, T. (1992), 'Unemployment and use of drugs and alcohol among young people: a longitudinal study in the general population', *British Journal of Addiction*, 87, pp. 1571–81.

Harding, S. (1988), 'Trends in permissiveness', in R. Jowell, S. Witherspoon and L. Brook (eds), *British Social Attitudes: The Fifth Report*, pp. 35–51, Aldershot, Gower.

Harding, S., Phillips, D. and Fogarty, M. (1986), *Contrasting Values in Western Europe: Unity, Diversity and Change*, Basingstoke, Macmillan.

Hare, B.R. (1980), 'Self-perception and academic achievement: variations in a desegregated setting', *American Journal of Psychiatry*, 137, pp. 683–9.

Harrison, A. (1984), 'Economic policy and expectation', in R. Jowell and C. Airey (eds), *British Social Attitudes: The 1984 Report*, pp. 47–73, Aldershot, Gower.

Haskey, J. (1990), 'Children in families broken by divorce', *Population Trends*, 61, pp. 34–42.

Hay, D. and Nye, R. (1998), *The Spirit of the Child*, London, Fount.

Heath, A. and Evans, G. (1988), 'Working-class conservatives and middle-class socialists', in R. Jowell, S. Witherspoon and L. Brook (eds), *British Social Attitudes: The Fifth Report*, pp. 53–69, Aldershot, Gower.

Heath, A., Taylor, B. and Toka, G. (1993), 'Religion, morality and politics', in R. Jowell, L. Brook, L. Dowds and D. Ahrendt (eds), *International Social Attitudes: The Tenth BSA Report*, pp. 49–80, Aldershot, Dartmouth.

Heaven, P.C.L. (1996), *Adolescent Health: The Role of Individual Differences*, London, Routledge.

Heelas, P. (1996), *The New Age Movement: The Celebration of the Self and the Sacralization of Modernity*, Oxford, Blackwell.

Hendry, L.B. (1983), *Growing Up and Going Out: Adolescents and Leisure*, Aberdeen, Aberdeen University Press.

Hendry, L.B., Kloep, M. and Olsson, S. (1998), 'Youth, lifestyles and society: a class issue?', *Childhood: A Global Journal of Child Research*, 5, pp. 133–50.

Hendry, L.B. and Patrick, H. (1977), 'Adolescents and television', *Journal of Youth and Adolescence*, 6, pp. 325–36.

Hendry, L.B., Shucksmith, J., Love, J.G. and Glendenning, A. (1993), *Young People's Leisure and Lifestyle*, London, Routledge.

Hendry, L.B. and Thornton, D.J.E. (1976), 'Games theory, television and leisure: an adolescent study', *British Journal of Social and Clinical Psychology*, 15, pp. 369–76.

Henriksson, B. (1983), *Not for Sale: Young People in Society*, Aberdeen, Aberdeen University Press.

Herek, G.M. and Birrell, K.T. (1992), *Hate Crimes: Confronting Violence against Lesbians and Gay Men*, Newbury Park, CA, Sage.

Hernandez, B., Gortmaker, S.L., Colditz, G.A., Peterson, K.E., Laird, N.M. and Parra-Cabrera, S. (1999), 'Association of obesity with physical activity, television programs and other forms of video viewing among children in Mexico City', *International Journal of Obesity*, 23, pp. 845–54.

Hess, L.E. (1995), 'Changing family patterns in Western Europe: opportunity and risk factors for adolescent development', in M. Rutter and D.J. Smith (eds), *Psychosocial Disorders in Young People: Time Trends and their Causes*, pp. 104–93, Chichester, John Wiley & Sons.

Heyer, D.L. and Nelson, E.S. (1993), 'The relationship between parental marital status and the development of identity and emotional autonomy in college students', *Journal of College Student Development*, 34, pp. 432–6.

Higgins, P.C. and Albrecht, G.L. (1977), 'Hellfire and delinquency revisited', *Social Forces*, 55, pp. 952–8.

Hill, J.M.M. and Scharff, D.E. (1976), *Between Two Worlds: Aspects of the Transition from School to Work*, London, Careers Consultants Ltd.

Hitchings, E. and Moynihan, P.J. (1998), 'The relationship between television food advertisements recalled and actual foods consumed by children', *Journal of Human Nutrition and Dietetics*, 11, pp. 511–17.

Hopf, H. and Weiss, R.H. (1996), 'Consumption of horror and violence videos by adolescents: study on samples of speech by video consumers using the Gottschalk–Gleser speech content analysis', *Praxis der Kinderpsychologie und Kinderpsychiatrie*, 45, pp. 179–85.

Hudson, F. and Ineichen, B. (1991), *Taking it Lying Down: Sexuality and Teenage Motherhood*, Hong Kong, Macmillan Education.

Huesmann, L.R. and Eron, L.D. (eds) (1986), *Television and the Aggressive Child: A Cross-national Comparison*, Hillsdale, NJ, Erlbaum.

Hughes, M. and Lloyd, E. (1996), 'Young people: stake holders in the educational system', in H. Roberts and D. Sachdev (eds), *Young People's Social Attitudes: The Views of 12–19 year olds*, pp. 99–117, Barkingside, Barnardos.

Jackson, R. (1997), *Religious Education: An Interpretive Approach*, London, Hodder & Stoughton.

Jenkins, J.E. and Zunguze, S.T. (1998), 'The relationship of family structure to adolescent drug use, peer affiliation, and perception of peer acceptance of drug use', *Adolescence*, 33, pp. 811–22.

Jennings, A.M., Salts, C.J. and Smith, T.A. Jr (1991), 'Attitudes toward marriage: effects of parental conflict, family structure, and gender', *Journal of Divorce and Remarriage*, 17(1), pp. 67–79.

Johnson, M. (1988), 'The price of honesty', in R. Jowell, S. Witherspoon and L. Brook (eds) *British Social Attitudes: The Fifth Report*, pp. 1–15, Aldershot, Gower.

Johnson, M. and Wood, D. (1985), 'Right and wrong in public and private life', in R. Jowell and S. Witherspoon (eds), *British Social Attitudes: The 1985 Report*, pp. 121–47, Aldershot, Gower.

Johnson-Smaragdi, V. (1983), *TV Use and Social Interaction in Adolescence: A Longitudinal Study*, Stockholm, Almquist & Wiksell International.

Johnston, W.M. and Davey, G.C.L. (1997), 'The psychological impact of negative TV news bulletins: the catastrophising of personal worries', *British Journal of Psychology*, 88, pp. 85–91.

Jones, S.H. and Francis, L.J. (1995), 'The relationship between Eysenck's personality factors and attitude towards truancy among 13–15 year olds in England and Wales', *Personality and Individual Differences*, 19, pp. 225–33.

Jowell, R. and Airey, C. (eds), (1984), *British Social Attitudes: The 1984 Report*, Aldershot, Gower.

Jowell, R., Brook, L. and Dowds, L. (1993), *International Social Attitudes: The Tenth BSA Report*, Aldershot, Dartmouth.

Jowell, R., Witherspoon, S. and Brook, L. (1988), *British Social Attitudes: The Fifth Report*, Aldershot, Gower.

Kanagy, C.L. and Nelsen, H.M. (1995), 'Religion and environmental concern: challenging the dominant assumptions', *Review of Religious Research*, 37, pp. 33–45.

Kanoy, K.W. and Cunningham, J.L. (1984), 'Consensus or confusion in research on children and divorce: conceptual and methodological issues', *Journal of Divorce*, 7(4), pp. 45–71.

Kay, W.K. (1997), 'Belief in God in Great Britain 1945–1996: moving the scenery behind the classroom RE', *British Journal of Religious Education*, 20, pp. 28–41.

Kay, W.K. and Francis, L.J. (1996), *Drift from the Churches: Attitude towards Christianity During Childhood and Adolescence*, Cardiff, University of Wales Press.

Keith, V.M. and Finlay, B. (1988), 'The impact of parental divorce on children's educational attainment, marital timing, and likelihood of divorce', *Journal of Marriage and the Family*, 50, pp. 797–809.

Kelley, P., Buckingham, D. and Davies, H. (1999), 'Talking dirty: children, sexual knowledge and television', *Childhood*, 6, pp. 221–42.

Kiernan, K.E. (1992a), 'Men and women at work and at home', in R. Jowell, L. Brook, G. Prior and B. Taylor (eds), *British Social Attitudes: The Ninth Report*, pp. 51–70, Aldershot, Dartmouth.

Kiernan, K.E. (1992b), 'The impact of family disruption in childhood on transitions made in young adult life', *Population Studies*, 46, pp. 213–34.

Kiernan, K.E. and Cherlin, A.J. (1999), 'Parental divorce and partnership dissolution in adulthood: evidence from a British cohort study', *Population Studies: A Journal of Demography*, 53, pp. 39–48.

Kiernan, K.E. and Eastaugh, V. (1993), *Cohabitation: Extra-marital Childbearing and Social Policy*, London, Family Policies Studies Centre.

Kilpatrick, D.G., Sutker, L.W. and Sutker, P.B. (1970), 'Dogmatism, religion, and religiosity: a review and re-evaluation', *Psychological Reports*, 26, pp. 15–22.

Kitwood, T. (1980), *Disclosures to a Stranger*, London, Routledge & Kegan Paul.

Koolstra, C.M. and van der Voort, T.H.A. (1996), 'Longitudinal effects of television on children's leisure-time reading: a test of three explanatory models', *Human Communication Research*, 23, pp. 4–35.

Koolstra, C.M., van der Voort, T.H.A. and van der Kamp, L.J.T. (1997), 'Television's impact on children's reading comprehension and decoding skills: a three year panel study', *Reading Research Quarterly*, 32, pp. 128–52.

Krcmar, M. and Valkenburg, P.M. (1999), 'A scale to assess children's moral interpretations of justified and unjustified violence and its relationship to television viewing', *Communication Research*, 26, pp. 608–34.

Kremer, J., Trew, K. and Ogle, S. (eds) (1997), *Young People's Involvement in Sport*, London, Routledge.

Krendl, K.A., Lasky, K. and Dawson, R. (1989), 'How television affects adolescents: their own perceptions', *Educational Horizons*, 67, pp. 88–91.

Kuh, D. and MacLean, M. (1990), 'Women's childhood experience of parental separation and their subsequent health and status in adulthood', *Journal of Biosocial Science*, 22, pp. 121–35.

Kulka, R.A. and Weingarten, H. (1979), 'The long term effects of parental divorce in childhood on adult adjustment', *Journal of Social Issues*, 35, 4, pp. 50–77.

Lader, D. and Matheson, J. (1991), *Smoking among Secondary School Children in 1990*, London, HMSO.

Lawrence, B. and Bennett, S. (1992), 'Shyness and education: the relationship between shyness, social class and personality variables in adolescence', *British Journal of Educational Psychology*, 62, pp. 257–63.

Lawrence, F.C. and Wozniak, P.H. (1989), 'Children's television viewing with family members', *Psychological Reports*, 65, pp. 395–400.

Leete, R. and Fox, J. (1997), 'Registrar General's social classes: origins and uses', *Population Trends*, 8, pp. 1–7.

Lester, D. (1992), *Why People Kill Themselves*, Springfield, IL, Charles C. Thomas.

Likert, R. (1932), 'A technique for the measurement of attitudes', *Archives of Psychology*, 140, pp. 1–55.

Linden, R. and Currie, R. (1977), 'Religiosity and drug use: a test of social control theory', *Canadian Journal of Criminology and Correction*, 19, pp. 346–55.

Livingston, R.B. and Kordinak, S.T. (1990), 'The long term effect of parental divorce: marital role expectations', *Journal of Divorce and Remarriage*, 14, 2, pp. 91–105.

Long, K.A. and Boik, R.J. (1993), 'Predicting alcohol use in rural children: a longitudinal study', *Nursing Research*, 42, 2, pp. 79–86.

Lonkey, E., Reihman, J. and Serlin, R. (1981), 'Political values and moral judgement in adolescence', *Youth and Society*, 12, pp. 423–41.

Lopez, F.G., Campbell, V.L. and Watkins, C.E. Jr (1988), 'The relation of parental divorce to college student development', *Journal of Divorce*, 12, 1, pp. 83–98.

Lubben, J.E., Chi, I. and Kitano, H.H.L. (1988), 'Exploring Filipino American drinking behaviour', *Journal of Studies on Alcohol*, 49, pp. 26–9.

MacDonald, A.P. (1970), 'Revised scale for ambiguity tolerance: reliability and validity', *Psychological Reports*, 26, pp. 791–8.

MacLean, M. and Wadsworth, M.E.J. (1988), 'The interests of children after parental divorce: a long-term perspective', *International Journal of Law and the Family*, 2, pp. 155–60.

McCabe, M.P. and Collins, J.K. (1990), *Dating, Relating and Sex*, Sydney, New South Wales, Horowitz Grahame.

McCann-Erickson Advertising Agency (1977), *You Don't Know Me: A Survey of Youth in Britain*, London, McCann-Erickson Advertising Agency.

McIntosh, W.A., Fitch, S.D., Wilson, J.B. and Nyberg, K.L. (1981), 'The effect of mainstream religious social controls on adolescent drug use in rural areas', *Review of Religious Research*, 23, pp. 54–75.

McLanahan, S. and Bumpass, L. (1988), 'Intergenerational consequences of family disruption', *American Journal of Sociology*, 94, pp. 130–52.

McLeish, J. (1970), *Student Attitudes and College Environments*, Cambridge, Institute of Education.

McNeish, D. (1996), 'Young people, crime, justice and punishment', in H. Roberts and D. Sachdev (eds), *Young People's Social Attitudes: The Views of 12–19 year olds*, pp. 71–98, Barkingside, Barnardos.

Maly, W.T. (1992), 'Socioeconomic status and early adolescent self-esteem', *Sociological Inquiry*, 62, pp. 374–82.

Mangleburg, T.F. and Bristol, T. (1998), 'Socialization and adolescents' skepticism toward advertising', *Journal of Advertising*, 27, pp. 11–21.

Mann, M. (1986), 'Work and work ethic', in R. Jowell, S. Witherspoon and L. Brook (eds), *British Social Attitudes: The 1986 Report*, pp. 17–38, Aldershot, Gower.

Market and Opinion Research International (1979), *Youth in Britain: Attitudes and Life Style*, London, MORI.

Martin, G. (1996), 'The influence of television suicide in a normal adolescent population', *Archives of Suicide Research*, 2, pp. 103–17.

Martin-Lebrun, E., Poussin, G., Barumandzadeh, T. and Bost, M. (1997), 'Psychological consequences of parental separation on children', *Archives de Pédiatrie*, 4, pp. 886–92.

Matthews, S.W. (1982), 'Rethinking sociology through a feminist perspective', *American Sociologist*, 17, pp. 29–35.

Max, D.A., Brokaw, B.F. and McQueen, N.M. (1997), 'The effects of marital disruption on the intergenerational transmission of religious values', *Journal of Psychology and Theology*, 25, pp. 199–207.

Meikle, S., Peitchinis, J.A. and Pearce, K. (1985), *Teenage Sexuality*, London, Taylor & Francis.

Menis, J. (1989), 'Attitudes towards school, chemistry students and science among upper secondary chemistry students in the United States', *Research in Science and Technological Education*, 7, pp. 183–90.

Metha, A. and McWhirter, E.H. (1997), 'Suicide ideation, depression and stressful life events among gifted adolescents', *Journal for the Education of the Gifted*, 20, pp. 284–304.

Moore, S. and Rosenthal, D. (1993), *Sexuality in Adolescence*, London, Routledge.

Morgan, D.H.J. (1986), 'Gender', in R.G. Burgess (ed.), *Key Variables in Social Investigation*, pp. 31–53, London, Routledge & Kegan Paul.

Mueller, C. and Pope, H. (1977), 'Marital instability: a study of its transmission between generations', *Journal of Marriage and the Family*, 39, pp. 83–93.

Mullen, K. and Francis, L.J. (1995), 'Religiosity and attitudes towards drug use among Dutch school-children', *Journal of Alcohol and Drug Education*, 41, pp. 16–25.

Murdock, G. and Phelps, G. (1973), *Mass Media and the Secondary School*, London, Macmillan.

Myrtek, M., Scharff, C., Brugner, G. and Muller, W. (1996), 'Physiological, behavioural and psychological effects associated with television viewing in schoolboys: an exploratory study', *Journal of Early Adolescence*, 16, pp. 301–23.

Neher, L.S. and Short, J.L. (1998), 'Risk and protective factors for children's substance use and antisocial behaviour following parental divorce', *American Journal of Orthopsychiatry*, 68, pp. 154–61.

Nelsen, H.M. and Rooney, J.F. (1982), 'Fire and brimstone, lager and pot: religious involvement and substance use', *Sociological Analysis*, 43, pp. 247–56.

Newman, T. (1996), 'Rights, rites and responsibilities: the age of transition to the adult world', in H. Roberts and D. Sachdev (eds), *Young People's Social Attitudes: The Views of 12–19 year olds*, pp. 6–22, Barkingside, Barnardos.

Nurco, D.N., Kinlock, T.W., O'Grady, K.E. and Hanlon, T.E. (1998), 'Differential contributions of family and peer factors to the etiology of narcotic addiction', *Drug and Alcohol Dependence*, 51, pp. 229–37.

Oakley, A. (1981), *Subject Women*, Oxford, Martin Robertson.

Oakley, A. (1996), 'Gender matters: man the hunter', in H. Roberts and D. Sachdev (eds), *Young People's Social Attitudes: The Views of 12–19 year olds*, pp. 23–43, Barkingside, Barnardos.

O'Connor, T.E., Thorpe, K., Dunn, J. and Golding, J. (1999), 'Parental divorce and adjustment in adulthood, findings from a community sample', *Journal of Child Psychology and Psychiatry and Allied Disciplines*, 40, pp. 777–89.

Office of Population Censuses and Surveys (1980), *Classification of Occupations 1980*, London, HMSO.

Office of Population Censuses and Surveys (1990), *Marriage and Divorce Statistics: England and Wales, 1837–1983*, London, HMSO.

Office of Population Censuses and Surveys (1991), *Standard Occupational Classification*, London, HMSO.

Office of Population Censuses and Surveys (1993), *Marriage and Divorce Statistics: England and Wales, 1990*, London, HMSO.

Owens, J., Maxim, R., McGuinn, M., Nobile, C., Msall, M. and Alario, A. (1999), 'Television-viewing habits and sleep disturbance in school children', *Pediatrics*, 104, A1–A8.

Page, R.M., Hammermeister, J., Scanlan, A. and Allen, O. (1996), 'Psychosocial and health-related characteristics of adolescent television viewers', *Child Study Journal*, 26, pp. 319–31.

Palosaari, U., Aro, H. and Laippala, P. (1996), 'Parental divorce and depression in young adulthood: adolescents' closeness to parents and self-esteem as mediating factor', *Acta Psychiatrica Scandinavica*, 93, pp. 20–6.

Parish, T.S. (1981), 'The impact of divorce on the family', *Adolescence*, 16, pp. 577–80.

Pearson, P.R., Lankshear, D.W. and Francis, L.J. (1989), 'Personality and social class among eleven year old children', *Educational Studies*, 15, pp. 107–13.

Peck, D.F. and Plant, M. (1986), 'Unemployment and illegal drug use: concordant evidence from a prospective study and national trends', *British Medical Journal*, 293, pp. 929–32.

Philips, D.P. and Carstensen, L.L. (1986), 'Clustering of teenage suicides after television news stories about suicide', *The New England Journal of Medicine*, 315, pp. 685–9.

Phillips, C.P. and Asbury, C.A. (1990), 'Relationship of parental marital dissolution and sex to selected mental health and self concept indicators in a sample of black university freshmen', *Journal of Divorce*, 13(3), pp. 79–91.

Phoenix, A. (1991), *Young Mothers?*, Cambridge, Polity Press.

Potter, W.J. (1990), 'Adolescents' perceptions of the primary values of television programming', *Journalism Quarterly*, 67, pp. 843–51.

Primavera, L.H., Tantillo, J. and DeLisio, T. (1980), 'Religious orientation, religious behaviour, and dogmatism as correlates of irrational beliefs', *Rational Living*, 15, pp. 35–7.

Qualifications and Curriculum Authority (1999), *Citizenship: The National Curriculum for England*, London, Department for Education and Employment and Qualifications and Curriculum Authority.

Qualifications, Curriculum and Assessment Authority for Wales (2000), *Personal and Social Education Framework*, Cardiff, Qualifications, Curriculum and Assessment Authority for Wales.

Quesnell, M.D. (2000), 'An analysis of selected beliefs and values among Czech fourteen and fifteen year old public school students', unpublished PhD dissertation, University of Wales, Trinity College, Carmarthen.

Reed, R.H. (1950), *Eighty Thousand Adolescents*, London, George Allen & Unwin.

Reid, I. (1998), *Class in Britain*, Cambridge, Polity Press.

Remafedi, G., Resnick, M., Blum, R. and Harris, L. (1992), 'Demography of sexual orientation in adolescence', *Pediatrics*, 89, pp. 714–21.

Richman, C.L., Clark, M.L. and Brown, K.P. (1985), 'General and specific self-esteem in late adolescent students: race x gender x sex effects', *Adolescence*, 20, pp. 555–66.

Richmond, P.G. (1985), 'The relationship of grade, sex, ability and socio-economic status to parent, peer and school affiliation', *British Journal of Educational Psychology*, 55, pp. 233–9.

Richter, P. and Francis, L.J. (1998), *Gone but not Forgotten: Church Leaving and Returning*, London, Darton, Longman & Todd.

Roberts, H. (1996), 'It wasn't like that in our day: young people, religion and right and wrong', in H. Roberts and D. Sachdev (eds), *Young People's Social Attitudes: The Views of 12–19 year olds*, pp. 128–40, Barkingside, Barnardos.

Roberts, H. and Sachdev, D. (eds) (1996), *Young People's Social Attitudes: The Views of 12–19 year olds*, Barkingside, Barnardos.

Robinson, T.N. (1999), 'Reducing children's television viewing to prevent obesity: a randomized controlled trial', *Journal of the American Medical Association*, 282, pp. 1561–7.

Robinson, T.N., Chen, H.L. and Killen, J.D. (1998), 'Television and music video exposure and risk of adolescent alcohol use', *Pediatrics*, 102, E541–E546.

Robinson, T.N. and Killen, J.D. (1995), 'Ethnic and gender differences in the relationships between television viewing and obesity, physical activity, and dietary fat intake', *Journal of Health Education*, 26, S91–S98.

Rokeach, M. (1960), *The Open and Closed Mind*, New York, Basic Books.

Rosenberg, M. (1965), *Society and the Adolescent Self-image*, Princeton, NJ, Princeton University Press.

Rosenberg, M. and Pearlin, L. (1978), 'Social class and self-esteem among children and adults', *American Journal of Sociology*, 84, pp. 53–7.

Rosenthal, D.A., Moore, S.M. and Brumen, I. (1990), 'Ethnic group differences in adolescents' responses to AIDS', *Australian Journal of Social Issues*, 25, pp. 220–39.

Rubenstein, J.L., Halton, A., Kasten, A., Rubin, C. and Stechler, G. (1998), 'Suicidal behaviour in adolescents: stress and protection in different family contexts', *American Journal of Orthopsychiatry*, 68, pp. 274–84.

Rutter, M., Maughan, B., Mortimore, P., Ouston, J. and Smith, A. (1979), *Fifteen Thousand Hours: Secondary Schools and their Effects on Children*, London, Open Books.

Sachdev, D. (1996), 'Racial prejudice and racial discrimination: whither British youth?', in H. Roberts and D. Sachdev (eds), *Young People's Social Attitudes: The Views of 12–19 year olds*, pp. 44–70, Barkingside, Barnardos.

Sampson, R.J. and Laub, J.H. (1993), *Crime in the Making: Pathways and Turning Points through Life*, Cambridge, MA, Harvard University Press.

Sarrel, L. and Sarrel, P. (1981), 'Sexual unfolding', *Journal of Adolescent Health Care*, 2, pp. 93–9.

Schlangen, J.A. and Davidson, J.D. (1985), 'Dogmatism and differential religious involvement', *Sociological Analysis*, 30, pp. 164–75.

School Curriculum and Assessment Authority (1995), *Spiritual and Moral Development*, London, School Curriculum and Assessment Authority.

School Curriculum and Assessment Authority (1996), *Education for Adult Life: The Spiritual and Moral Development of Young People*, London, School Curriculum and Assessment Authority.

Scott, J. (1990), 'Women and the family', in R. Jowell, S. Witherspoon and L. Brook (eds), *British Social Attitudes: The Seventh Report*, pp. 51–76, Aldershot, Gower.

Scott, J., Braun, M. and Alwin, D. (1993), 'The family way', in R. Jowell, L. Brook, L. Dowds and D. Ahrendt (eds), *International Social Attitudes: The Tenth BSA Report*, pp. 23–47, Aldershot, Dartmouth.

Selnow, G.A. and Reynolds, H. (1984), 'Some opportunity costs of television viewing', *Journal of Broadcasting*, 28, pp. 315–22.

Shanahan, J. (1995), 'Television viewing and adolescent authoritarianism', *Journal of Adolescence*, 18, pp. 271–88.

Shanahan, J. (1998), 'Television and authoritarianism: exploring the concept of mainstreaming', *Political Communication*, 15, pp. 483–95.

Sheehan, P.W. (1983), 'Age trends and correlates of children's television viewing', *Australian Journal of Psychology*, 35, pp. 417–31.

Sheiham, A., Marmot, M., Rawson, D. and Ruck, N. (1987), 'Food values: health and diet', in R. Jowell, S. Witherspoon and L. Brook (eds), *British Social Attitudes: The 1987 Report*, pp. 92–119, Aldershot, Gower.

Sheiham, A., Marmot, M., Taylor, B. and Brown, A. (1990), 'Recipes for health', in R. Jowell, S. Witherspoon and L. Brook (eds), *British Social Attitudes: The Seventh Report*, pp. 145–65, Aldershot, Gower.

Shucksmith, J. and Hendry, L.B. (1998), *Health Issues and Adolescence: Growing Up, Speaking Out*, London, Routledge.

Signorielli, N. and Lears, M. (1992), 'Children, television and conceptions about chores: attitudes and behaviours', *Sex Roles*, 27, pp. 157–70.

Signorielli, N. and Staples, J. (1997), 'Television and children's conceptions of nutrition', *Health Communication*, 9, pp. 289–301.

Silverman-Watkins, L.T. and Sprafkin, J.N. (1983), 'Adolescents' comprehension of televised sexual innuendos', *Journal of Applied Developmental Psychology*, 4, pp. 359–69.

Simmons, C. and Wade, W. (1984), *I Like to Say What I Think: A Study of the Attitudes, Values and Beliefs of Young People Today*, London, Kogan Page.

Singer, M.I., Miller, D.B., Guo, S.Y., Flannery, D.J., Frierson, T. and Slovak, K. (1999), 'Contributors to violent behaviour among elementary and middle school children', *Pediatrics*, 104, pp. 878–84.

Singer, M.I., Slovak, K., Frierson, T. and York, P. (1998), 'Viewing preferences, symptoms of psychological trauma and violent behaviours among children who watch television', *Journal of the American Academy of Child and Adolescent Psychiatry*, 37, pp. 1041–8.

Sloane, D.M. and Potvin, R.H. (1986), 'Religion and delinquency: cutting through the maze', *Social Forces*, 65, pp. 87–105.

Smith, C. and Nutbeam, D. (1992), 'Adolescent drug use in Wales', *British Journal of Addiction*, 87, pp. 227–33.

Smith, D.J. (1995a), 'Living conditions in the twentieth century', in M. Rutter and D.J. Smith (eds), *Psychosocial Disorders in Young People: Time Trends and their Causes*, pp. 194–295, Chichester, John Wiley & Sons.

Smith, D.J. (1995b), 'Youth crime and conduct disorders: trends, patterns, and causal explanations', in M. Rutter and D.J. Smith (eds), *Psychosocial Disorders in Young People: Time Trends and their Causes*, pp. 389–489, Chichester, John Wiley & Sons.

Smith, P.K., Morita, Y., Junger-Tas, J., Olweus, D., Catalano, R. and Slee, P. (eds) (1999), *The Nature of School Bullying: A Cross-national Perspective*, London, Routledge.

Spencer, L. and Snape, D. (1994), *The Gospel, the Poor and the Churches*, London, Christian Aid.

Spruijt, E. and deGoede, M. (1997), 'Transitions in family structure and adolescent well-being', *Adolescence*, 32, pp. 897–911.

Steinberg, L. (1990), 'Autonomy, conflict, and harmony in the family relationship', in S.S. Feldman and G.R. Elliott (eds), *At the Threshold: The Developing Adolescent*, pp. 125–30, Philadelphia, PA, W. B. Saunders.

Steininger, M.P., Durso, B.E. and Pasquariello, C. (1972), 'Dogmatism and attitudes', *Psychological Reports*, 30, pp. 151–7.

Stephenson, J., Ling, L., Burman, E. and Cooper, M. (eds) (1998), *Values in Education*, London, Routledge.

Stevenson, T.H.C. (1928), 'The vital statistics of wealth and poverty', *Journal of the Royal Statistical Society*, 91, pp. 207–30.

Stratford, N., Marteau, T. and Bobrow, M. (1999), 'Tailoring genes', in R. Jowell, J. Curtice, A. Park and K. Thomson (eds), *British Social Attitudes: The Sixteenth Report*, pp. 157–78, Aldershot, Ashgate.

Suh, T., Schutz, C.G. and Johanson, C.E. (1996), 'Family structure and initiating non-medical drug use among adolescents', *Journal of Child and Adolescent Substance Abuse*, 5(3), pp. 21–36.

Tan, A.S. (1979), 'TV beauty ads and role expectations of adolescent female viewers', *Journalism Quarterly*, 56, pp. 283–8.

Taylor, M.J. (1994a), *Values Education in the UK: A Directory of Research and Resources*, Slough, NFER.

Taylor, M.J. (1994b), *Values Education in Europe: A Comparative Overview of a Survey of 26 Countries in 1993*, Dundee, SCC for UNESCO/CIDREE.

Taylor, M.J. (1998), *Values Education and Values in Education*, London, Association of Teachers and Lecturers.

Taylor, M.J. (2000), 'Values education: issues and challenges in policy and practice', in M. Leicester, C. Modgil and S. Modgil (eds), *Values, Culture and Education: Institutional Issues*, pp. 151–65, London, Falmer Press.

Taylor-Gooby, P. (1987), 'Citizenship and welfare', in R. Jowell, S. Witherspoon and L. Brook (eds), *British Social Attitudes: The 1987 Report*, pp. 1–28, Aldershot, Gower.

Telfer, R.J. and Kann, R.S. (1984), 'Reading achievement, free reading, watching TV, and listening to music', *Journal of Reading*, 27, pp. 536–9.

Thompson, E.H. (1991), 'Beneath the status characteristics: gender variations in religiousness', *Journal for the Scientific Study of Religion*, 30, pp. 381–94.

Tidhar, C.E. and Peri, S. (1990), 'Deceitful behaviour in situation comedy:

effects on children's perceptions of social reality', *Journal of Educational Television*, 16, pp. 61–76.

Tiggemann, M. and Pickering, A.S. (1996), 'Role of television in adolescent women's body dissatisfaction and drive for thinness', *International Journal of Eating Disorders*, 20, pp. 199–203.

Topf, R., Mohler, P. and Heath, A. (1989), 'Pride in one's country: Britain and West Germany', R. Jowell, S. Witherspoon and L. Brook (eds), *British Social Attitudes: The Sixth Report*, pp. 121–42, Aldershot, Gower.

Troiden, R.R. (1989), 'The formation of homosexual identities', *Journal of Homosexuality*, 17, pp. 43–73.

Trowbridge, N. (1970), 'Effects of socio-economic class on self concept of children', *Psychology in the School*, 7, pp. 304–6.

Trowbridge, N. (1972), 'Self-concept and socio-economic status in elementary school children', *American Educational Research Journal*, 9, pp. 525–37.

Tucker, J.S., Friedmand, H.S., Schwartz, J.E., Criqui, M.H., Tomlinson-Keasey, C., Wingard, D.L. and Martin, L.R. (1997), 'Parental divorce: effects on individual behaviour and longevity', *Journal of Personality and Social Psychology*, 73, pp. 381–91.

Tucker, L.A. and Hager, R.L. (1996), 'Television viewing and muscular fitness of children', *Perceptual and Motor Skills*, 82, pp. 1316–18.

van Driel, L. and Kole, I.A. (1987), *Bij-tijds Leren Geloven: Verkenning van het Educatief Klimaat in een Drietal Kerkelijke Gemeenten*, Kampen, J.H. Kok.

Vess, J.D., Schwebel, A.I. and Moreland, J. (1983), 'The effects of early parental divorce on the sex role development of college students', *Journal of Divorce*, 7(1), pp. 83–95.

Wadsworth, M.E.J. (1984), 'Early stress and association with adult health behaviour and parenting', in N.R. Butler and B.D. Corner (eds), *Stress and Disability in Childhood*, pp. 100–4, Bristol, John Wright & Sons.

Walker, D. (1996), 'Young people, politics and the media', in H. Roberts and D. Sachdev (eds), *Young People's Social Attitudes: The Views of 12–19 year olds*, pp. 44–70, Barkingside, Barnardos.

Wallace, J.M. and Forman, T.A. (1998), 'Religion's role in promoting health and reducing risk among American youth', *Health Education and Behaviour*, 25, pp. 721–41.

Ward, L.M. and Rivadeneyra, R. (1999), 'Contributions of entertainment television to adolescents' sexual attitudes and expectations: the role of viewing amount versus viewer involvement', *Journal of Sex Research*, 36, pp. 237–49.

Wellings, K. and Wadsworth, J. (1990), 'AIDS and the moral climate', in

R. Jowell, S. Witherspoon and L. Brook (eds) *British Social Attitudes: The Seventh Report*, pp. 109–26, Aldershot, Gower.

White, L. (1967), 'The historical roots of our ecological crisis', *Science*, 155, pp. 1203–7.

Whiteley, P. (1985), 'Attitudes to defence and international affairs', in R. Jowell and S. Witherspoon (eds), *British Social Attitudes: The 1985 Report*, pp. 95–119, Aldershot, Gower.

Wiegman, O., Kuttschreuter, M. and Baarda, B. (1992), 'A longitudinal study of the effects of television viewing on aggressive and prosocial behaviours', *British Journal of Social Psychology*, 31, pp. 147–64.

Wielandt, H. and Boldsen, J. (1989), 'Age of first intercourse', *Journal of Biological Science*, 21, pp. 169–77.

Wilson, R.W. (1985), 'Christianity, biased and unbiased: dogmatism's relationships to different Christian commitments, including conversion', *High School Journal*, 68, pp. 374–88.

Witherspoon, S. (1985), 'Sex roles and gender issues', in R. Jowell and S. Witherspoon (eds), *British Social Attitudes: The 1985 Report*, pp. 55–94, Aldershot, Gower.

Witherspoon, S. (1988), 'Interim report: a woman's work', in R. Jowell, S. Witherspoon and L. Brook (eds), *British Social Attitudes: The Fifth Report*, pp. 175–200, Aldershot, Gower.

Wober, M. and Gunter, B. (1982), 'Television and personal threat: fact or artifact? A British survey', *British Journal of Social Psychology*, 21, pp. 239–47.

Wolfinger, N.H. (1998), 'The effects of parental divorce on adult tobacco and alcohol consumption', *Journal of Health and Social Behaviour*, 39, pp. 254–69.

Woodroffe, C., Glickman, M., Barker, M. and Power, C. (1993), *Children, Teenagers and Health: The Key Data*, Buckingham, Open University Press.

Woodrum, E. and Hoban, T. (1994), 'Theology and religiosity effects on environmentalism', *Review of Religious Research*, 35, pp. 193–206.

Woodward, D.R., Cumming, F.J., Ball, P.J., Williams, H.M., Hornsby, H. and Boon, J.A. (1997), 'Does television affect teenagers' food choices?', *Journal of Human Nutrition and Dietetics*, 10, pp. 229–35.

Wright, J.D. and Pearl, L. (1981), 'Knowledge and experience of young people regarding drug abuse between 1969 and 1979', *British Medical Journal*, 282, pp. 793–6.

Yankelovich, D. (1974), *The New Morality: A Profile of American Youth in the 1970s*, New York, McGraw-Hill.

Young, K. (1984), 'Political attitudes', in R. Jowell and C. Airey (eds),

British Social Attitudes: The 1984 Report, pp. 11–45, Aldershot, Gower.

Young, K. (1985a), 'Local government and the environment', in R. Jowell and S. Witherspoon (eds), *British Social Attitudes: The 1985 Report*, pp. 149–76, Aldershot, Gower.

Young, K. (1985b), 'Shades of opinion', in R. Jowell and S. Witherspoon (eds), *British Social Attitudes: The 1985 Report*, pp. 1–32, Aldershot, Gower.

Young, K. (1986), 'A green and pleasant land?', in R. Jowell, S. Witherspoon and L. Brook (eds), *British Social Attitudes: The 1986 Report*, pp. 59–88, Aldershot, Gower.

Young, K. (1987a), 'Nuclear reactions', in R. Jowell, S. Witherspoon and L. Brook (eds), *British Social Attitudes: The 1987 Report*, pp. 71-94, Aldershot, Gower.

Young, K. (1987b), 'Interim report: the countryside', in R. Jowell, S. Witherspoon and L. Brook (eds), *British Social Attitudes: The 1987 Report*, pp. 121–52, Aldershot, Gower.

Young, K. (1988), 'Interim report: rural prospects', in R. Jowell, S. Witherspoon and L. Brook (eds), *British Social Attitudes: The Fifth Report*, pp. 155–74, Aldershot, Gower.

Young, K. (1990), 'Living under threat', in R. Jowell, S. Witherspoon and L. Brook (eds), *British Social Attitudes: The Seventh Report*, pp. 77–109, Aldershot, Gower.

Young, K. (1991), 'Shades of green', in R. Jowell, L. Brook and B. Taylor (eds), *British Social Attitudes: The Eighth Report,* pp. 155–74, Aldershot, Dartmouth.

Youniss, J. and Smollar, J. (1985), *Adolescents' Relations with Mothers, Fathers and Friends*, Chicago, IL, University of Chicago Press.

Zimet, G., Bunch, D., Anglin, T., Lazebnik, R., Williams, P. and Krowchuk, D. (1992), 'Relationship of AIDS-related attitudes to sexual behaviour changes in adolescents', *Journal of Adolescent Health*, 13, pp. 493–8.

Zubrick, S., Silburn, S., Garton, A., Burton, P., Dalby, R., Carlton, J., Shepherd, C. and Lawrence, D. (1995), *Western Australian Child Health Survey: Developing Health and Well-being in the Nineties*, Perth, Western Australia, Australian Bureau of Statistics and the Institute for Child Health Research.

Zuckerman, D.M., Singer, D.G. and Singer, J.L. (1980), 'Children's television viewing, racial and sex-role attitudes', *Journal of Applied Social Psychology*, 10, pp. 281–94.

INDEX

SUBJECT INDEX